Robert Hays Cunningham

Amusing Prose Chap-Books

Chiefly of Last Century

Robert Hays Cunningham

Amusing Prose Chap-Books
Chiefly of Last Century

ISBN/EAN: 9783337077655

Printed in Europe, USA, Canada, Australia, Japan

Cover: Foto ©Thomas Meinert / pixelio.de

More available books at **www.hansebooks.com**

Amusing

Prose Chap-Books

Chiefly of Last Century

Edited by
ROBERT HAYS CUNNINGHAM

LONDON: HAMILTON, ADAMS, & CO
GLASGOW: THOMAS D. MORISON
1889

EDITORIAL NOTE.

Of late years there has been a largely increasing interest on the subject of folklore in its various departments. In such respects there has been a very considerable change in the feelings and tastes of the educated middle-class population of this country, from what there was several generations ago. Formerly the educated classes appeared to think that anything relating to the tastes or ideas of the common people was of very little interest. And in the course of some two hundred years back, leaving out the present time, the number of writers who thought it worth their while to deal with such topics were not much more than a dozen in number, including such men as Aubrey, Bourne, Brand, Hone, Strut, Halliwell, etc. Now, all that is changed, and it has been discovered that much of extreme interest can be learned from the superstitions, habits, beliefs, tastes, customs, ideas, amusements, and general social life of the uneducated or lower classes of previous times.

Not the least interesting or least important of the many sources from which information on these and similar matters, can be obtained, is that of the *people's* earliest popular literature—namely, the chap-book. Beginning at little after the commencement of the eighteenth century, and continuing for over a hundred years afterwards, right up to the general introduction and use of cheap magazines and cheap newspapers, the chap-book was almost the only kind of reading within the reach of the poorer portion of the nation.

What adds greatly both to the interest attaching to the chap-book literature and to its importance, is the fact, that these literary productions, if they may be so termed, were almost entirely written by the people themselves; that is, they were written by the people for the people. This fact intensifies the conviction that they give a true and unvarnished description of the lower orders and their ways. Then, as now, every district had its proportion of local geniuses, who had a gift above their fellows in the matter of story-telling, or some other such way. And in many instances these narratives became chap-books, and were printed and reprinted times without number at the various printing establishments over the country devoted to business of that description.

With regard to this feature in chap-book literature already referred to—namely, that it was composed by the people for the people, and thus gives a true portraiture of many features in their social life—still more may be said. It being the case that not a few of those who hawked these cheap volumes over the country were themselves the authors of some of them, and in the composition of the chaps, to a considerable extent, just reproduced circumstances, incidents, and narratives that they had met with in their wanderings over the country.

To a very marked degree was this the case in the most prominent of all the Scottish chap-book writers—namely, Dougal Graham. See his works, two volumes octavo, collected and edited by George MacGregor in 1883. It would appear that at an early period of Graham's peregrinations he accompanied Prince Charlie's army in 1745-46 throughout its various fortunes, pursuing his trade as a hawker of sundry articles that might be in demand by the prince's retainers. After that event was over, Graham continued the calling of hawker and chapman, at the same time becoming the author of a number of chap-books. But after a while he got a step or two further on; for, finding such an immense demand for his extremely amusing, though coarse, volumes, he ultimately set up a printing press of his own, for the purpose of producing his chaps and supplying the chapmen with them, by whom they were spread broadcast over the country. The knowledge of such instances as this lends much additional value to the chap-book, as containing a forcible description of the social life and ideas of the masses in former times.

A slight study of this department of literature will show that there was, then as now, much variety in the tastes of the people. And we also find that in this respect the various tastes could be fairly well met from among the stores of the chap-book publisher. In these days, just as at the present time, there had been any amount of enterprise on the part of authors and publishers in furnishing readers with whatever their fancy might desire. The *Litteratura Vulgi* may be fairly well divided into the following or similar classifications :—Historical, biographical, religious, romantic, poetical, humorous, fabulous, supernatural, diabolical, legendary, superstitious, criminal, jest-books, etc.

The strictly religious appear to be the fewest in number. The supernatural and the superstitious elements appear to have been more in demand, as the supply of such classes seems to have been greater,—in these days the marvellous had evidently very great charms. The romantic likewise had been in great request,—the old romances handed down from the days long before printing was invented continued up till last century to be of undiminished interest. Also, from the number of poetical chaps that have come down to us, it is evident that the demand for them had been great all over the country. The most popular of all, however, appears to have been the humorous section, which again might be subdivided into a variety of departments, each with numerous representatives. The love of fun and frolic was apparently as deeply implanted in the feelings and tastes of previous generations as of the present.

Printing establishments devoted to the production of

chap-books were pretty well scattered all over the country In England the principal places appear to have been London, York, Birmingham, and Newcastle. In Scotland, the towns of Glasgow, Stirling, Falkirk, and Montrose appear to have carried off the palm in that respect. In Ireland there had been few places besides Dublin and Belfast.

The immense volume of business done in the production of the chap-book, and its importance as an article of trade all over the country, has been a matter of surprise; and the more one investigates into the facts of the case, the more is one impressed with the magnitude of the institution. It appears to have given employment to many thousands of chapmen and printers' employees. As an instance of the profits derivable from the business as an article of trade, one publisher of chap-books, and that not in an especially large way, is known to have retired with accumulated profits amounting to £30,000, which in these days would represent a much larger sum than it does now.

Notwithstanding the immense quantities of chap-books circulated broadcast over the country, comparatively early copies are now extremely rare. And the desire on the part of the public for their possession is now so great that about sixty times their original price is readily given—that is, what originally was sold for one penny, now frequently fetches five shillings, and sometimes more.

In the present collection, which is chiefly of last century, the reader will find considerable variety, containing as it does interesting specimens of several classes or divisions of the popular literature, mostly, however, of an amusing and humorous nature; and from the perusal of the majority of the chaps herein contained, a good deal of entertainment may be derived.

As a companion volume, it is the Editor's intention to issue shortly a collection of AMUSING POETICAL CHAP-BOOKS.

CONTENTS.

THE COMICAL HISTORY OF THE   PAGE
KING AND THE COBBLER
Containing the Entertaining and Merry Tricks and Droll Frolics played by the Cobbler, how he got acquainted with the King, became a Great Man and lived at Court ever after, - - 13

THE MERRY TALES OF THE
WISE MEN OF GOTHAM,   23

THE HISTORY OF
THOMAS HICKATHRIFT,   35

THE HISTORY OF
JACK THE GIANT-KILLER
Containing his Birth and Parentage; His Meeting with the King's Son; His Noble Conquests over many Monstrous Giants; and his rescuing a Beautiful Lady, whom he afterwards married, - - - - - - - - - 53

SIMPLE SIMON'S MISFORTUNES
AND HIS
WIFE MARGERY'S CRUELTY
Which began the very next Morning after their Marriage, - 69

THE ADVENTURES OF
BAMFYLDE MOORE CAREW,
Who was for more than forty years King of the Beggars, - 78

CONTENTS.

THE COMICAL SAYINGS OF
PADDY FROM CORK

With his Coat Buttoned behind, being an Elegant Conference between English Tom and Irish Teague; with Paddy's Catechism, and his Supplication when a Mountain Sailor, - 95

THE HISTORY OF
DICK WHITTINGTON
AND HIS CAT, 117

THE MAD PRANKS OF
TOM TRAM,

Son in Law to Mother Winter; to which are added his Merry Jests and Pleasant Tales, - - - - - - - 127

A YORK DIALOGUE BETWEEN
NED AND HARRY:

Or Ned giving Harry an Account of his Courtship and Marriage State, - - - - - - - - - 141

DANIEL O'ROURKE'S WONDERFUL
VOYAGE TO THE MOON. 150

MOTHER BUNCH'S CLOSET
NEWLY BROKE OPEN;

Containing Rare Secrets of Nature and Art, tried and experienced by Learned Philosophers, and recommended to all ingenious young men and maids, teaching them, in a natural way, how to get good wives and husbands. Approved by several that have made trial of them; it being the product of forty-nine years' study. By our loving Friend Poor Tom, for the King, a lover of Mirth but a hater of Treason. In Two Parts, - 159

THE COMICAL HISTORY OF THE
COURTIER AND TINKER. 178

CONTENTS. 11

The History of the
FOUR KINGS
Of Canterbury, Colchester, Cornwall, and Cumberland, their Queens and Daughters; being the Merry Tales of Tom Hodge and his School-Fellows, - - - - - - - 187

THE PENNY
BUDGET OF WIT
AND PACKAGE OF DROLLERY, 200

The Merry Conceits of
TOM LONG THE CARRIER,
Being many Pleasant Passages and Mad Pranks which he observed in his Travels. Full of Honest Mirth and Delight, - 219

The Story of
BLUE BEARD
Or the Effects of Female Curiosity, - - - 230

The Life of
MANSIE WAUCH
Tailor in Dalkeith, - - - - - - - - 236

The Life and Astonishing Adventures of
PETER WILLIAMSON
Who was carried off when a Child from Aberdeen and sold for a Slave, - - - - - - - - - 254

The Famous Exploits of
ROBIN HOOD,
LITTLE JOHN, AND HIS MERRY MEN ALL,
Including an Account of his Birth, Education, and Death, - - 269

CONTENTS.

PAGE

HISTORY OF
DR. FAUSTUS

Showing his wicked Life and horrid Death, and how he sold himself to the Devil, to have power for twenty-four years to do what he pleased, also many strange things done by him with the assistance of

MEPHISTOPHELES,

With an account how the Devil came for him at the end of twenty-four years, and tore him to pieces, - - - - 286

THE WHOLE LIFE AND DEATH OF
LONG MEG

Of Westminster, - - - - - - - - - 299

THE FAMOUS HISTORY OF THE LEARNED
FRIAR BACON

Giving a Particular Account of his Birth, Parentage, with the many Wonderful Things he did in his Lifetime, to the amazement of all the World, - - - - - - 309

THE HISTORY OF
THE BLIND BEGGAR
OF BETHNAL GREEN,

Containing his Birth and Parentage; how he went to the Wars and Lost his Sight, and turned Beggar at Bethnal Green; how he got Riches, and educated his Daughter; of her being Courted by a rich, young Knight; how the Blind Beggar dropt Gold with the Knight's Uncle; of the Knight and the Beggar's Daughter being Married; and, lastly, how the famous Pedigree of the Beggar was discovered, and other Things worthy of Note, - - - - - - 324

THE PLEASANT HISTORY OF
POOR ROBIN
THE MERRY SADDLER OF WALDEN

Showing the Merry Pranks he played during his Apprenticeship, and how he Tricked a Rich Miser, etc. Very diverting for a Winter Evening Fireside, - - - - - - 337

Amusing Prose Chap-Books.

THE
COMICAL HISTORY
OF THE
KING AND THE COBBLER

CONTAINING

The Entertaining and Merry Tricks and Droll Frolics
played by the Cobbler
How he got acquainted with the King,
became a Great Man and lived at Court ever after.

Chapter I.

*How King Henry VIII. used to visit the watches in the city
and how he became acquainted with a
merry, jovial cobbler.*

It was the custom of King Henry the Eighth to walk late in the night into the city disguised, to observe and take notice how the constables and watch performed their duty, not only in guarding the city gates, but also in diligently watching the inner parts of the city, that so they might, in a great measure, prevent those disturbances and casualties which too often happen in great and populous cities in the night; and this he did oftentimes, without the least discovery who he was, returning home to Whitehall early in the morning.

Now, on his return home through the Strand, he took notice of a certain cobbler who was constantly up at work whistling and singing every morning. The king was resolved to see him and be acquainted with him, in order to which he immediately knocks the heel off his shoe by hitting it against a stone, and having so done, he bounced at the cobbler's stall.

"Who's there?" cries the cobbler.

"Here's one," cries the king. With that the cobbler opened the stall door, and the king asked him if he could put the heel on his shoe.

"Yes, that I can," says the cobbler; "come in, honest fellow, and sit thee down by me and I will do it for thee straight," the cobbler scraping his awls and old shoes to one side to make room for the king to sit down.

The king being hardly able to forbear laughing at the kindness of the cobbler, asked him if there was not a house hard by that sold a cup of ale and the people up.

"Yes," said the cobbler, "there is an inn over the way, where I believe the folks are up, for the carriers go from thence very early in the morning."

With that the king borrowed an old shoe off the cobbler and went over to the inn, desired the cobbler would bring his shoe to him thither as soon as he had put on the heel again. The cobbler promised he would; so making what haste he could to put on the heel, he carries it over to the king, saying, "Honest blade, here is thy shoe again, and I warrant thee it will not come off in such haste again."

"Very well," says the king; "what must you have for your pains?"

"A couple of pence," replied the cobbler.

"Well," said the king, "seeing thou art an honest merry fellow, there is a tester for thee; come, sit down by me, I will drink a full pot with thee; come, here's a good health to the king."

"With all my heart," said the cobbler, "I'll pledge thee were it in water."

So the cobbler sat down by the king and was very merry, and drank off his liquor very freely; he likewise sung some of his merry songs and catches, whereat the king laughed heartily and was very jocund and pleasant with the cobbler, telling him withal that his name was Harry Tudor, that he belonged to the court, and that if he would come and see him there, he would make him very welcome, because he was a merry companion, and charged him not to forget his name, and to ask any one for him about the court and they would soon bring him to him; "For," said the king, "I am very well known there."

Now the cobbler little dreamt that he was the king that spake to him, much less that the king's name was Harry Tudor. Therefore, with a great deal of confidence, he stands up and puts off his hat, makes two or three scrapes with his foot and gives the king many thanks, also telling him that he was one of the most honest fellows he ever met with in all his lifetime, and although he never had been at court, yet he should not be long before he would make a holiday to come and see him.

Whereupon the king paying for what they had drunk, would have taken his leave of the cobbler; but he, not being willing to part with him, took hold of his hand and said, "By my faith you must not go, you shall not go, you shall first go and see my poor habitation. I have there a tub of good brown ale that was never tapped yet, and you must go and taste it, for you are the most honest blade I ever met withal, and I love an honest merry companion with all my heart."

Chapter II.

How the cobbler entertained the king in his cellar, and of the disturbance they had like to have had by his wife Joan.

So the cobbler took the king with him over the way, where he had his cellar adjoining the stall, which was handsomely and neatly furnished for a man of his profession. Into the cellar he took the king. "There," said he, "sit down, you are welcome; but I must desire you to speak softly, for fear of waking my wife Joan, who lies hard by (showing the king a close bed made neatly up at one corner of the cellar, much like a closet), for if she should wake she will make our ears ring again."

At which speech of the cobbler the king laughed and told him he would be mindful and follow his directions.

Whereupon the cobbler kindled up a fire and fetched out a brown loaf, from which he cut a lusty toast, which he sat baking at the fire; then he brought out his Cheshire cheese. "Now," says he, "there is as much fellowship in eating as in drinking."

Which made the king admire the honest freedom of the cobbler. So having eaten a bit the cobbler began. "A health to all true hearts and merry companions;" at which the king smiled, saying, "Friend, I'll pledge thee."

In this manner they ate and drank together till it was almost break of day; the cobbler being very free with his liquor, and delighting the king with several of his old stories, insomuch that he was highly pleased with the manner of his entertainment: when, on a sudden, the cobbler's wife Joan began to awake. "I'faith," says the cobbler, "you must begone, my wife Joan begins to grumble, she'll awake presently, and I would not for half the shoes in my shop she should find you here.

Then taking the king by the hand, he led him up the

stairs, saying, "Farewell, honest friend, it shan't be long before I make a holiday to come and see thee at court."

"Thou shalt be kindly welcome," replied the king.

So they parted, the king on his way to Whitehall and the cobbler to his cellar, and there putting all things to rights before his wife Joan got up, he went to work again, whistling and singing as merry as he used to be, being much satisfied that he happened on so good and jovial a companion, still pleasing himself in his thoughts how merry he should be when he came to court.

Chapter III.

How the cobbler prepared himself to go to court and how he was set out in the best manner by his wife Joan.

Now as soon as the king came home, he sent out orders about the court, that if any one inquired for him by the name of Harry Tudor, they should immediately bring him before him, whatever he was, without any further examination.

The cobbler thought every day a month till he had been at court to see his new acquaintance, and was troubled how he should get leave of his wife Joan, for he could not get without her knowledge, by reason he did resolve to make himself as fine as he could, for his wife always keeped the keys of his holiday clothes; whereupon one evening, as they sat at supper, finding her in a very good humour, he began to lay open his mind to her, telling her the whole story of their acquaintance, repeating it over and over again, that he was the most honest fellow that ever he met withal. "Husband," quoth she, "because you have been so ingenious as to tell me the whole truth, I will give you leave to make a holiday, for this once you shall go to court, and I will make you as fine as I can."

So it was agreed that he should go to court the next day;

whereupon Joan rose betime the next morning to brush up her husband's holiday clothes and make him as fine as she could. She washed and ironed the lace-band, and made his shoes shine that he might see his face in them; having done this she made her husband rise and pull off his shirt. Then she washed him with warm water from head to foot, putting on him a clean shirt; afterwards she dressed him in his holiday clothes, pinning his laced band in prim.

CHAPTER IV.

The cobbler's reception at court with the manner of his behaviour before the king.

The cobbler being thus set forth, he strutted through the street like a crow in a gutter, thinking himself as fine as the best of them all.

In this manner he came to the court, staring on this body and on that body as he walked up and down, and not knowing how to ask for Harry Tudor. At last he espied one as he thought, in the habit of a servant-man, to whom he made his address, saying—

"Dost thou hear, honest fellow, do you know one Harry Tudor who belongs to the court?"

"Yes," said the man, "follow me and I will bring you to him."

With that he had him presently up into the guard chamber, telling one of the yeomen of the guard there was one that inquired for Harry Tudor.

The yeoman replied: "I know him very well, if you please to go along with me, I'll bring you to him immediately."

So the cobbler followed the yeoman, admiring very much the prodigious finery of the rooms which he carried him through. He thought within himself that the yeoman was mistaken in the person whom he inquired for; for, said he, "He whom I look for is a plain, merry, honest fellow, his name is Harry Tudor; we drank two pots together not long since. I suppose he may belong to some lord or other about the court?"

"I tell you, friend," replied the yeoman, "I know him very well, do you but follow me and I shall bring you to him instantly."

So going forward, he came into the room where the king was accompanied by several of his nobles, who attended him.

As soon as the yeoman had put up by the arras, he spoke aloud, "May it please your majesty, here is one that inquires for Harry Tudor."

The cobbler hearing this, thought he had committed no less than treason, therefore he up with his heels and ran for it; but not being acquainted with the several turnings and rooms through which he came, he was soon overtaken and brought before the king, whom the cobbler little thought to be the person he inquired after, therefore in a trembling condition he fell down on his knees, saying—

"May it please your grace, may it please your highness, I am a poor cobbler, who inquired for one Harry Tudor, who is a very honest fellow; I mended the heel of his shoe not long since, and for which he paid me nobly and gave me two pots to boot; but I had him afterwards to my cellar, where we drank part of a cup of nappy ale and we were very merry till my wife Joan began to grumble, which put an end to our merriment for that time; but I told him I would come to the court and see him as soon as conveniently I could.

"Well," said the king, "don't be troubled, would you know this honest fellow again if you could see him?"

The cobbler replied, "Yes; that I will among a thousand."

"Then," said the king, "stand up and be not afraid, but look well about you, peradventure you may find the fellow in this company."

Whereupon the cobbler arose and looked wistfully upon

the king and the rest of the nobles, but it was to little or no purpose; for, though he saw something in the king's face which he thought he had seen before, yet he could not be Harry Tudor, the heel of whose shoe he had mended and who had been so merry a companion with him at the inn and at his own cellar.

He therefore told the king he did not expect to find Harry Tudor among such fine folks as he saw there, but that the person he looked for was a plain, honest fellow. Adding withal, that he was sure that did Harry Tudor but know he was come to court, he would make him very welcome, "For," says the cobbler, "when we parted he charged me to come to court soon and see him, which I promised I would, and accordingly I have made a holiday on purpose to have a glass with him."

At which speech of the cobbler's the king had much ado to forbear laughing out, but keeping his countenance as steady as he could before the cobbler, he spoke to the yeoman of the guard.

"Here," said he, "take this honest cobbler down into my cellar and let him drink my health, and I will give orders that Harry Tudor shall come to him presently."

So away they went, the cobbler being fit to leap out of his skin for joy, not only that he had come off so well, but that he should see his friend Harry Tudor.

Chapter V.
The cobbler's entertainment in the king's cellar.

The cobbler had not been long in the king's cellar, before the king came to him in the same habit that he had on when the cobbler mended his shoe; whereupon the cobbler knew him immediately and ran and kissed him, saying, "Honest Harry, I have made an holiday on purpose to see you, but I had much ado to get leave of my wife Joan, who was loath to lose so much time from my work: but I was resolved to see you and therefore I made myself as fine as I could; but I'll tell thee, Harry, when I came to court I was in a peck of troubles how to find you out; but at last I met with a man who told me he knew you very well and that he would bring me to you, but instead of doing so he brought me before the king, which almost frightened me out of my seven senses; but faith, I'm resolved to be merry with you now, since I have met you at last."

"Aye, that we shall," replied the king; "we shall be as merry as princes."

Now after the cobbler had drunk about four or five good healths, he began to be merry and fell a-singing his old songs and catches, which pleased the king very much and made him laugh heartily.

When on a sudden several of the nobles came into the cellar, extraordinary rich in apparel, and all stood uncovered before Harry Tudor, which put the cobbler into great amazement at first, but presently recovering himself, he looked more wistfully upon Harry Tudor, and soon knowing him to be the king, whom he saw in his presence chamber, though in another habit, he immediately fell upon his knees saying—

"May it please your grace, may it please your highness, I am a poor honest cobbler and mean no harm."

"No, no," said the king, "nor shall receive any here, I assure you."

He commanded him therefore to rise and be merry as he was before, and, though he knew him to be the king, yet he should use the same freedom with him as he did before, when he mended the heel of his shoe.

This kind speech of the king's and three or four glasses of wine made the cobbler be in as good humour as before, telling the king several of his old stories and singing some of his best songs, very much to the satisfaction of the king and all his nobles.

THE COBBLER'S SONG IN THE KING'S CELLAR.

Come let us drink the other pot,
  Our sorrows to confound;
We'll laugh and sing before the king,
  So let his health go round.
For I am as bold as bold can be,
  No cobbler e'er was ruder;
Then here, good fellow, here's to thee,
  (Remembering Harry Tudor.)

When I'm at work within my stall,
  Upon him I will think;
His kindness I to mind will call,
  Whene'er I eat or drink.
His kindness was to me so great,
  The like was never known,
His kindness I shall still repeat,
  And so shall my wife Joan.

I'll laugh when I sit in my stall,
  And merrily will sing;
That I with my poor last and awl,
  Am fellow with the king.
But it is more I must confess,
  Than I at first did know;
But Harry Tudor, ne'ertheless,
  Resolves it shall be so.

And now farewell unto Whitehall,
  I homeward must retire;
To sing and whistle in my stall,
  My Joan will me desire.
I do but think how she shall laugh,
  When she hears of this thing,
That he that drank her nut-brown ale,
  Was England's Royal King.

Chapter VI.
How the cobbler became a courtier.

Now the king considering the pleasant humour of the cobbler, how innocently merry he was and free from any design; that he was a person that laboured very hard, and took a great deal of pains for a small livelihood, was pleased, out of his princely grace and favour, to allow him a liberal annuity of forty merks a year, for the better support of his jolly humour and the maintenance of his wife Joan, and that he should be admitted one of his courtiers, and that he might have the freedom of his cellar whenever he pleased.

Which being so much beyond expectation, did highly exalt the cobbler's humour, much to the satisfaction of the king.

So after a great many legs and scrapes, he returned home to his wife Joan, with the joyful news of his reception at court, which so well pleased her that she did not think much at the great pains she took in decking him for the journey.

THE MERRY TALES

OF THE

WISE MEN OF GOTHAM.

Tale I.

There were two men of Gotham, and one of them was going to Nottingham market to buy sheep, and both met together on Nottingham bridge. "Well met," said one to the other;

"whither are you going?" said he that came from Nottingham. "Marry," said he that was going thither, "I am going to the market to buy sheep." "Buy sheep!" said the other, "which way will you bring them home?" "Marry," said the other, "I will bring them over this bridge." "By Robin Hood," said he that came from Nottingham, "but thou shalt not." "By my maid Margery," said the other, "but I will." "You shall not," said the one. "I will," said the other. Then they beat their staves one against the other and then against the ground, as if a hundred sheep had been betwixt them. "Hold there," said the one. "Beware of my sheep leaping over the bridge," said the other. "I care not," said the one. "They shall all come this way," said the other. "But they shall not," said the one. "Then," said the other, "if thou makest much ado, I will put my finger in thy mouth." "A groat thou wilt," said the other. And as they were in contention, another wise man that belonged to Gotham, came from the market with a sack of meal on his horse, and seeing his neighbours at strife about sheep and none betwixt them, said he, "Ah! fools, will you never learn wit? Then help me," continued he, "to lay this sack upon my shoulder." They did so and he went to the side of the bridge and shook out the meal into the river, saying, "How much meal is there in my sack, neighbour?" "Marry," said one, "there is none." "Indeed," replied this wise man, "even so much wit is there in your two heads, to strive for what you have not." Now which was the wisest of these three I leave thee to judge.

TALE II.

THERE was a man of Gotham that rode to the market with two bushels of wheat, and, lest his horse should be damaged by carrying too great a burden, he was determined to carry the corn himself upon his own neck, and still kept riding upon his horse till he arrived at the end of his journey. I will leave you to judge which was the wisest, his horse or himself.

Tale III.

On a time the men of Gotham fain would have pinned in the cuckoo that she might sing all the year, and in the midst of the town they had a hedge made round in compass, and got a cuckoo and put her into it, and said, "Sing here and thou shalt lack neither meat nor drink all the year." The cuckoo, when she found herself encompassed by the hedge, flew away. "A vengeance on her," said these wise men, "we did not make our hedge high enough."

Tale IV.

There was a man of Gotham who went to Nottingham market to sell cheese, and going down the hill to Nottingham bridge, one of his cheeses fell out of his wallet and ran down the hill. "Prithee," said the man, "can you run to the market alone? I'll now send one after another." Then laying his wallet down and taking out the cheeses, he tumbled them down the hill one after another. Some ran into one bush and some into another. He charged them, however, to meet him at the market place. The man went to the market to meet the cheeses and staying till the market was almost over, then went and inquired of his neighbours if they saw his cheeses come to the market. "Why, who should bring them?" says one. "Marry, themselves," said the fellow, "they knew the way very well. A vengeance on them, they ran so fast I was afraid they would run beyond the market; I am sure they are by this time as far as York." So he immediately rode to York, but was much disappointed. And to add to it he never found nor heard of one of his cheeses.

Tale V.

A man of Gotham bought, at Nottingham market, a trevet of bar iron, and going home with it his feet grew weary with the carriage. He set it down and seeing it had three feet said, "Prithee, thou hast three feet and I but two; thou shalt bear me home if thou wilt," so he set himself down upon it and said to it, "Bear me as long as I have done thee, for if thou dost not thou shalt stand still for me." The man of Gotham saw his trevet would not move. "Stand still," said he, "in the mayor's name and follow me if thou wilt and I can show you the right way." When he went home his wife asked where the trevet was. He said it had three legs and he had but two and he had taught him the ready way to his house, therefore he might come himself if he would. "Where did you leave the trevet?" said the woman. "At Gotham bridge," said he. So she immediately ran and fetched the trevet herself, otherwise she must have lost it on account of her husband's want of wit.

Tale VI.

A CERTAIN smith of Gotham had a large wasp's nest in the straw at the end of the forge, and there coming one of his neighbours to have his horse shod, and the wasps being exceeding busy the man was stung by one of them. The man, being grievously affronted, said, "Are you worthy to keep a forge or not, to have men stung with these wasps?" "O neighbour," said the smith, "be content, and I will put them from their nest presently." Immediately he took a coulter and heated it red hot, and thrust it into the straw at the end of his forge, and set it on fire and burnt it up. Then, said the smith, "I told thee I'd fire them out of their nest."

Tale VII.

On Good Friday the men of Gotham consulted together what to do with their white herrings, sprats, and salt fish, and agreed that all such fish should be cast into a pond or pool in the midst of the town, that the number of them might increase the next year. Therefore everyone that had any fish left did cast them immediately into the pond. "Then," said one, "I have gotten left so many red herrings." "Well," said another, "and I have left so many whitings." Another cried out, "I have as yet gotten so many sprats left." "And," said the last, "I have gotten so many salt fishes, let them go together in the great pond, without any distinction, and we may be sure to fare like lords the next year." At the beginning of the next Lent, they immediately went about drawing the pond, imagining they should have the fish, but were much surprised to find nothing but a great eel. "Ah!" said they, "a mischief on this eel, for he hath eaten up our fish." "What must we do with him?" said one. "Chop him in pieces," said another. "Nay, not so," said another; "but let us drown him." "Be it accordingly so," replied they all. So they went immediately to another pond and cast the eel into the water. "Lay there," said these wise men, "and shift for thyself, since you may not expect help from us." So they left the eel to be drowned.

Tale VIII.

On a time the men of Gotham had forgotten to pay their rents to their landlord; so one said to the other, "To-morrow must be pay-day, by whom can we send our money?" So one said, "I have this day taken a hare and she may carry it, for she is very quick-footed." "Be it so," replied the rest; "she shall have a letter and a purse to put our money in, and we can direct her the way." When the letter was written and the money put into a purse, they tied them about the hare's neck, saying, "You must first go to Loughborough and then to Leicester, and at Newark is our landlord; then commend us to him and there is his due." The hare, as soon as she got out of their hands, ran quite a contrary way. Some said, "Thou must first go to Loughborough." Others said, "Let the hare alone, for she can tell a nearer way than the best of us, let her go."

Tale IX.

A man of Gotham, that went mowing in the meadow, found a large grasshopper. He instantly threw down his scythe and ran home to his neighbour and said that the devil was at work in the field, and was hopping among the grass. Then was every man ready with their clubs, staves, halberts, and other weapons to kill the grasshopper. When they came to the place where the grasshopper was, said one to the other, "Let every man cross himself from the devil, for we will not meddle with him." So they returned again and said, "We are blest this day that we went no farther." "O, ye cowards!" said he that left the scythe in the meadow, "help me to fetch my scythe." "No," answered they, "it is good to sleep in a whole skin. It is much better for thee to lose thy scythe than to mar us all."

Tale X.

On a certain time there were twelve men of Gotham that went to fish; some waded in the water and some stood on dry land. In going home, one said to the other, "We have ventured wonderfully in wading, I pray God that none of us did come from home to be drowned." "Nay, marry," said one to the other, "let us see that, for there did twelve of us come out." Then they told themselves and every one told eleven. Said the one to the other, "There is one of us drowned." Then they went back to the brook where they'd been fishing, and sought up and down for him that was drowned, making a great lamentation. A courtier coming by asked what it was they sought for and why they were sorrowful. "Oh," said they, "this day we went to fish in the brook; twelve of us came out together and one is drowned." The courtier said, "Tell how many there be of you." One of them told eleven, but he did not tell himself. "Well," said the courtier, "what will you give me and I will find the twelfth man?" "All the money we have got," said they. "Give me the money." said he. He began with the first and gave him a stroke over the shoulders with his whip, that made him groan, saying, "Here is one," and so he served them all, and they groaned at the matter. When he came to the last, he paid him well, saying, "Here is the twelfth man." "God's blessings on thee," said they, "for finding our brother."

Tale XI.

A MAN of Gotham, riding along the highway, saw a cheese, so drew his sword and pricked it with the point in order to pick it up. Another man who came by alighted, picked it up and rode away with it. The man of Gotham rides to Nottingham to buy a long sword to pick up the cheese, and returning to the place where it did lie, he pulled out his sword, pricked the ground and said, "If I had had but this sword I should have had the cheese myself, but now another has come before me and got it."

Tale XII.

A MAN in Gotham that did not love his wife, and she having fair hair he said divers times he would cut it off, but durst not do it when she was awake, so he resolved to do it when she was asleep; therefore, one night he took a pair of shears and put them under his pillow, which his wife perceiving, said to her maid, "Go to bed to my husband to-night, for he intends to cut off my hair; let him cut off thy hair and I will give thee as good a kirtle as ever thou didst see." The maid did so and feigned herself asleep, which the man perceiving, cut off her hair, wrapped it about the shears, and laying them under the pillow, fell asleep. The maid arose and the wife took the hair and shears and went to the hall and burnt the hair. The man had a fine horse that he loved, and the goodwife went into the stable, cut off the hair of the horse's tail, wrapped the shears up in it and laid them under the pillow again. Her husband, seeing her combing her head in the morning, marvelled thereat. The girl, seeing her master in a deep study, said, "What ails the horse in the stable, he has lost his tail?" The man ran into the stable and found the horse's tail was cut off; then going to the bed, he found the shears wrapped up in his horse's tail. He then went to his wife, saying, "I crave thy mercy, for I intended to cut off thy hair, but I have cut off my own horse's tail." "Yea," said she, "self do self have." Many men think to do a bad turn, but it turneth oftimes to themselves.

TALE XIII.

A MAN of Gotham laid his wife a wager that she could not make him a cuckold. "No," said she, "but I can." "Do not spare me," said he, "but do what you can." On a time she had hid all the spigots and faucets, and going into the buttery, set a barrel of broach, and cried to her spouse, "Pray, bring me a spigot and faucet or else the ale will all run out." He sought up and down but could not find one. "Come here then," said she, "and put thy finger in the taphole." Then she called a tailor with whom she made a bargain. Soon after she came to her husband and brought a spigot and a faucet, saying, "Pull thy finger out of the taphole, good cuckold. Beshrew your heart for your trouble," said she, "make no such bargain with me again."

TALE XIV.

A MAN of Gotham took a young buzzard and invited four or five gentlemen's servants to the eating of it; but the wife killed an old goose, and she and two of her gossips ate up the buzzard, and the old goose was laid to the fire for the gentlemen's servants. So when they came the goose was set before them. "What is this?" said one of them. The goodman said, "A curious buzzard." "A buzzard! why it is an old goose, and thou art an knave to mock us," and so departed in great anger. The fellow was sorry that he had affronted them, and took a bag and put the buzzard's feathers in it; but his wife desired him, before he went, to fetch a block of wood, and in the interim she pulled out the buzzard's feathers and put in the goose's. The man, taking the bag, went to the gentlemen's servants and said, "Pray, be not angry with me, you shall see I had a buzzard, for here be the feathers." Then he opened the bag and took out the goose's feathers; upon which one of them took a cudgel and gave him a dozen of stripes, saying, "Why, you knave, could you not be content to mock us at home, but you are come here to mock us also."

Tale XV.

A man's wife of Gotham was brought to bed of a male child, and the father invited the gossips who were children of eight or ten years of age. The eldest child's name was Gilbert, the second's name was Humphrey, and the godmother was called Christabel. Their relations admonished them divers times, that they must all say after the parson. And when they were come to the church, the priest said, "Be you all agreed of the name?" "Gilbert, Humphrey, and Christabel," said the same. The priest then said, "Wherefore came you hither?" They immediately said the same. The priest being amazed could not tell what to say, but whistled and said, "Whey," and so did they. The priest being angry, said, "Go home, you fools, go home." Then Gilbert, Humphrey, and Christabel did the same. The priest then provided godfathers and godmothers himself.

Tale XVI.

A young man of Gotham went a wooing a fair maid: his mother warned him beforehand, saying, "Whenever you look at her, cast a sheep's eye at her, and say, 'How dost thou, my sweet pigmy?'" The fellow went to a butcher and bought seven or eight sheep eyes. And when this lusty wooer was at dinner, he would look upon the fair wench and cast in her face a sheep's eye, saying, "How dost thou do, my sweet pigmy?" "How do I do," said the wench; "swine's face, what do you mean by casting a sheep's eye at me?" "O! sweet pigmy, have at thee with another." "I defy thee, swine's face," said the wench. "What my sweet old pigmy, be content, for if you live to next year you will be a foul sow." "Walk, knave, walk," said she, "for if you live till next year you will be a fool."

Tale XVII.

There was a man of Gotham who would be married, and when the day of marriage was come they went to the church. The priest said, "Do you say after me." The man said "Do you say after me." The priest said, "Say not after me such like, but say what I shall tell you; thou dost play the fool to mock the holy scriptures concerning matrimony." The fellow said, "Thou dost play the fool to mock the holy scriptures concerning matrimony." The priest wist not what to say, but answered, "What shall I do with this fool?" and the man said, "What shall I do with this fool?" So the priest took his leave and would not marry them. The man was instructed by others how to do, and was afterwards married. And thus the breed of the Gothamites has been perpetuated even unto this day.

Tale XVIII.

There was a Scotsman who dwelt at Gotham, and he took a house a little distance from London and turned it into an inn, and for his sign he would have a boar's head. Accordingly he went to a carver and said, "Can you make me a bare head?" "Yes," said the carver. "Then," said he, "make me a bare head, and thou'se hae twenty shillings for thy hire." "I will do it," said the carver. On St. Andrew's day before Christmas (called Yule in Scotland) the Scot came to London for his boar's head. "I say, speak," said the Scotsman, "hast thou made me a bare head?" "Yes," said the carver. He went and brought a man's head of wood that was bare, and said, "Sir, there is your bare head." "Ay," said the Scot, "the meikle de'il! is this a bare head?" "Yes," said the carver. "I say," said the Scotsman, "I will have a bare head like the head that follows a sow with gryces. What, fool, know you not a sow that will greet and groan and cry a-week, a-week." "What," said the carver, "do you mean a pig?" "Yes," said the Scotsman, "let me have her head made of timber, and set on her a scalp and let her sing, 'Whip whire.'" The carver said he could not. "You fool," said he, "gar her as she'd sing whip whire."

Tale XIX.

In old times, during these tales, the wives of Gotham were got into an alehouse, and said they were all profitable to their husbands. "Which way, good gossips?" said the ale-wife. The first said, "I will tell you all, good gossips, I cannot brew nor bake, therefore I am every day alike, and go to the ale-house because I cannot go to church; and in the ale-house I pray to God to speed my husband, and I am sure my prayers will do him more good than my labour." Then said the second, "I am profitable to my husband in saving of candle in winter, for I cause my husband and all my people to go to bed by daylight and rise by daylight." The third said, "I am profitable in sparing bread, for I drink a gallon of ale, and I care not much for meat." The fourth said, "I am loath to spend meat and drink at home, so I go to the tavern at Nottingham and drink wine and such other things as God sends me there." The fifth said, "A man will ever have more company in another's house than his own, and most commonly in the ale-house." The sixth said, "My husband has flax and wool to spare if I go to other folk's houses to do their work." The seventh said, "I spare my husband's wood and clothes, and sit all day talking at other folks' fires." The eighth said, "Beef, mutton, and pork are dear, I therefore take pigs, chickens, conies, and capons, being of a lesser price." The ninth said, "I spare my husband's soap, for instead of washing once a week, I wash but once a quarter." Then said the ale-wife, "I keep all my husband's ale from souring; for as I was wont to drink it almost up, now I never leave a drop."

TALE XX.

On Ash Wednesday, the minister of Gotham would have a collection from his parishioners, and said unto them. "My friends, the time is come that you must use prayer, fasting, and alms, but come ye to shrift, I will tell you more of my mind, but as for prayer I don't think that two men in the parish can say their paternoster. As for fasting, ye fast still, for ye have not a good meal's meat in the year. As for alm-deeds, what should they give that have nothing? In Lent you must refrain from drunkenness and abstain from drink." "No, not so," said one fellow, "for it is an old proverb, 'That fish should swim.'" "Yes," said the priest, "they must swim in the water." "I crave thy mercy," quoth the fellow, "I thought it should have swam in fine ale, for I have been told so." Soon after the men of Gotham came to shrift, and being seven the priest knew not what penance to give. He said, "If I enjoin you to pray, you cannot say your paternoster. And it is but folly to make you fast, because you never eat a meal's meat. Labour hard and get a dinner on Sunday, and I will partake of it." Another man he enjoined to fare well on Monday, and another on Tuesday, and another on Wednesday, and so on one after another, that one or other should fare well once in the week, that he might have part of their meat, on every day during the week. "And as for your alm-deeds," the priest said, "ye be but beggars all, except one or two, therefore bestow your alms on yourselves."

THE HISTORY

OF

THOMAS HICKATHRIFT

PART THE FIRST.

Chapter I.
Tom's Birth and Parentage.

In the reign of William the Conqueror, having read in ancient records, there lived in the Isle of Ely, in Cambridgeshire, a man named Thomas Hickathrift, a poor labourer, yet he was an honest, stout man, and able to do as much work in a day as two ordinary men. Having only one son, he called him after his own name, Thomas. The old man put his son to school, but he would not learn anything.

It pleased God to call the old man aside, and his mother being tender of her son, she maintained him by her own labour as well as she could; but all his delight was in the corner; and he ate as much at once as would serve five ordinary men.

At ten years old he was near six feet high, and three in thickness; his hand was much like to a shoulder of mutton, and every other part proportionable; but his great strength was yet unknown.

Chapter II.
How Thomas Hickathrift's Great Strength Came to be Known.

Tom's mother, being a poor widow, went to a rich farmer's house to beg a bundle of straw to shift herself and her son Thomas. The farmer, being an honest charitable man, bid her take what she wanted. She going home to her son Thomas, said, "Pray go to such a place, and fetch me a bundle of straw; I have asked leave." He swore he would not go. "Nay, prithee go," said the good old mother. He again swore he would not go, unless she would borrow him a cart rope. She being willing to please him, went and borrowed one.

Then taking up the cart rope, away he went, and coming to the farmer's house, the master was in the barn, and two other men threshing.

Said Tom, "I am come for a bundle of straw." "Tom," said the farmer, "take as much as thou can'st carry." So he laid down his cart rope, and began to make up his bundle.

"Your rope, Tom," said they, "is too short," and jeered him. But he fitted the farmer well for his joke; for when he had made up his burden, it was supposed to be near a thousand weight. "But," said they, "what a fool thou art; for thou can'st not carry the tithe of it." But, however, he took up his burden, and made no more of it than we do of an hundred pounds weight, to the great astonishment of both master and men.

Now Tom's strength beginning to be known in the town, they would not let him lie basking in the chimney corner, every one hiring him to work, seeing he had so much strength, all telling him it was a shame for him to lie idle as he did from day to day; so that Tom finding them bait at him as they did, went first to one to work and then to another.

One day a man came to him, desiring him to bring a tree home. So Tom went with him and four other men.

Now when they came to the wood they set the cart by the tree, and began to draw it by pulleys; but Tom seeing them not able to stir it, said, "Stand aside, fools," and so set on the one end, and then put it into the cart. "There," said he, "see what a man can do!" "Marry," said they, "that is true indeed."

Having done, and coming through the wood, they met the woodman; and Tom asked him for a stick to make his mother a fire with.

"Aye," says the woodman, "take one."

So Tom took up a bigger than that on the cart, and putting it on his shoulder, walked home with it faster than the six horses in the cart drew the other.

Now this was the second instance of Tom showing his strength; by which time he began to think that he had more natural strength than twenty common men, and from that time Tom began to grow very tractable; he would jump, run, and take delight in young company, and would ride to fairs and meetings, to see sports and diversions.

One day going to a wake where the young men were met, some went to wrestling, and some to cudgels, some to throwing the hammer, and the like.

Tom stood awhile to see the sport, and at last he joined the company in throwing the hammer: at length he took the hammer in his hand, and felt the weight of it, bidding them stand out of the way, for he would try how far he could throw it.

"Ay," says the old smith, "you will throw it a great way, I warrant you."

Tom took the hammer, and giving it a swing, threw it into a river four or five furlongs distant, and bid them go and fetch it out.

After this Tom joined the wrestlers, and though he had no more skill than an ass, yet by main strength he flung all he grasped with; if once he but laid hold they were gone; some he threw over his head, and others he laid gently down.

He did not attempt to look or strike at their heels, but threw them two or three yards from him, and sometimes on their heads, ready to break their necks. So that at last none durst enter the ring to wrestle with him, for they took him to be some devil among them.

Thus was the fame of Tom's great strength spread more and more about the country.

Chapter III.

How Tom became a Brewer's Servant; how he killed a Giant, and came to be called Mr. Hickathrift.

Tom's fame being spread, no one durst give him an angry word; for being foolhardy, he cared not what he did, so that those who knew him would not displease him. At last a brewer of Lynn, who wanted a lusty man to carry beer to the Marsh and to Wisbeach, hearing of Tom, came to hire him; but Tom would not hire himself till his friends persuaded him, and his master promised him a new suit of clothes from top to toe, and also that he should be his man; and the master showed him where he should go, for there was a monstrous giant who kept part of the Marsh, and none dared to go that way; for if the giant found them he would either kill them or make them his servants.

But to come to Tom and his master, Tom did more in one day than all the rest of his men did in three: so that his master seeing him so tractable and careful in his business, made him his head man, and trusted him to carry beer by himself, for he needed none to help him. Thus Tom went each day to Wisbeach, a journey of near twenty miles.

Tom going this journey so often, and finding the other road the giant kept nearer by the half, and Tom having increased his strength by being so well kept, and improving his courage by drinking so much strong ale; one day as he was going to Wisbeach, without saying anything to his master or any of his fellow servants, he resolved to make the nearest road or lose his life; to win the horse or lose the saddle; to kill or be killed, if he met with this giant.

Thus resolved, he goes the nearest way with his cart, flinging open the gates in order to go through; but the giant soon spied him, and seeing him a daring fellow, vowed to stop his journey and make a prize of his beer; but Tom cared not a groat for him, and the giant met him like a roaring lion, as though he would have swallowed him up.

"Sirrah," said he, "who gave you authority to come this way? Do you not know that I make all stand in fear of my sight? and you, like an impudent rogue, must come and fling open my gates at pleasure. Are you so careless of your life that you do not care what you do? I will make you an example to all rogues under the sun. Dost thou not see how many heads hang upon yonder tree that have offended my laws? Thine shall hang higher than any of them all."

"A tod in your teeth," said Tom, "you shall not find me like them."

"No," said the giant; "why, you are but a fool if you come to fight me, and bring no weapon to defend thyself."

Cries Tom, "I have got a weapon here that shall make you know I am your master."

"Aye, say you so, sirrah," said the giant, and then ran to his cave to fetch his club, intending to dash his brains out at a blow.

While the giant was gone for his club, Tom turned his cart upside down, taking the axle tree and wheel for his sword and buckler; and excellent weapons they were on such an emergency.

The giant coming out again began to stare at Tom, to see him take the wheel in one of his hands and the axle tree in the other.

"Oh, oh!" said the giant, "you are like to do great things with those instruments; I have a twig here that will beat thee, thy axle tree, and wheel to the ground."

Now that which the giant called a twig was as thick as a mill post; with this the giant made a blow at Tom with such force as made his wheel crack.

Tom, not in the least daunted, gave him as brave a blow on the side of the head, which made him reel again.

"What," said Tom, "have you got drunk with my small

beer already?" The giant recovering, made many hard blows at Tom; but still as they came he kept them off with his wheel, so that he received but very little hurt.

In the meantime Tom plied him so well with blows that sweat and blood ran together down the giant's face, who, being fat and foggy, was almost spent with fighting so long, so begged Tom to let him drink, and then he would fight him again.

"No," said Tom, "my mother did not teach me such wit. Who is fool then?" Whereupon, finding the giant grew weak, Tom redoubled his blows till he brought him to the ground.

The giant, finding himself overcome, roared hideously, and begged Tom to spare his life and he would perform anything he should desire, even yield himself unto him and be his servant.

But Tom, having no more mercy on him than a dog upon a bear, laid on him till he found him breathless, and then cut off his head, after which he went into his cave, and there found great store of gold and silver, which made his heart leap for joy.

When he had rummaged the cave, and refreshed himself a little, he restored the wheel and axle tree to their places, and loaded his beer on his cart, and went to Wisbeach, where he delivered his beer, and returned home the same night as usual.

Upon his return to his master, he told him what he had done, which, though he was rejoiced to hear, he could not altogether believe, till he had seen if it were true.

Next morning Tom's master went with him to the place, to be convinced of the truth, as did most of the inhabitants of Lynn.

When they came to the place they were rejoiced to find the giant quite dead; and when Tom showed them the head and what gold and silver there was in the cave, all of them leaped for joy; for the giant had been a great enemy to that part of the country.

News was soon spread that Tom Hickathrift had killed the giant, and happy was he that could come to see the giant's cave; and bonfires were made all round the country for Tom's success.

Tom, by the general consent of the country, took possession of the giant's cave and riches. He pulled down the cave, and built himself a handsome house on the spot. He gave part of the giant's lands to the poor for their common, and the rest he divided and enclosed for an estate to maintain him and his mother.

Now Tom's fame was spread more and more through the country, and he was no longer called plain Tom, but Mr. Hickathrift, and they feared his anger now almost as much as they did that of the giant before.

Tom now finding himself very rich, resolved his neighbours should be the better for it. He enclosed himself a park and kept deer; and just by his house he built a church, which he dedicated to St. James, because on that saint's day he killed the giant.

CHAPTER IV.

How Tom kept a pack of Hounds, and of his being attacked by some Highwaymen.

Tom not being used to such a stock of riches, could hardly tell how to dispose of it; but he used means to do it, for he kept a pack of hounds and men to hunt them; and who but Tom; he took much delight in sports and exercises, and he would go far and near to a merry making.

One day as Tom was riding he saw a company at football, and dismounted to see them play for a wager; but he spoiled all their sport, for meeting the football, he gave it such a kick that they never found it more; whereupon they began to quarrel with Tom, but some of them got little good by it; for he got a spar, which belonged to an old house that had been blown down, with which he drove all opposition before him, and made a way wherever he came.

After this, going home late in the evening, he was met by four highwaymen, well mounted, who had robbed all the passengers that travelled on that road.

When they saw Tom, and found that he was alone, they were cock sure of his money, and bid him stand and deliver.

"What must I deliver?" cries Tom. "Your money, sirrah," said they. "Aye," said Tom, "but you shall give me better words for it first, and be better armed too."

"Come, come," said they, "we came not here to prate, but for your money, and money we must have before we go." "Is it so?" said Tom; "then get it and take it."

Whereupon one of them made at him with a rusty sword, which Tom immediately wrenched out of his hand, and attacked the whole four with it, and made them set spurs to their horses; but seeing one had a portmanteau behind him, and supposing it contained money, he more closely pursued them, and soon overtook them and cut their journey short, killing two of them and sadly wounding the other two, who, begging hard for their lives, he let them go, but took away all their money, which was about two hundred pounds, to bear his expenses home.

When Tom came home he told them how he had served the poor football players and the four thieves, which produced much mirth and laughter amongst all the company.

CHAPTER V.

Tom meets with a Tinker and of the Battle they Fought.

SOME time afterwards, as Tom was walking about his estate to see how his workmen went on, he met upon the skirts of the forest a very sturdy tinker, having a good staff on his shoulder and a great dog to carry his budget of tools.

So Tom asked the tinker from whence he came and

whither he was going, as that was no highway? Now the tinker being a very sturdy fellow, bid him go look, what was that to him? But fools must always be meddling.

"Hold," said Tom, "before you and I part I will make you know who I am."

"Aye," says the tinker, "it is three years since I had a combat with any man; I have challenged many a one, but none dare face me, so I think they are all cowards in this part of the country; but I hear there is a man lives hereabouts named Thomas Hickathrift, who has killed a giant, him I'd willingly see to have a bout with him."

"Aye," said Tom, "I am the man. What have you to say to me?"

"Truly," said the tinker, "I am very glad we are so happily met, that we may have one touch."

"Surely," said Tom, "you are but in jest."

"Marry," said the tinker, "but I am in earnest."

"A match," said Tom.

"It is done," said the tinker.

"But," said Tom, "will you give me leave to get me a twig?"

"Aye," said the tinker, "I hate him that fights with a man unarmed."

So Tom stepped to a gate and took a rail for a staff. So to it they fell. The tinker at Tom, and Tom at the tinker, like two giants. The tinker had a leather coat on, so that every blow Tom gave him made it roar again, yet the tinker did not give way an inch till Tom gave him such a bang on the side of the head that felled him to the ground.

"Now, tinker, where art thou?" said Tom. But the tinker being a nimble fellow, leaped up again, and gave Tom a bang, the which made him reel, and following his blows, took Tom on the other side, which made him throw down his weapon and yield the mastery to the brave tinker.

After this Tom took the tinker home to his house, where

we shall leave them to improve their acquaintance, and get themselves cured of the bruises they gave each other. And for a further account of the merry pranks of Tom and the tinker, the reader is referred to the Second Part, which is far more entertaining than this.

PART THE SECOND.

CHAPTER I.

Tom Hickathrift and the Tinker conquer Ten Thousand Rebels.

IN and about the Isle of Ely, many disaffected persons, to the number of ten thousand or upwards, drew themselves together in a body, pretending to contend for their rights and privileges, which they said had been greatly infringed; insomuch that the civil magistrates of the country thought themselves in great danger of their lives.

Whereupon the sheriff by night came to the house of Mr. Thomas Hickathrift, as a secure place of refuge in so eminent a time of danger, where he laid open to Mr. Hickathrift the unreasonableness of the complaint of these rebels, and begged his protection and assistance.

"Sheriff," said Tom, "what service my brother," meaning the tinker, "and I can perform shall not be wanting."

This said, in the morning, by break of day, with trusty clubs, they both went out, desiring the sheriff to be their guide in conducting them to the place where the rebels were.

When they came there, Tom and the tinker marched boldly up to the head of them, and demanded the reason why they disturbed the government? To which they replied, "That their will was their law, and by that only we will be governed."

"Nay," said Tom, "if it be so, these are our weapons, and by them ye shall be chastised." These words were no sooner out of his mouth, but the tinker and he threw themselves both together into the crowd, where with their clubs they beat down all before them. Nay, remarkable it was, the tinker struck a tall man upon the neck with such force that his head flew off and was carried ten yards from him, and struck the chief leader with such violence as levelled him to the ground.

Tom, on the other hand, pressing forward, beat down all before him, making great havoc, till by an unfortunate blow he broke his club; yet he was not in the least dismayed, for he presently seized a lusty, stout, raw-boned miller, and so made use of him for a weapon, till at last they cleared the field, that not one of them durst lift up their hand against them.

Shortly after Tom took some of them and exposed them to public justice; the rest being pardoned at the request of Tom and the tinker.

CHAPTER II.

Tom Hickathrift and the Tinker are sent for up to Court; and of their kind Entertainment.

THE king being truly informed of the faithful services performed by these his loving subjects, Tom Hickathrift and the tinker, he was pleased to send for them and the nobility.

Now after the banquet the king said, "These are my trusty and well-beloved subjects, men of known courage and valour, who conquered ten thousand persons who were met together to disturb the peace of my realm.

According to the characters given of Thomas Hickathrift and Henry Nonsuch, persons here present, which cannot be matched in the world; all were it possible to have an army of 20,000 such, I durst immediately venture to act the part of great Alexander.

As a proof of my favour, kneel down and receive the order of knighthood, Mr. Hickathrift; and as for Henry Nonsuch I will settle upon him a reward of forty pounds a year during life."

4

So said, the king withdrew, and Sir Thomas Hickathrift and Henry Nonsuch, the tinker, returned to their home. But, to the great grief of Sir Thomas Hickathrift, he found his mother dead and buried.

Chapter III.

Tom, after the Death of his Mother, goes a-wooing; and of a Trick he served a Gallant, who had offended him.

Tom's mother being dead, and he left alone in a spacious house, he found himself strange; therefore began to consider with himself that it would not be amiss to seek a wife; so, hearing of a rich and young widow in Cambridge, he goes to her and makes his addresses, and at the first coming she seemed to show him much favour; but between that and his coming again she gave entertainment to an airy, brisk, and young spark that happened to come in while Tom was there a second time.

He looked very wistfully at Tom, and Tom stared as fiercely at him again; so at last the young spark began to abuse Tom with very affronting language, saying he was a lubberly welp and a scoundrel.

"A scoundrel!" said Tom. "Better sayings would become you; and if you do not instantly mend your manners, you will meet with correction."

At which the young man challenged him; so to the yard they went—the young man with his sword, and Tom with neither stick nor staff.

Said the spark, "Have you nothing to defend yourself? Then I shall the sooner despatch you."

So he made a pass at Tom, but that he butt by; and then, wheeling round unto his back, Tom gave him such a nice kick in the breech as sent the spark like a crow up in the air, whence he fell upon the ridge of a thatched house, and came down into a fish-pond, where he had certainly been drowned if it had not been for a poor shepherd, who was walking by that road, and, seeing him floating on the water, dragged him out with his hook, and home he returned like a drowned rat; whilst Tom enjoyed the kind embraces of his lady.

Chapter IV.
How Tom served Two Troopers, whom the Spark had hired to beset him.

Now the young gallant vexed himself to think how Tom had conquered him before his new mistress, so was resolved on speedy revenge, and, knowing he was not able to cope with Tom, he hired two lusty troopers, well mounted, to lie in ambush under a thicket, which Tom was to pass on his way home, and so accordingly they both attempted to set upon him.

"How now, rascals!" said Tom; "what would you be at? Are you indeed so weary of your lives that you so unadvisedly set upon one who is able to crush you like a cucumber?" The two troopers, laughing at him, said they were not to be daunted at his high words. "High words!" said Tom; "nay, now I will come to action," and so ran between them, catching them in his arms, horses and men, as easy as if they had been but two baker's bavins.

In this manner he steered homewards, but, as he passed through a company of haymakers, the troopers cried, "Stop him! stop him! He runs away with two of the king's troopers." But they laughed to see Tom hugging them, frequently upbraiding them for their baseness, saying he'd make mince meat of them for crows and jackdaws.

This was a dreadful lecture to them, and the poor rogues begged he would be merciful to them, and they would discover the whole plot, and who was the person that employed them, which they accordingly did, and gained favour in the sight of Tom, who pardoned them on promise that they would never be concerned in so villainous an action as that was for the future.

Chapter V.

Tom, going to be Married, is set upon by Twenty-one Ruffians; and of the Havock he made.

In regard Tom had been hindered hitherto by the troopers, he delayed his visit to his lady and love till the next day, and, coming to her, he gave her a full account of what had happened.

She was much pleased at this relation, and received him with joy and satisfaction, knowing it was safe for a woman to marry with a man who was able to defend her against any assault whatever; and so brave a man as Tom was found to be.

The day of marriage being appointed, and friends and relations invited, yet secret malice, which is never satisfied but with revenge, had like to have prevented it; for, having near three miles to go to church, the aforementioned gentleman had provided one-and-twenty ruffians to destroy Tom, for to put them to consternation.

Howbeit, it so happened in a private place, all bolted out upon Tom, and with a spear gave him a slight wound, which made his sweetheart shriek out lamentably. Tom endeavoured to pacify her, saying, "Stand you still, and I will soon show you some pleasant sport."

Here he catched hold of a broad-sword from the side of one of the company, and behaved so gallantly with it that at every stroke he took off a joint. He spared their lives, but lopped off their legs and arms, that in less than a quarter of an hour there was not one in the company but had lost a limb. The grass was all stained with a purple gore, and the ground was covered with legs and arms.

His lover and the rest of the company were all this while standing by and admiring his valour, crying out, "O, what a sight of cripples has he made in a short time!"

"Yes," said Tom, "I verily believe that for every drop of blood I have lost I have made the rascals pay me a limb, as a just tribute."

This said, he steps to a farmer's house, and hired a servant, by giving him twenty shillings to carry the several cripples home to their respective habitations in his cart, and then posted to church with his love, when they were heartily merry with their friends after this encounter.

Chapter VI.
Tom provides a Feast for all the poor Widows in the adjacent Towns; and how he served an Old Woman who Stole a Silver Cup.

Now Tom, being married, made a plentiful feast, to which he invited all the poor widows in the parish, for the sake of his mother, who had been lately buried.

This feast was carried on with the greatest solemnity, and, being ended, a silver cup was missing, and being asked about it they all denied it.

At last, all being searched, the cup was found on an old woman named Strumbelow. Then all the rest were in a rage; some were for hanging her, others for chopping the old woman in pieces for ingratitude to such a generous benefactor.

But he entreated them all to be quiet, saying they should not murder a poor old woman, for he would appoint a punishment for her, which was this:—He bored a hole through her nose, and put a string in it, and then ordered her to be stripped; so commanding the rest of the old women to lead her through all the streets and lanes in Cambridge, which comical sight caused a general laughter.

This being done, she had her clothes again, and so was acquitted.

Chapter VII.
Sir Thomas and his Lady are sent for up to Court; and of what happened at that Time.

Now, tidings of Tom's wedding was soon raised at court, insomuch that they had a royal invitation there, in order that the king might have a sight of his newly-married lady.

Accordingly, they came, and were received with much joy and triumph.

Whilst they were in the midst of their mirth news was brought the king by the Commons of Kent that a very dreadful giant was landed in one of the islands, and had brought with him a great number of bears, and also young lions, with a dreadful dragon, upon which he always rode, which said monster and ravenous beasts had much frighted all the inhabitants of the said island. And, moreover, they said, if speedy course was not taken to suppress them in due time, they would destroy the country.

The king, hearing of this relation, was a little startled; yet he persuaded them to return home, and make the best defence they could for the present, assuring them that he would not forget them, and so they departed.

Chapter VIII.

Tom is made Governor of East Angles, now called the Isle of Thanet; and of the wonderful Achievements he there performed.

The king, hearing these dreadful tidings, immediately sat in council to consider what was best to be done for the conquering this giant and wild beasts.

At length Tom Hickathrift was pitched upon as being a stout and bold subject, for which reason it was judged necessary to make him Governor of that island, which place of trust he readily accepted; and accordingly he went down with his wife and family to take possession of the same, attended by a hundred and odd knights and gentlemen at least; they taking leave of him, and wishing him all health and prosperity.

Many days he had not been there before it was his fortune to meet this monstrous giant, for thus it was:—Sir Thomas, looking out at his own window, espied this giant mounted on a dreadful dragon, and on his shoulder he bore a club of iron. He had but one eye, which was in the middle of his forehead, and was as large as a barber's basin, and seemed like flaming fire, the hair of his head hanging down like snakes, and his beard like rusty wire.

Lifting up his eye, he saw Sir Thomas, who was viewing him from one of the windows of the castle. The giant then began to knit his brows, and to breathe forth some threatening words to the Governor, who, indeed, was a little surprised at the approach of such a monstrous and ill-favoured brute.

The monstrous giant, finding that Tom did not make much haste to get down to him, alighted from his dragon, and chained him to an oak tree, then marched to the castle, setting his broad shoulders against the corner of the wall as if he intended to overthrow the whole bulk of the building at once. Tom, perceiving it, said, "Is this the game you would be at? Faith, I shall spoil your sport, for I have a tool to pick your teeth with."

He then took the two-handed sword the king gave him, down he went, and, flinging open the gate, he there finds the giant, who, by an unfortunate slip in his thrusting, was fallen along, and there lay, not able to defend himself.

"How now!" said Tom: "do you come here to take up your lodging? This is not at all to be suffered." And with that he ran his long broad sword between the giant's tawny buttocks, and made the brute give a groan almost as loud as thunder.

Then Sir Thomas, pulling out his sword again, and at six or seven blows he severed his head, which, when cut off, seemed like the root of a great oak; then, turning to the dragon, which was all this time chained to a tree, without any more ado, at a few blows cut off that also.

This adventure being over, he sent for a waggon and horses, and loaded them with the heads, and then summoned all the constables of the county for a safeguard, and sent them to the court, with a promise to his Majesty that in a short time he would clear the island of all the bears, lions, etc., etc.

CHAPTER IX.

The Tinker, hearing of Tom's Fame, he goes to his Partner; and of his being unfortunately slain by a Lion.

Tom's victories rang so loud that they reached the ears of his old acquaintance the tinker, who, being desirous of honour, resolved to go down and visit him in his government; and coming there he was kindly entertained.

After a few days' pleasure, Tom told him he must go in search of some bears and lions in the island.

"Then," said the tinker, "I will go with you."

"With all my heart," said Tom, "for I must own I shall be glad of your company." On this they went forward—Tom with his great sword and the tinker with his pike staff.

After they had travelled four or five hours, it was their fortune to meet all the wild beasts together, being in number fourteen, six of which were bears, the other eight young lions. When these creatures had set their eyes on them they ran furiously, as if they would have devoured them at a mouthful, but Tom and the tinker stood side by side, with their backs against an oak, until the lions and bears came within their reach. Tom, with his sword, clave all their heads asunder, until they were all destroyed, except one young lion, who, seeing the rest of his fellow-creatures dead, he was making his escape; but the tinker, being too venturous, ran hastily after him, and gave the lion a blow. The beast turned upon him, and seized him with such violence by the throat as soon ended his life.

Tom's joy was now mingled with sorrow, for, though he had cleared the island of those ravenous beasts, yet his grief was intolerable for the loss of his friend.

Home he returned to his lady, where, in token of joy for the success he'd had in his dangerous enterprizes, he made a very noble and splendid feast, to which he invited all his friends and acquaintances, and then made the following promises:—

> "My friends, while I have strength to stand,
> Most manfully I will pursue
> All dangers, till I clear the land
> Of lions, bears, and tigers too."

THE HISTORY
OF
JACK
THE
GIANT-KILLER

CONTAINING

His Birth and Parentage
His Meeting with the King's Son; His Noble
Conquests over many Monstrous Giants
And his rescuing a Beautiful Lady, whom he
afterwards married.

In the reign of King Arthur, near the Land's-End of England, in the county of Cornwall, there lived a wealthy farmer, who had only one son, commonly known by the name of Jack. He was brisk, and of a lively, ready wit, so that whatever he could not perform by strength he completed by wit and policy. Never was any person heard of that could worst him; nay, the learned he baffled by his cunning and ready inventions.

For instance, when he was no more than seven years of

age, his father sent him into the field to look after his oxen. A country vicar, by chance one day coming across the field, called Jack, and asked him several questions; in particular, "How many commandments were there?" Jack told him there were nine. The parson replied, "There are ten." "Nay," quoth Jack, "master parson, you are out of that; it is true there were ten, but you have broken one of them." The parson replied, "Thou art an arch wag, Jack." "Well, master parson," quoth Jack, "you have asked me one question, and I have answered it; let me ask you another. "Who made these oxen?" The parson replied, "God." "You are out again," quoth Jack, "for God made them bulls, but my father and his man Hobson made oxen of them." The parson, finding himself fooled, trudged away, leaving Jack in a fit of laughter.

In those days the mount of Cornwall was kept by a huge and monstrous giant of 27 feet high and of 3 yards in compass, of a grim countenance, to the terror of all the neighbouring towns. His habitation was a cave in the midst of the mount; neither would he suffer any living creature to inhabit near him. His feeding was upon other men's cattle; for whensoever he had occasion for food he would wade over to the main land, where he would furnish himself with whatever he could find; for the people at his approach would forsake their habitations; then he would take their cows and oxen, of which he would make nothing to carry over on his back half a dozen at a time; and as for sheep and hogs, he would tie them round his waist. This he had for many years practised in Cornwall.

But one day Jack, coming to the Town Hall, when the Magistrates were sitting in consternation about the giant, he asked what reward they would give to any person that would destroy him. They answered, "He shall have all the giant's treasure in recompense." Quoth Jack, "Then I myself will undertake the work."

Jack furnished himself with a horn, a shovel, and a pick-axe, and over to the mount he goes in the beginning of a dark winter evening, where he fell to work, and before morning had digged a pit 22 feet deep, and as broad, and covered the same over with long sticks and straw; then strewed a little mould upon it, so that it appeared like the plain ground.

This done, Jack places himself on the contrary side of the pit just about the dawning of the day, when, putting his horn to his mouth, he then blew, "Tan twivie, tan twivie," which unexpected noise roused the giant, who came roaring towards Jack, crying out, "You incorrigible villain, are you come hither to break my rest? You shall dearly pay for it; satisfaction I will have, and it shall be this—I will take you wholly and broil you for my breakfast," which words were no sooner out of his mouth but he tumbled headlong into the deep pit, whose heavy fall made the very foundation of the mount to shake.

"Oh! giant, where are you now? Faith, you are got into Lobb's Pond, where I shall plague you for your threatening words. What do you think now of broiling me for your breakfast? Will no other diet serve you but poor Jack?" Thus having tantalized the giant for a while, he gave him a most weighty knock on the crown of his head with his pick-axe, so that he immediately tumbled down, gave a most dreadful groan, and died. This done, Jack threw the earth in upon him, and so buried him; then, going and searching the cave, he found a great quantity of treasure.

Now, when the Magistrates who employed him heard the work was over, they sent for him, declaring that he should henceforth be called Jack the Giant-Killer. And in honour thereof, they presented him with a sword, together with a fine rich embroidered belt, on which these words were wrought in letters of gold—

"Here's the right valiant Cornish man
Who slew the giant Cormillan."

The news of Jack's victory was soon spread; when another huge giant, named Blunderboar, hearing of it, vowed to be revenged on Jack if ever it was his fortune to light upon him. This giant kept an enchanted castle, situated in the midst of a lonesome wood. Now, Jack, about four months after, walking near the borders of the said wood, on his journey towards Wales, grew weary, and therefore sat himself down by the side of a pleasant fountain, where a deep sleep suddenly seized on him, at which time the giant coming for water, found him; and by the line on his belt knew him to be Jack that killed his brother; and, without any words, threw him upon his shoulder, to carry him to his enchanted castle.

Now, as they passed through a thicket, the rustling of the boughs awaked poor Jack, who, finding himself in the clutches of the giant, was strangely surprised; for, at the entering within the first walls of the castle, he beheld the ground all covered with bones and skulls of dead men, the giant telling Jack that his bones would enlarge the number that he saw. This said, he brought him into a large parlour, where he beheld the bloody quarters of some who were lately slain, and in the next room were many hearts and livers, which the giant, in order to terrify Jack, told him " that men's hearts and livers were the choicest of his diet, for he commonly ate them with pepper and vinegar, and he did not question but his heart would make him a dainty bit." This said, he locks up poor Jack in an upper room, while he went to fetch another giant living in the same wood, that he might partake in the destruction of poor Jack.

Now, while he was gone, dreadful shrieks and cries affrighted poor Jack, especially a voice which continually cried—

" Do what you can to get away,
Or you'll become the giant's prey;
He's gone to fetch his brother, who
Will kill and likewise torture you."

This dreadful noise so amazed poor Jack he was ready to run distracted. Seeing from the window afar off the two giants coming, "Now," quoth Jack to himself, "my death or deliverance is at hand."

There were strong cords in the room by him, of which he takes two, at the end of which he makes a noose, and, while the giant was unlocking the gate, he threw the ropes over each of the heads, and, drawing the other end across the beam, he pulled with all his strength until he had throttled them; and then, fastening the rope to the beam, turning towards the window he beheld the two giants to be black in their faces. Sliding down by the rope, he came close to their heads, where the helpless giants could not defend themselves, and, drawing out his sword, slew them both, and delivered himself from their intended cruelty: then, taking out a bunch of keys, he unlocked the rooms, where he found three fair ladies, tied by the hair of their heads, almost starved to death, who told Jack that their husbands were slain by the giant, and that they were kept many days without food, in order to force them to feed upon the flesh of their husbands.

"Sweet ladies," quoth Jack, "I have destroyed this monster, and his brutish brother, by which I have obtained your liberties." This said, he presented them with the keys of the castle, and so proceeded on his journey to Wales.

Jack, having but very little money, thought it prudent to make the best of his way by travelling as fast as he could, but, losing his road, was benighted, and could not get a place of entertainment until he came to a valley placed between two hills, where stood a large house in a lonesome place. He took courage to knock at the gate, and to his great surprise there came forth a monstrous giant, having two heads; yet he did not seem so fiery as the others had been, for he was a Welsh giant, and what he did was by secret malice, for Jack telling his condition he bid him welcome, showing him a room with a bed in it, whereon he might take his night's repose; therefore Jack undressed himself, and, as the giant was walking to another apartment, Jack heard him mutter forth these words to himself—

"Though here you lodge with me this night,
You shall not see the morning light;
My club shall dash your brains out quite."

"Sayest thou so," quoth Jack; "this is like your Welsh tricks; yet I hope to be cunning enough for you." Then getting out of bed he put a billet in his stead, and hid himself in a corner of the room; and in the dead time of the night the Welsh giant came with his great knotty club, and struck several heavy blows upon the head where Jack had laid the billet, and then returned to his own chamber, supposing he had broken all the bones in his body.

In the morning Jack gave him hearty thanks for his lodging. The giant said to him, "How have you rested? Did you not feel something in the night?" "Nothing," quoth Jack, "but a rat which gave me three or four slaps with her tail." Soon after the giant arose and went to breakfast with a bowl of hasty pudding, containing nearly four gallons, giving Jack the like quantity, who, being loath to let the giant know he could not eat with him, got a large leathern bag, putting it very artfully under his loose coat, into which he secretly conveyed his pudding, telling the giant he could show him a trick; then, taking a large knife, he ripped open the bag, which the giant supposed to be his belly, when out came the hasty pudding, at which the Welsh giant cried, "Cotsplut, hur can do dat trick hurself." Then, taking his sharp knife, he ripped up his own belly from the bottom to the top; and out dropped his bowels, so that he fell down for dead. Thus Jack outwitted the giant, and proceeded on his journey.

About this time King Arthur's son only desired of his father to furnish him with a certain sum of money, that he might go and seek his fortune in Wales, where a beautiful lady lived, whom he heard was possessed with seven evil spirits; but the king his father advised him utterly against it, yet he would not be persuaded of it; so he granted what he requested, which was one horse loaded with money, and another for himself to ride on; thus he went forth without any attendants.

Now, after several days' travel, he came to a market town in Wales, where he beheld a large concourse of people gathered together. The king's son demanded the reason of it, and was told that they had arrested a corpse for many large sums of money which the deceased owed when he died. The king's son replied, "It is a pity that creditors should be so cruel; go bury the dead, and let his creditors come to my lodging, and their debts shall be discharged." Accordingly they came in great numbers, so that he left himself moneyless.

Now, Jack the Giant-Killer being there, and, seeing the generosity of the king's son, he was taken with him, and desired to be his servant. It was agreed upon the next morning, when, riding out at the town-end, the king's son, turning to Jack, said, "I cannot tell how I will subsist in my intended journey." "For that," quoth Jack, "take you no care: let me alone; I warrant you we will not want."

Now, Jack, having a spell in his pocket, which served at noon for a refreshment, when done, they had not one penny left betwixt them. The afternoon they spent in travel and discourse, till the sun began to grow low, at which time the king's son said, "Jack, since we have no money, where can we think to lodge this night?" Jack replied, "We'll do well enough, for I have an uncle living within two miles of this. He is a monstrous giant with three heads; he will fight 500 men in armour, and make them to fly before him." "Alas!" saith the king's son, "what shall we do there? He will certainly chop us both up at one mouthful!" "It is no matter for that," quoth Jack; "I will go before and prepare the way for you. Tarry here."

He waits, and Jack rides full speed; when he came to the castle, he knocked with such a force that he made all the neighbouring hills to resound. The giant, with a voice like thunder, roared out, "Who's there?" He answered, "None but your own cousin Jack. Dear uncle, heavy news, God wot." "Prithee, what heavy news can come to me? I am a giant with three heads, and besides thou knowest I can fight five hundred men." "O! but," quoth Jack, "here's the king's son coming with 1,000 men to kill you." "Oh! Jack, this is heavy news indeed. I have a large vault under ground, where I will hide myself, and thou shalt lock, bolt, and bar me in, and keep the keys till the king's son is gone."

Jack having secured the giant, he returned and fetched his master. They were both heartily merry with the wine and other dainties which were in the house; so that night they rested in very pleasant lodgings, whilst the poor uncle the giant lay trembling in the vault under ground.

Early in the morning Jack furnished his master with a supply of gold and silver, and set him three miles forward on his journey, concluding he was then pretty well out of the smell of the giant, and then returned to let his uncle out of the hole, who asked Jack what he would give him in reward, since his castle was not demolished. "Why," quoth Jack, "I desire nothing but the old coat and cap, together with the old rusty sword and slippers which are at your bed-head." "Jack, thou shalt have them, and pray keep them for my sake, for they are things of excellent use. The coat will keep you invisible; the cap will furnish you with knowledge; the sword cuts asunder whatever you strike, and the shoes are of extraordinary swiftness: these may be serviceable to you, and therefore pray take them with all my heart." Jack takes them, thanking his uncle, and follows his master.

Jack, having overtaken his master, soon after arrived at the lady's house, who, finding the king's son to be a suitor, prepared a banquet for him, and, being ended, she wiped his mouth with her napkin, saying, "You must show this to-morrow, or else lose your head," and she put it safely into her bosom.

The king's son went to bed sorrowful, but Jack's cap of knowledge instructed him how to obtain it. In the middle of the night she called upon her familiar spirit to carry her to Lucifer. Jack put on his coat of darkness, with his shoes of swiftness, and was there as soon as her; by reason of his coat they could not see him. When she entered the place she gave the handkerchief to old Lucifer, who laid it carefully upon a shelf, from whence Jack brought it to his master, who showed it to the lady the next day.

The next night she saluted the king's son, telling him he must show her to-morrow morning the lips that she kissed last this night, or lose his head. "Ah," replied he, "if you kiss none but mine I will." "It is neither here nor there," said she; "if you do not, death's your portion." At midnight she went as before, and was angry with Lucifer for letting the handkerchief go. "But now," said she, "I will be too hard for the king's son, for I will kiss thee, and he's to show thy lips." Jack, standing near him with his sword of sharpness, cut off the devil's head, and brought it under his invisible coat to his master, who was in bed, and laid it at the end of his bolster. In the morning, when the lady came up, he pulled it out by the horns, and showed her the devil's lips, which she kissed last.

Thus, having answered her twice, the enchantment broke, and the evil spirits left her, at which time she appeared a beautiful and virtuous creature. They were married next morning in great pomp and solemnity, and returned with a numerous company to the court of King Arthur, where they were received with the greatest joy and loud acclamations

Jack, for the many and great exploits he had done for the good of his country, was made one of the Knights of the Round Table.

Jack, having resolved not to be idle, humbly requested of the king to fit him with a horse and money to travel, "for," said he, "there are many giants alive in the remotest parts of the kingdom, to the unspeakable damage of your Majesty's liege subjects; wherefore, may it please your Majesty to give me encouragement to rid the realm of these cruel and devouring monsters of nature, root and branch.

Now, when the king had heard these noble propositions, and had duly considered the mischievous practices of these blood-thirsty giants, he immediately granted what Jack requested; and, being furnished with all necessaries for his progress, he took his leave of King Arthur, taking with him the cap of knowledge, sword of sharpness, shoes of swiftness, and likewise the invisible coat, the better to perfect and complete the dangerous enterprises that lay before him.

Jack travelled over vast hills and mountains, when, at the end of three days, he came to a large and spacious wood, where, on a sudden, he heard dreadful shrieks and cries, whereupon, casting his eyes around, he beheld a giant rushing along with a worthy knight and his fair lady, whom he held by the hair of their heads in his hands, wherefore he alighted from off his horse, and then, putting on his invisible coat, under which he carried his sword of sharpness, he came up to the giant, and, though he made several passes at him, yet he could not reach the trunk of his body, by reason of his height, though it wounded his thighs in several places; but at length, giving him a swinging stroke, he cut off both his legs just below the knee, so that the trunk of his body made the ground shake with the force of his fall, at which the knight and the lady escaped; then had Jack time to talk with him, and, setting his foot upon his neck, said, "You savage and barbarous wretch, I am come to execute upon you the just reward of your villainy." And with that, running him through and through, the monster sent forth a hideous groan, and yielded up his life, while the noble knight and virtuous lady were joyful spectators of his sudden downfall and their own deliverance.

This being done, the courteous knight and his fair lady returned him hearty thanks for their deliverance, but also invited him home, there to refresh himself after the dreadful encounter, as likewise to receive ample reward, by way of gratitude for his good service. "No," quoth Jack, "I cannot be at ease till I find out the den which was this monster's habitation." The knight hearing this waxed sorrowful, and replied, "Noble stranger, it is too much to run a second risk, for this monster lived in a den under yon mountain, with a brother of his, more fierce than himself; therefore, if you go thither and perish in the attempt, it would be the heartbreaking of both me and my lady. Let me persuade you to go with us." "Nay," quoth Jack, "if there were twenty I would shed the last drop of my blood before one of them should escape my fury; but when I have finished this task I will come and pay my respects to you." So, taking directions to their habitation, he mounted his horse, and went in pursuit of the deceased giant's brother.

Jack had not rode past a mile before he came in sight of the cave's mouth, at the entrance of which he beheld the other giant sitting upon a huge block of timber, with a knotty iron club by his side, waiting for his brother's return with his cruel prey. His goggle eyes appeared like terrible flames of fire, his countenance grim and ugly, and his cheeks appeared like a couple of large flitches of bacon; the bristles of his head seemed to resemble rods of iron wire; his locks hung down on his broad shoulders like curled snakes.

Jack alighted from his horse, and put him into a thicket; then, with his coat of darkness, he came near to behold his figure, and said, "Oh! are you here? It will not be long before I take you by the beard." The giant could not see him by reason of his invisible coat: so Jack, fetching a blow at his head with his sword of sharpness, and missing somewhat of his aim, cut off the giant's nose, whose nostrils were wider than a pair of jack-boots. The pain was terrible; he put up his hand to feel for his nose, and when he could not find it he raved and roared louder than thunder; and, though he turned up his large eyes, he could not see from whence the blow came; nevertheless, he took up his iron-headed club, and began to thrash about him like one stark mad. "Nay," quoth Jack, "if you be for that sport, then I will despatch you quickly, for fear of an accidental blow." Then Jack makes no more to do, but runs his sword up to the hilt in the giant's body, where he left it sticking for a while, and stood himself laughing to see the giant caper and dance with the sword in him, crying out he should die with the pain in his body. Thus did the giant continue raving for an hour or more, and at length fell down dead.

This being done, Jack cut off both the giants' heads, and sent them to King Arthur by a waggoner, whom he hired for the purpose.

Jack, having despatched these two monsters, resolved to enter the cave in search of the giant's treasure. He passed through many turnings and windings, which led him at length to a room paved with freestone, at the upper end of which was a boiling cauldron; on the right hand stood a large table, where the giants used to dine; then he came to an iron gate, where was a window secured with bars of iron, through which he looked, and beheld a vast many captives, who, seeing Jack, said, "Young man, art thou come to be one among us in this miserable den?" "Ay," quoth Jack, "I hope I shall not tarry long here; but what is the meaning of your captivity?" "Why," said one of them, "we have been taken by the giants, and here we are kept till they have a feast, then the fattest among us is slaughtered for their devouring jaws. It is not long since they took three of us for the purpose." "Say you so," quoth Jack; "well, I have given them both such a dinner that it will be long enough ere they need any more. You may believe me, for I have slain them both; and as for their monstrous heads, I sent them to the court of King Arthur as trophies of my victory." Then, leading them to the aforesaid room, he placed them round the table, and set before them two quarters of beef, also bread and wine, so that they feasted there very plentifully. Supper being ended, they searched the giant's coffers, where, finding a vast store of gold, Jack divided it equally among them. They all returned him hearty thanks for their treasure and miraculous deliverance. That night they went to their rest, and in the morning they arose and departed to their respective places of abode, and Jack to the knight's house.

Jack mounted his horse, and by his direction he came to the knight's house, where he was received with all demonstrations of joy by the knight and his lady, who, in respect to Jack, prepared a feast, which lasted for many days, inviting all the gentry in the adjacent parts. He presented him with a ring of gold, on which was engraven by curious art the picture of the giant dragging a distressed knight and his fair lady by the hair of the head.

Now, there were five aged gentlemen who were fathers to some of those miserable captives whom Jack had set at liberty, who immediately paid him their respects. The smiling bowl was then pledged to the victorious conqueror, but during their mirth a dark cloud appeared, which daunted the assembly.

A messenger brought the dismal tidings of the approach of one Thunderful, a huge giant with two heads, who, having heard of the death of his kinsmen, the above-named giants, was come in search of Jack, to be revenged on him for their terrible downfall, and was within a mile of the knight's seat, the people flying before him from their habitations. When they had related this, Jack said, "Let him come. I am prepared with a tool to pick his teeth, and you, gentlemen and ladies, walk forth into the garden, and you shall be the joyful spectators of this monstrous giant's death." To which they consented, wishing him good fortune in that great enterprise.

The situation of the knight's house was in a small island, encompassed with a vast moat, thirty feet deep and twenty feet wide, over which lay a drawbridge. Wherefore Jack employed two men to cut it on both sides, and then, dressing himself in his coat of darkness, putting on his shoes of swiftness, he marched against the giant, with his sword of sharpness ready drawn. When he came close up, the giant could not see Jack, by reason of his invisible coat; nevertheless, he was sensible of approaching danger, which made him cry out—

"Fe, Fi, Fo, Fum, I smell the blood of an Englishman; be he living or be he dead, I'll grind his bones to mix my bread."

"Sayest thou so," quoth Jack; "then thou art a monstrous miller. But how? If I serve thee as I did the two giants of late, I should spoil your practice for the future."

At which time the giant spoke with a voice as loud as thunder—"Art thou that villain which destroyed my kinsmen? Then I will tear thee with my teeth, and suck thy blood. I will grind thy bones to powder."

"Catch me first," quoth Jack; and he threw off his coat of darkness that the giant might see him, and then ran from him as through fear, the giant, with glaring eyes, following after like a walking castle, making the earth to shake at every step. Jack led him a dance three or four times round the moat, that the ladies and gentlemen might take a full view of this huge monster who followed Jack, but could not overtake him by reason of his shoes of swiftness. At length Jack took over the bridge, the giant, with full speed, pursuing after him, with his iron club; but, coming to the middle of the draw-bridge, the weight of his body, and the most dreadful steps which he took, it broke down, and he tumbled into the water, where he rolled and wallowed like a whale. Jack, standing at the side of the moat, laughed at the giant, and said, "You would grind my bones to powder? You have water; pray, where is your mill?" The giant foamed to hear him scoffing at that rate, though he plunged from place to place in the moat. Jack at length got a cart rope, and cast it over the giant's two heads with a slip knot, and, by the help of horses, he dragged him out again, nearly strangled. Before he would let him loose, he cut off both his heads with his sword of sharpness, in the view of all the assembly of knights and ladies, who gave a shout when they saw the giant despatched. Then, before he would either eat or drink, he sent these heads also to the court of King Arthur.

After some mirth and pastime, Jack, taking leave of the noble knights and ladies, set off in search of new adventures. Through many woods and groves he passed, till, coming to the foot of a high mountain late at night, he knocked at the door of a lonesome house, at which a man, with a head as white as snow, arose and let him in.

"Father," said Jack, "have you any entertainment for a benighted traveller that has lost his way?"

"Yes," said the old man; "if thou wilt accept of such as my poor cottage afford, thou shalt be welcome." Jack returned him thanks. They sat together, and the old man began to discourse as follows—"Son, I am sensible thou art the great conqueror of giants, and it is in thy power to free this place; for there is an enchanted castle kept by a monstrous giant, named Galligantus, who, by the help of a conjurer, betrays knights and ladies into this strong castle, where, by magic art, they are transformed into sundry shapes; but, above all, I lament the misfortune of a duke's daughter, whom they fetched from her father's garden, carrying her through the air in a charion drawn by fiery dragons. She was immediately transformed into the shape of a white hind. Many knights have endeavoured to break the enchantment for her deliverance, yet none could accomplish it, by reason of two griffins, who are at the entrance of the castle gate, who destroy them as they see them; but you, being furnished with an invisible coat, may pass them undiscovered, where, on the gates of the castle, you will find engraven in characters the means the enchantment may be broken."

Jack gave him his hand, with a promise that in the morning he would break the enchantment and free the lady.

Having refreshed themselves with a morsel of meat, they laid down to rest. In the morning Jack arose, and put on his invisible coat, his cap of knowledge, and shoes of swiftness, and so prepared himself for the dangerous enterprise.

Now, when he had ascended the mountain he discovered the two fiery griffins. He passed between them, for they could not see him by reason of his invisible coat. When he had got beyond them, he found upon the gate a golden trumpet, hung in a chain of fine silver, under which were engraven—

"Whoever shall this trumpet blow
Shall soon the giant overthrow,
And break the black enchantment straight,
So all shall be in happy state."

Jack had no sooner read this inscription, but he blew the trumpet, at which the foundation of the castle trembled, and the giant, with the conjurer, were tearing their hair, knowing their wicked reign was at an end. At which time the giant was stooping to take up his club;

Jack, at one blow with his sword of sharpness, cut off his head. The conjurer mounted into the air, and was carried away by a whirlwind. Thus was the enchantment broken, and every knight and lady who had been transformed into birds and beasts returned to their proper shapes, and the castle, though it seemed to be of a vast strength and bigness, vanished away like a cloud, whereon universal joy appeared among the released knights and ladies. This being done, the head of Galligantus was conveyed to the court of King Arthur the next day. Having refreshed the knights and ladies at the old man's habitation, Jack set forward to the court of King Arthur with those knights and ladies whom he delivered.

Coming to his Majesty, his fame rung through the court, and, as a reward of his services, the duke bestowed his daughter in marriage to Jack. The whole kingdom was filled with joy at the wedding; after which the king bestowed upon him a noble house, with a large estate, where he and his lady passed their days in great joy and happiness.

SIMPLE SIMON'S MISFORTUNES

AND HIS

WIFE MARGERY'S CRUELTY

WHICH BEGAN

The very next Morning after their Marriage.

CHAPTER I.

An Account of Simon's Wedding, and his Wife's Behaviour the Day after their Marriage.

Simon, the subject of our ensuing discourse, was a man very unfortunate many years after marriage, not only by crosses, but by the cruelty of Margery his severe wife—his wedding day being the best he saw in seven years after, for then he had all his friends about him. Rough Ralph the Fiddler and Will the Piper were appointed to make him and his guests merry.

Singing, dancing, and good feasting attended the day, which being ended, this loving couple went to bed, where their friends all left them.

But the morning was ushered in with a mighty storm, only because Simon put on his roast-meat clothes.

Thus she began the matter—" Why, how now, pray, and what is to-day, that you must put on your holiday clothes, with a pye-crust to you? What do you intend to do, say you, tell me quickly."

"Nothing," said Simon, " but to walk abroad with you, sweet wife, as it is common on the day after marriage."

"No, no," said Margery, " this must not, nor shall not be. It is very well known that I have brought you a very considerable fortune—forty shillings in money, and a good milch cow, four fat wethers, with half a dozen ewes and lambs; likewise, geese, hens, and turkeys; also a sow and pigs, with other moveables, worth more than any of your crook-back generation is able to give you. And do you think you shall lead as lewd a life now as you did before you married; but if you do, then say my name is not Margery. Now I've got you in the bands of matrimony I will make you know what it is to be married; therefore, to work you rascal, and take care that what I brought is not consumed; for, if you do not, what will become of your wife and children?"

Now, Simon looked liked one that had neither sense nor reason, but stood amazed, as if there had been a whole army of Billingsgate shrews. However, recollecting what he had heard about scolds, he muttered to himself, " Udswagers, I think I have got a woeful one now."

"What is that you say, sirrah?" said she.

"Nothing, dear wife, but what you say I allow to be true."

And so, taking his bag and bottle, he went forward to his daily labour: but, coming towards the lower end of the town, he chanced to meet old Jobson, a cobbler, a merry blade, who loved a cup of good ale.

"What! honest Simon," said Jobson, "I am glad to see you, for since our last meeting I hear you are married, and now I wish thee much happiness."

Now, old Jobson, being a merry fellow, invited Simon to take a flaggon of the best liquor that the next ale-house would afford, and there to drink to Margery's health.

Being merry in discourse, talking of the tricks and pranks they had played when bachelors.

Jobson, taking up the flaggon in his hand, said, "Come, here's to thee, honest Simon, and I wish thee better luck than Randal, thy old father-in-law, had with his wife; for she was such a scold that happy were they who lived out of the clamour of her noise. But without doubt thy dear wife may be of a milder spirit, and have more of her father's meekness than her mother's fury in her; but come, Simon, here's to thee and to thy dearly-beloved Margery."

Cries Simon, "If she was present how merry we should be; but, I fear, on the wrong side of the mouth."

"Well," said Jobson, "I vow I long to see her; and I verily believe she would be as glad to see me. I dare to say she will prove a very good wife."

"Truly, neighbour Jobson, I don't know; but if I have no better ending than beginning, I wish I had ended my life at the plough tail."

No sooner were these words out of his mouth but in comes Margery, with her gossips, whom Simon wished to see, forsooth. He wished her much joy, but Margery, in a woeful fury, snatched up Jobson's oaken staff from off the table, and gave poor Simon such a clank upon the noddle which made the blood spin out, saying, "Is this your work, sirrah!" Jobson, seeing so sudden an alteration, was affrighted, not knowing how to escape.

She then truned about to the left, saying, "Thou rogue and rascal, it is you that ruins all the good women's husbands in the town; therefore you shall not go unrewarded," giving him such strokes over his back and shoulders as caused poor Jobson to lay in bed almost a fortnight.

Simple Simon all this while not having any power to run away, but stood like one half frighted out of his wits, and trembling before his bride, with his hat in one hand and the flaggon in the other, begging her that she would be patient, and he would never offend her any more.

But she gave him a frown, and bid him begone about his business, which he immediately did. So then Margery and her friendly gossips had the whole apartment to themselves, where they sat till they were all as drunk as fish-women.

CHAPTER II.
She drags him up into the Chimney, and hangs him a Smoke-drying.

AT night, when he returned to his own home, Margery, by the help of a nap she had taken, was a little restored to her senses again; but yet, not forgetting the fault he had committed, she invented a new kind of punishment; for, having a wide chimney, wherein they used to dry bacon, she, taking him at a disadvantage, tied him hand and foot, bound him in a basket, and, by the help of a rope, drew him up to the beam in the chimney, and left him there to take his lodging the second night after his wedding, with a small, smoky fire under him, so that in the morning he almost reezed like to a red-herring. But in length of time he prevailed with his wife to show him so much pity as to let him down again.

"In love release me from this horrid smoke,
    And I will never more my wife provoke;
  She then did yield to let him down from thence,
    And said, " Be careful of the next offence."

Chapter III.
Simon loses a Sack of Corn that he was carrying to the Mill to have ground.

Not long after she sent him to the mill with a sack of corn, and bade him remember what she said to him, or else he should not go unpunished.

"Well," said Simon, "I hope I shall never offend thee any more."

For this promise she gave him a mess of milk, and when he had eaten all up he took the sack of corn upon his back, and went towards the mill, which stood about two miles from the house.

When Simon was got about half way he began to be weary, which was the forerunner of a great misfortune, for a man riding by, leading an empty horse towards the mill, perceived Simon weary of his load, told him he might lay it upon his spare horse, to which Simon willingly consented.

The man riding on, Simon could not pace with him, so desired him to leave it for him at the mill. He promised he would, but never intended to perform his promise.

Simon, thus loosing his sack of corn, knew not how to go home, or show his face before his wife, until he got two or three of his neighbours to go with him to beg for his pardon, and to help to make up the difference between them, which they did after a long parley. So that for this crime he passed unpunished.

Chapter IV.
Simon goes to the Market with his Basket of Eggs, breaks them all by the Way, and is set in the Stocks.

But, although he was not punished according to the severe correction he had formerly received, yet he did not escape the continual railings in his ears for several days after, ever and anon she crying out, "You sot, will you never be wise?"

"Yes, sweet Margery, dear Margery, I hope I shall some time."

"Well," says she, "I'll now try you once more. Here, take this basket of eggs, and go to the market and sell them, but be sure don't break them nor spend the money, for if you do, sorrow will be your sops, and you may expect to feel the weight of my hands more than ever you have done before.

At which harsh words he trembled much, and looked as white as his dear Margery's shift, for fear that he should miscarry with his basket of eggs, for he well knew that his wife would be sure to be as good as her promise.

Then Simon, taking his basket of eggs, trudged away to the market, but was no sooner come there than, seeing a vast crowd of people, he was resolved to see what was the matter.

When he came to the place he found that two butter-women had fallen out, and to that degree that they had taken one another by the que of their hair, and their fillets all flying about their ears; which Simon seeing he was moved with compassion, and ran to part them, but in vain; poor Simon was still unfortunate, and came off with a great loss, for one of the women pushed him down and broke his eggs.

Poor Simon was now almost distracted to see the ground, but whether it was the fear of the anger of his wife, or whether it was courage, thus it was, Simon ran in amongst them, and resolved to be revenged on them for the loss of his eggs.

Whilst they were in the fray the constable came, and, supposing them drunk, gave orders that they should all be set in the stocks together—Simon in the middle, and the women on each side—which was accordingly done; but they rang such a peal in Simon's ears that he was deaf for a fortnight after.

Being released, he ventured home again, dreading the

impending storm; but this was his comfort in the midst of all his hard fortune, that, though he might feel the force of her blows, still he would be deaf to her noise, being stunned by the women in the stocks.

CHAPTER V.
Simon's Wife Cudgels him severely for losing his Money.

AT length Simon coming home he met with his beloved wife Margery, who, seeing his dejected countenance, she began to mistrust something, and so, taking hold of his arm, she hauled him in for examination.

When Simon saw this he could not forbear weeping, and began to tell her a dismal story concerning the stocks; but she wanted the money for the eggs; but Simon, being deaf, could not hear her, which made her fall on him with such fury that he was obliged to run up stairs and jump out of the chamber window, which, when she saw, she followed him down the town, with a hundred boys and girls after them, Simon still crying out to the people, " You may see what it is to be married."

And her tone was, " You rascal; the money for my eggs," often giving him a crack on the crown.

At length it was his good hap to get away from her.

Night drawing on, and Simon not having one penny to help himself, was forced to make the best of a bad bargain, resolved for to lodge that night in a hog-stye amongst the swine.

And so the next morning, in the presence of some of his dearest friends, he begged pardon on his knees of his sweet, kind, and loving wife, Margery.

CHAPTER VI.
Simon loses his Wife's Pail, and at the same time burns out the Bottom of her Kettle.

MARGERY, being reconciled again on his humble petition, she charged him to be careful for the future that he did not offend her as he had done before, which he promised to observe. "Then, Simon," said she, "I am this day to go to a gossiping, and shall leave you at home to make a fire and hang on the kettle."

"Yes, sweet wife."

Now, Margery was no sooner gone but he made a fire and hung on the kettle. Then, taking the pail, he goes to the well to fetch some water, when there came an ox running down, and a butcher and his boy close after him, who called out to Simon to stop the ox, which he endeavoured to do, but the ox, giving them the slip, Simon ran in pursuit of him for the space of three or four miles, and, having secured him, the butcher gave him many thanks for his kindness.

So Simon returned back to the well, but his pail was lost, and he made sad lamentation for it, inquiring about it, but could not hear nothing of it; and as the old proverb says, "One sorrow never comes alone," for on going in doors the fire was flaming, and the bottom of the kettle was quite burnt out.

At the sight of this he fell to wringing his hands and crying out with a lamentable tone, "None was so unfortunate as poor Simon. What shall I say to my wife when she comes? First, I have lost my pail; and, second, I have let the bottom of the kettle be burnt out. Here will be a sad reckoning for these misfortunes."

Just in the middle of these lamentations in comes Margery, who, having heard him, came armed and fitted for the fray.

"How now, sirrah," said she, "has this been the care you promised of my business?" and with that let fly an earthen pot at his head, which caused the blood to run about his ears.

This done, she took him by the collar, and cuft him about the kitchen at a most terrible rate, Simon crying for mercy, but cruel Margery still increased his misery, till the neighbours came, persuading Margery to be satisfied, "for," said they, "it was but a mischance."

"A rascal," said she, "for I can set him about nothing, but thus he serves me."

They still interceded for Simon, until at length she excused him.

CHAPTER VII.

Simon's Wife sends him to buy Soap, but, going over a Bridge, he lets his Money fall into the River; and of a Ragman's running away with his Clothes.

MARGERY, calling Simon to her, said, "Will you never be careful in anything I set you about?"

"Yes, dear wife, I hope I shall."

"Why, then," said she, "take this money. I have tied it in a clout, that you may not lose it. Therefore, go you to the market, and make all the haste you can, and get me some soap."

"I will, sweet wife," quoth he, and with that he went as fast as he could.

Now, on his way he was to pass over a bridge, and, coming to the middle of it, a flight of crows flew over his head, which so frightened him that he let fall his money.

This was the beginning of a new sorrow. He stood awhile, and knew not what course to take. At length he resolved to pull off his clothes and jump into the water and search for it. Now, as he was searching for his money, an old ragman came by, and put his clothes into a bag.

Simon, seeing this, pursued him, but in vain, and was forced to return home naked, which his wife seeing fell in a most horrible sweat, and, taking the dog-whip, she so jerked poor Simon about, making him to dance the canaries for two hours, till he cried out, "Good wife, forbear!" but she cried out, "You rascal! where is my money, and your clothes?" Thus she continued until she was tired, and he heartily begged her pardon.

THE ADVENTURES

OF

BAMFYLDE MOORE CAREW,

WHO WAS FOR MORE THAN FORTY YEARS

KING OF THE BEGGARS.

CHAPTER I.

Carew's Boyhood. And how he became a Gipsy.

MR. BAMFYLDE MOORE CAREW was the son of a clergyman near Tiverton, in Devonshire, and born in 1693. He was tall and majestic, his limbs strong and well-proportioned, his features regular, and his countenance open and ingenious, bearing the resemblance of a good-natured mind. At twelve years old he was put to Tiverton school, where he soon got a considerable knowledge of the Latin and Greek tongues, so as to be fitted for the University, that in due time he might be fitted for the church, for which his father designed him; but here a new exercise engaged his attention, namely, that of hunting, in which he soon made a prodigious progress. The Tiverton scholars had command of a fine cry of hounds, which gave Carew a frequent opportunity of exercising his beloved employment, and getting acquainted with John Martin, Thomas Coleman, and John Escott, young gentlemen of the best rank and fortune. One day a farmer came to the school and complained of a deer, with a collar round its neck, that he had seen running through his grounds, and had done him much damage, desiring them to hunt it down and kill it. They, wishing for no better sport, on the next day put the old farmer's request into execution, in doing of which they did much damage to the neighbouring grounds, whose owners, together with Colonel Nutcombe, to whom the deer belonged, came and complained to the schoolmaster of the injuries they had suffered by his scholars; they were very severely reprimanded and hard threatened for the same. The resentment of the present reproof and the fear of future chastisement made them abscond from the school; and going into a brick alehouse, about half a mile from Tiverton, there they accidentally fell in company with some gipsies, who were then feasting and carousing. This company consisted of seventeen, who were met on purpose for festivity and jollity; which, by plenty of meat, fowl, flowing cups of beer, cider, etc., they seemed to enjoy to their hearts' content. In short, the freedom, mirth, and pleasure that appeared among them, invited our youngsters to enlist into their company: which, on communicating to the gipsies, they would not believe them, as thinking they jested; but on tarrying with them all night and continuing in the same mind next morning, they at length thought them serious and encouraged them; and, after going through the requisite ceremonials and administering to them the proper oath, they admitted them into their number.

The reader will, no doubt, wonder to hear of the ceremonials and oaths among gipsies and beggars, but that will cease on being informed, that these people are subject to a form of government and laws peculiar to themselves, and pay due obedience to one who is styled their king; to which honour Carew in a short time arrived, after having by many acts proved himself worthy of it. The substance of them is this—Strong love and mutual regard for each member in particular, and the whole community in general; which, being taught them in their infancy, grows up with them, prevents oppression, frauds, and over-reaching one another, which is common among other people, and tends to the very worst of evils. This happiness and temper of mind so wrought on Carew as to occasion the strongest attachment to them for forty years, refusing very large offers that had been made to him to quit their society.

Being thus initiated into the ancient society of gipsies, who take their name from Egypt—a place well known to abound in learning, and the inhabitants of which country travel about from place to place to communicate knowledge to mankind—Carew did not long continue in it before he was consulted in important matters; particularly Madam Musgrove, of Monkton, near Taunton, hearing of his fame, sent for him to consult him in an affair of difficulty. When he was come, she informed him that she suspected a large quantity of money was buried somewhere about her house, and if he would acquaint her with the particular place, she would handsomly reward him. Carew consulted the secrets of his art on this occasion, and, after a long study, he informed the lady that under a laurel tree in the garden lay the treasure she sought for; but that she must not seek it till such a day and hour. The lady rewarded him with twenty guineas; but, whether Carew mistook his calculations or the lady mistook her lucky hour, we cannot tell, but truth obliges us to say, the lady having dug below the root of the laurel tree she could not find the treasure.

When he was further initiated, he was consulted in important matters and met with better success; generally giving satisfaction by his wise and sagacious answers. In the meantime his parents sorrowed after him, as one that was no more, having advertised him in all the public papers and sent messengers after him to almost every part of the kingdom; till about a year and a half afterwards, when Carew, hearing of their grief, and being struck with tenderness thereat, repaired to his father's house. He was so disguised they did not know him, but when they did their joy was beyond expressing, tenderly embracing him, bedewing his cheeks with tears and kisses, and all his friends and neighbours showed every demonstration of joy at his return. His parents did everything to render home agreeable to him; but the uncommon pleasure he had enjoyed in the community he had left, their simplicity, freedom, sincerity, mirth, and frequent change of habitation, and the secret presages of the honour he has since arrived at, sickened and palled all other diversions, and at last prevailed over his filial duty, for one day, without taking leave of his friends or parents, he went back to them again, where he was heartily welcomed, both to his own and their satisfaction, they being glad to regain one who was likely to become so useful a member of their community.

CHAPTER II.

Carew's First Adventure in his New Profession.

Carew being again initiated among them, at the first general assembly of the gipsies, took the oaths of allegiance to their sovereign, by whom he was soon sent out on a cruise against their enemies. Carew now set his wits to work how to succeed: so equipping himself with an old pair of trousers, a piece of a jacket, just enough to cover his nakedness, stockings full of holes, and an old cap, he forgot both friends and family and became nothing more or less than an unfortunate shipwrecked seaman. In this, his first excursion, he gained much credit, artfully imitating passes and certificates that were necessary for him to travel unmolested. After a month's travel he happened to meet with his old school-fellow Coleman, who had once left the gipsies' society, but, for the same reason as himself, returned to them again. Great was their joy at meeting, and they agreed to travel some time together; so entering Exeter, they, in one day, raised a contribution of several pounds.

Having obtained all he could from this stratagem, he then became a plain, honest farmer, whose grounds had been overflowed, and cattle drowned; his dejected countenance and mournful tale, together with a wife and seven helpless infants being partakers of his misfortunes, gained him both pity and profit.

Having obtained a considerable booty by these two stratagems, he returned to his companions, where he was received with great applause; and, as a mark of their respect, seated him next the king. He soon became a great man in the profession and confined not himself from doing good to others, when it did not infringe upon the community of which he was a member.

His next stratagem was to become a madman; so stripping himself quite naked, he threw a blanket over him and then he was, " Poor mad Tom, whom the foul fiend had led through fire and through flame! through fire and whirlpool, over bog and quagmire; that hath laid knives under his pillow, and halters in his pew; set ratsbane for his porridge, and made him proud at heart to ride on a bay trotting-horse over four-inch bridges; to curse his own shadow for a traitor; who eats the swimming-frog, the toad, the tadpole, the wall-newt, and the water-newt; that in the fury of his heart, when the foul fiend rages, swallows the old rat and ditch dog; drinks the green mantle of the standing pool:

And mice and rats, and such like gear,
Have been Tom's food for seven long year.
O do de, do de, do de! bless thee! from whirlwind, star-blasting, and taking! Do poor Tom some charity, whom the foul fiend vexes. There I could have him now—and there!—and there!—and here again!—and there!—Through the sharp hawthorn blows the cold wind—Tom's a cold!—who gives anything to poor Tom?"

In this character, with such like expressions, he entered the houses of both small and great, claiming kindred to them, and committing all kinds of frantic actions, such as beating himself, offering to eat coals of fire, running against the wall, and tearing to pieces whatever garments were given to him to cover his nakedness; by which means he raised considerable contributions.

He never was more happy than when he was engaged in some adventure; therefore he was always very diligent to inquire when any accident happened, especially fire, to which he would immediately repair, and, getting information of the causes, names, trades, and circumstances of the unhappy sufferers, he would assume one of them, and burning some part of his clothes, by way of demonstration, run to some place distant, pass for one of them, gain credit and get much profit. Under this character he had once the boldness to address a justice, who was the terror and professed enemy to all the gipsies, yet he so well managed the affair, that in a long examination he made him believe he was an honest miller, whose house, mill and substance had been consumed by fire, occasioned by the negligence of the apprentice; and accordingly, got a bountiful sum for his relief, the justice not in the least suspecting a defraud.

He had such wonderful facility in every character he assumed, that he even deceived those who thought themselves so well acquainted with him, that it was impossible for him to impose on them.

Coming one day to Squire Portman's house at Blandford, in the character of a rat-catcher, with a hair cap on his head, a buff girdle about his waste, a little box by his side, and a tame rat in his hand, he goes boldly up to the house, where he had been well known before, and meeting the squire, Parson Bryant, and one Mr. Pleydell, of Milbourn, and some other gentlemen, he asked them if they had any rats to kill. "Do you understand the business well?" says the squire. "Yes, an please your honour," replied Carew, "I have been a rat-catcher for many years, and I have been employed in his majesty's yards and ships." "Well," says the squire, "go in and get some vituals, and after dinner we will try your abilities." He was accordingly called into the parlour, where were a large company of gentlemen and ladies. "Well, honest rat-catcher," says the squire, "can you lay any scheme to kill the rats without hurting my dogs?" "Yes, yes," cries Carew, "I can lay it where even the rats cannot climb to reach it." "What countryman are you?" "A Devonshire man, an please your honour." "What is your name?" Here our hero began to perceive that he was discovered, by the smilings and whisperings of several gentlemen, and he very composedly answered, "My name is Bamfylde Moore Carew." This occasioned much mirth, and Mr. Pleydell expressed extraordinary pleasure. He had often wished to see him but never had. "Yes, you have," replied Carew, "and given me a suit of clothes. Do you not remember meeting a poor wretch one day at your stable door, with a stocking round his head, an old mantle over his shoulders, without shirt, stockings, or scarce any shoes, who told you he was a poor unfortunate man, cast away upon the coast, with sixteen more of the crew who were all drowned; you, believing the story, generously relieved me with a guinea and a good suit of clothes." "I well remember it," said Mr. Pleydell, "but, on this discovery, it is impossible to deceive me so again, come in whatever shape you will." The company blamed him for thus boasting, and secretly prevailed upon Carew to put his art in practice to convince him of the fallacy thereof: to which he agreed, and in a few days after appointing the company present to be at Mr. Pleydell's house, he put the following scheme into execution.

He shaved himself closely, and clothed himself in an old woman's apparel, with a high-crowned hat, and a large dowdy under his chin; then, taking three children from among his fraternity, he tied two on his back and one under his arm. Thus accoutred, he comes to Mr. Pleydell's door, and pinching one of the brats, set it a roaring; this gave the alarm to the dogs, who came out with open mouths, so that the whole company was soon alarmed. Out came the maid saying, "Carry away the children, good woman, they disturb the ladies." "God bless their ladyships," said Carew, "I am the poor unfortunate grandmother of these helpless infants, whose mother and all they had were burnt at the dreadful fire at Kirkton, and hope the good ladies, for Heaven's sake, will bestow something on the poor, famishing, starving infants." In goes the maid with this affecting story to the ladies, while Carew keeps pinching the children to make them cry, and the maid soon returned with half-a-crown and some good broth, which he thankfully received, and went into the courtyard to sit down and sup them, as perceiving the gentlemen were not at home. He had not long been there before they came, when one of them accosted him thus—"Where do you come from, old woman?" "From Kirkton, please your honours," said he, "where the poor unhappy mother of these helpless infants was burnt in the flames and all she had consumed." "There has been more money collected for Kirkton than ever Kirkton was worth," said the gentleman. However, they gave the supposed old grandmother a shilling, commiserating the hard case of her and her poor helpless infants, which he thankfully received, pretending to go away; but the gentlemen were hardly got into the house, before their ears were suddenly saluted with a "tantivy, tantivy," and a "halloo" to the dogs; on which they turned about, supposing it to be some other sportsmen; but seeing nobody, they imagined it to be Carew, in the disguise of the old Kirkton grandmother; so bidding the servants fetch him back, he was brought into the parlour among them all, and confessed himself to be the famous Mr. Bamfylde Moore Carew, to the astonishment and mirth of them all; who well rewarded him for the diversion he had afforded them.

In like manner he raised a contribution twice in one day of Mr. Jones, near Bristol. In the morning, with a sooty face, leather apron, a dejected countenance, and a woollen cap, he was generously relieved as an unfortunate blacksmith, whose all had been consumed by fire. In the afternoon he exchanged his legs for crutches, and, with a dejected countenance, pale face, and every sign of pain, he became a disabled tinner, incapable of maintaining a wife and seven small children, by the damps and hardships he had suffered in the mines; and so well acted his part, that the tinner got as well relieved in the afternoon as the blacksmith in the morning.

These successful stratagems gained him high applause and honour in the community of gipsies. He soon became the favourite of their king, who was very old and decrepid, and had always some honourable mark of distinction assigned him at their assemblies.

Being one morning near the seat of his good friend, Sir William Courtney, he was resolved to pay him three visits that day. He therefore puts on a parcel of rags, and goes to him with a piteous, mean, dismal countenance, and deplorable tale, and got half-a-crown from him, telling him he had met with great misfortunes at sea. At noon he puts on a leather apron scorched with fire, and with a dejected countenance goes to him again, and was relieved as an unfortunate shoemaker, who had been burnt out of his house and all he had. In the afternoon he goes again in trimmed clothes, and desiring admittance to Sir William, with a modest grace and submissive eloquence, he repeats his misfortunes, as the supercargo of a vessel which had been cast away and his whole effects lost.

Sir William, seeing his genteel appearance and behaviour, treated him with respect and gave him a guinea at his departure. There were several gentlemen at dinner with Sir William at that time, none of whom had any knowledge of him except the Rev. Mr. Richards, who did not discover him till he was gone; upon which a servant was despatched to desire him to come back, which he did; and when he entered the room they were very merry with him and requested him to give an account how he got his fine clothes, and of his stratagems, with the success of them. He asked Sir William if he had not given half-a-crown in the morning to a beggar, and about noon relieved a poor unfortunate shoemaker. "I did," said Sir William. "Behold him before you," said Carew, " in this fine embroidered coat, as a broken merchant." The company would not believe him; so to convince them, he re-assumed those characters again, to their no small mirth and satisfaction.

Chapter III.
Carew made King of the Beggars.

On the death of the king of the gipsies, named Clause Patch, our hero was a candidate to succeed him, and exhibited to the electors a long list of bold and ingenious stratagems which he had executed, and made so graceful and majestic an appearance in his person, that he had a considerable majority of voices, though there were ten candidates for the same honour; on which he was declared duly elected and hailed by the whole assembly—King of the Gipsies. The public register of their acts being immediately committed to his care, and homage done him by all the assembly, the whole concluded by rejoicings.

Though Mr. Carew was now privileged, by the dignity of his office, from going on any cruise, and was provided with everything necessary by the joint contribution of the community, yet he did not give himself up to indolence. Our hero, though a king, was as active in his stratagems as ever, and ready to encounter any difficulty which seemed to promise success.

Mr. Carew being in the town of South Molton, in Devonshire, and having been ill-used by an officer there called the bellman, resolved on the following stratagem by way of revenge. It was at that time reported that a gentleman of the town, lately buried, walked nightly in the churchyard; and as the bellman was obliged by his nightly duty to go through it just at the very hour of one, Mr. Carew repaired thither a little before the time, and stripping in his shirt, lay down upon the gentleman's grave. Soon after, hearing the bellman approach, he raised himself up with a solemn slowness, which the bellman beholding, by the glimmerings of the moon through a dark cloud, was terribly frightened, so took to his heels and ran away. In his fright he looked behind him, and seeing the ghost following him, dropped his bell and ran the faster; which Carew seized on as a trophy, and forbore any further pursuit. The bellman did not stop till he reached home, where he obstinately affirmed he had seen the gentleman's ghost, who had taken away the bell, which greatly alarmed the whole town.

Coming to the seat of Squire Rhodes, in Devonshire, and knowing he had lately married a Dorsetshire lady, he thought proper to become a Dorsetshire man of Lyme, the place of the lady's nativity; and meeting the squire and his bride, he gave them to understand that he was lost in a vessel belonging to Lyme, Captain Courtney, commander. The squire and his lady gave him half-a-crown each, for country sake, and entertained him at their house.

Our hero, exercising his profession at Milbury, where the squire's father lived, and to whom the son was come on a visit, Mr. Carew made application to him, and knocking at the door, on its being opened, saw the young squire sitting alone, whom Mr. Rhodes interrupted by saying he "was twice in one day imposed on by that rogue Carew, of whose gang you may likely be; besides, I do not live here, but am a stranger." In the meantime comes the old squire, with a bottle of wine in his hand, giving Carew a wink to let him understand he knew him, and then very gravely inquired into the circumstances of his misfortunes, and also of the affairs and inhabitants of Dartmouth, from whence he pretended to have sailed several times, of all which he gave a full and particular account, whereupon the old squire gave him half-a-crown, and the young one the same; on which Carew and the old man burst into laughter, and discovered the whole affair, at which Squire Rhodes was a little chagrined at being imposed on a third time; but, on recollecting the expertness of the performer, was well satisfied, and they spent the remainder of the day in mirth and jollity.

At Bristol he dressed himself like a poor mechanic, and then going out into the streets, acted the religious madman, talking in a raving manner about Messrs. Whitfield and Wesley, as though he was disordered in his mind by their preaching; calling in a furious manner, every step, upon the Virgin Mary, Pontius Pilate, and Mary Magdalene, and acting every part of a man religiously mad; sometimes walking with his eyes fixed upon the ground, and then on a sudden he would break out in some passionate expressions about religion. This behaviour greatly excited the curiosity and compassion of the people; some of them talked to him, but he answered everything they said in a wild and incoherent manner; and, as compassion is generally the forerunner of charity, he was relieved by most of them.

Next morning he appeared in a morning gown, still acting the madman, and addressed himself to all the posts of the street, as if they were saints, lifting up his hands and eyes to heaven, in a fervent but distracted manner, and making use of so many extravagant gestures, that he astonished the whole city. Going through Castle Street he met the Rev. Mr. Bone, whom he accosted with his arms thrown around him, and insisted, in a raving manner, he should tell him who was the father of the morning star; which frightened the parson so much, that he took to his heels and ran for it, Carew running after him, till the parson was obliged to take shelter in a house.

Having well recruited his pocket by this stratagem, he

left Bristol next day, and travelled towards Bath, acting the madman all the way till he came to Bath: as soon as he came there, he inquired for Dr. Coney's, and being directed to his house, found two brother mendicants at the door. After they had waited some time, the servant brought out each of them a halfpenny, for which his brother mendicants were very thankful. But Carew gave his halfpenny to one of them; then knocking at the door, and the maid coming out again, "Tell your master," says he, "I am not a halfpenny man, but that my name is Bamfylde Moore Carew, king of the mendicants;" which being told, the doctor came out with one of his daughters and gave him sixpence and a mug of drink, for which he returned them thanks.

Mr. Carew happening to be in the city of Wells on a Sunday, was told the bishop was to preach that morning, on which he slipped on a black waistcoat and morning gown, and ran out to meet the bishop as he was walking in procession, and addressed himself to him as a poor unhappy man, whose misfortunes had turned his brains; which the bishop hearing gave him half-a-crown.

It was in Newcastle-upon-Tyne that he became enamoured with the daughter of Mr. Glady, an eminent apothecary and surgeon there. This young lady had charms sufficient to captivate the heart of any man susceptible of love; and they made so deep an impression upon him, that they wholly effaced every object which before had created any desire in him, and never permitted any other to raise them afterwards; for, wonderful to tell, we have, after about thirty years' enjoyment, seen him lament her occasional absence, almost with tears, and talk of her with all the fondness of one who has been in love with her but three days. Our hero tried all love's persuasions with his fair one in an honourable way, and, as his person was very engaging and his appearance genteel, he did not find her greatly averse to his proposals. As he was aware that his being of the community of gipsies might prejudice her against him, without examination, he passed with her for the mate of a collier's vessel, in which he was supported by Captain Lawn, in whose vessel they set sail; and the very winds being willing to favour these happy lovers, they had an exceedingly quick passage to Dartmouth, where they landed. In a few days they set out for Bath, where they lawfully solemnized their nuptials with great gaiety and splendour; and nobody at that time could conjecture who they were, which was the cause of much speculation and false surmises.

Some time after this he took his passage at Folkstone, in Kent, for Boulogne, in France, where he arrived safe and proceeded to Paris and other noted cities of that kingdom. His habit was now tolerably good, his countenance grave, his behaviour sober and decent—pretending to be a Roman Catholic, who had left England, his native country, out of an ardent zeal for spending his days in the bosom of the Catholic church. This story readily gained belief: his zeal was universally applauded, and handsome contributions made for him. But, at the time he was so zealous a Roman Catholic, with a little change of habit, he used to address those English he heard of in any place, as a Protestant and shipwrecked seaman; and had the good fortune to meet with an English physician at Paris, to whom he told this deplorable tale, who not only relieved him very handsomely, but recommended him to that noble pattern of unexhausted benevolence, Mrs. Horner, who was then on her travels, from whom he received ten guineas, and from some other company with her five more.

It was about this time he became acquainted with the Hon. Sir William Weem, in the following manner:—Being at Watchett, in Somersetshire, near the seat of that gentleman, he resolved to pay him a visit. Putting on, therefore, a jacket and a pair of trousers, he made the best of his way to Sir William's seat, and luckily met Sir William,

Lord Bolingbroke, and several other gentlemen and clergy, with some commanders of vessels, walking in the park. Carew approached Sir William with a great deal of seeming fearfulness and respect, and with much modesty acquainted him he was a Silverton man, that he was the son of one of his tenants named Moore—had been to Newfoundland, and in his passage homeward, the vessel was run down by a French ship in a fog, and only he and two more were saved; but being put on board an Irish vessel, were carried into Ireland, and from thence landed at Watchett. Sir William hearing this, asked him a great many questions concerning the inhabitants of Silverton, who were most of them his own tenants, and of the principal gentlemen in the neighbourhood; all whom Carew was well acquainted with and therefore gave satisfactory answers. Sir William at last asked him if he knew Bickley, and if he knew the parson thereof. Carew replied that he knew him very well, and so indeed he might as it was no other than his own father. Sir William then inquired what family he had, and whether he had not a son named Bamfylde, and what became of him. "Your honour," replied he, "means the beggar and dog-stealer—I don't know what has become of him, but it is a wonder if he is not hanged by this time." "No, I hope not," replied Sir William, "I should be glad, for his family's sake, to see him at my house." Having satisfactorily answered many other questions, Sir William generously relieved him with a guinea, and Lord Bolingbroke followed his example; the other gentlemen and clergy contributed according to their different ranks. Sir William then ordered him to go to his house and tell the butler to entertain him, which he accordingly did, and set himself down with great comfort.

Having heard that young Lord Clifford, his first cousin (who had just returned from his travels abroad), was at his seat at Callington, about four miles from Bridgewater, he resolved to pay him a visit. In his way thither resided parson Carson, who, being one whom nature had made up in a hurry without a heart, Mr. Carew had never been able to obtain anything off him, even under the most moving appearance of distress, but a small cup of drink. Stopping now in his way, he found the parson was gone to Lord Clifford's; but, being saluted at the door by a fine black spaniel, with almost as much crustiness as he would have been had his master been at home, he thought himself under no stronger obligation of observing the strict laws of honour, than the parson did of hospitality; and therefore soon charmed the crossness of the spaniel and made him follow him to Bridgewater.

Having secured the spaniel and passed the night merrily at Bridgewater, he set out the next morning for Lord Clifford's, and in his way called upon the parson again, who very crustily told him he had lost his dog, and supposed some of his gang had stolen him; to which Mr. Carew very calmly replied, "What was he to his dog, or what was his dog to him? if he would make him drink it was well, for he was very dry." At last, with the use of much rhetoric, he got a cup of small drink; then, taking leave of him, he went to the Red Lion, in the same parish, where he stayed some time. In the meantime, down ran the parson to my Lord Clifford's, to acquaint him that Mr. Carew was in the parish and to advise him to take care of his dogs; so that Mr. Carew, coming down immediately after, found a servant with one dog in his arms, and another with another, here one stood whistling and another calling, and both my lord and his brother were running about to seek after their favourites.

Mr. Carew asked my lord what was the meaning of this hurry, and if his dogs were cripples, because he saw several carried in the servants' arms, adding, he hoped his lordship did not imagine he was come to steal any of them. Upon which his lordship told him, that parson Carson had advised him to be careful, as he had lost his spaniel but the day before. "It may be so," replied he, "the parson knows but little of me, or the laws of our community, if he is ignorant that with us ingratitude is unknown, and the property of our friends always sacred." His lordship, hearing this, entertained him very handsomely, and both himself and his brother made him a present.

On his return home, he reflected how idly he had spent the prime of life; and recovering from a severe illness, he came to a resolution of resigning the Egyptian sceptre. The assembly, finding him determined, reluctantly acquiesced, and he departed amidst the applause and sighs of his subjects.

Our adventurer, finding the air of the town not rightly to agree with him, and the death of some of his relations rendering his circumstances quite easy, he retired to the western parts, to a neat purchase he had made, and there he ended his days, beloved and esteemed by all; leaving his daughter (his wife dying some time before him) a genteel fortune, who was married to a neighbouring young gentleman.

THE COMICAL SAYINGS

OF

PADDY FROM CORK

WITH HIS

COAT BUTTONED BEHIND

Being an Elegant Conference between English Tom and Irish Teague;

WITH PADDY'S CATECHISM,

And his Supplication when a Mountain Sailor.

PART I.

Tom. Good morrow, sir. This is a very cold day.

Teag. Arra, dear honey, yesternight was a very cold morning.

Tom. Well, brother traveller, of what nation art thou?

Teag. Arra, dear shoy, I came from my own kingdom.

Tom. Why, I know that; but where is thy kingdom?

Teag. Allelieu, dear honey, don't you know Cork in Ireland?

Tom. You fool, Cork is not a kingdom, but a city.

Teag. Then, dear shoy, I'm sure it is in a kingdom.

Tom. And what is the reason you have come and left your own dear country?

Teag. Arra, dear honey, by Shaint Patrick, they have got such comical laws in our country that they will put a man to death in perfect health; so, to be free and plain with you, neighbour, I was obliged to come away, for I did not choose to stay among such a people that can hang a poor man when they please, if he either steals, robs, or kills a man.

Tom. Ay, but I take you to be more of an honest man than to steal, rob, or kill a man.

Teag. Honest, I am perfectly honest. When I was but a child my mother would have trusted me with a house full of mill-stones.

Tom. What was the matter? Was you guilty of nothing?

Teag. Arra, dear honey, I did harm to nobody, but fancied an old gentleman's gun, and afterwards made it my own.

Tom. Very well, boy, and did you keep it so?

Teag. Keep it? I would have kept it with all my heart while I lived. Death itself could not have parted us; but the old rogue, the gentleman, being a justice of peace himself, had me tried for the rights of it, and how I came by it, and so took it again.

Tom. And how did you clear yourself without punishment?

Teag. Arra, dear shoy, I told him a parcel of lies, but they would not believe me, for I said that I got it from my father when it was a little pistol, and I had kept it till it had grown a gun, and was designed to use it well until it had grown a big cannon, and then sell it to the military. They all fell a-laughing at me as I had been a fool, and bade me go home to my mother and clean the potatoes.

Tom. How long is it since you left your own country?

Teag. Arra, dear honey, I do not mind whether it be a fortnight or four months; but I think myself it is a long time. They tell me my mother is dead since, but I won't believe it until I get a letter from her own hand, for she is a very good scholar, suppose she can neither write nor read.

Tom. Was you ever in England before?

Teag. Ay, that I was, and in Scotland too.

Tom. And were they kind to you when you were in Scotland?

Teag. They were that kind that they kicked me, and the reason was because I would not pay the whole of the liquor that was drunk in the company, though the landlord and his two sons got mouthful about of it all, and I told them it was a trick upon travellers first to drink his liquor, and then to kick him out of doors.

Tom. I really think they have used you badly, but could you not beat them.

Teag. That's what I did, beat them all to their own contentment; but there was one of them stronger than me who would have killed me if the other two had not pulled me away, and I had to run for it till his passion was over. Then they made us drink and gree again; we shook hands, and made a bargain never to harm other more; but this bargain did not last long, for, as I was kissing his mouth, by Shaint Patrick I bit his nose, which caused him to beat me very sore for my pains.

Tom. Well, Paddy, what calling was you when in Scotland?

Teag. Why, sir, I was no business at all, but what do you call the green tree that's like a whin bush, people makes a thing to sweep the house of it?

Tom. O, yes, Paddy, they call it the broom.

Teag. Ay, ay, you have it, I was a gentleman's broom, only waited on his horses, and washed the dishes for the cook; and when my master rode a-hunting I went behind with the dogs.

Tom. O, yes, Paddy, it was the groom you mean. But I fancy you was cook's mate or kitchen boy.

Teag. No, no, it was the broom that I was; and if I had stayed there till now I might have been advanced as high as my master, for the ladies loved me so well that they laughed at me.

Tom. They might admire you for a fool.

Teag. What, sir, do you imagine that I am not a fool?

No, no; my master asked counsel of me in all his matters, and I always give him a reason for everything. I told him one morning that he went too soon to the hunting, that the hares were not got out of their beds, and neither the barking of horns nor the blowing of dogs could make them rise, it was such a cold morning that night; so they all ran away that we catched, when we did not see them. Then my master told my words to several gentlemen that were at dinner, and they admired me for want of judgment, for my head was all of a lump, adding they were going a-fishing along with my master and me in the afternoon; but I told them that it was a very unhappy thing for any man to go a-hunting in the morning and a-fishing in the afternoon. They would try it, but they had better stayed at home, for it came on a most terrible fine night of south-west rain, and even down wind; so the fishes got all below the water to keep themselves dry from the shower, and we catched them all, but got none.

Tom. How long did you serve that gentleman, Paddy?

Teag. Arra, dear honey, I was with him six weeks, and he beat me seven times.

Tom. For what did he beat you? Was it for your madness and foolish tricks?

Teag. Dear shoy, it was not, but for being too inquisitive, and going sharply about business. First, he sent me to the post office to inquire if there were any letters for him; so when I came there, said I, "Is there any letters here for my master to day?" Then they asked who was my master. "Sir," said I, "it is very bad manners in you to ask any gentleman's name." At this they laughed, mocking me, and said they could give me none if I would not tell my master's name; so I returned to my master and told him the impudence of the fellow, who would give me no letters unless I would tell him your name, master. My master at this flew in a passion, and kicked me down stairs, saying, "Go, you rogue, and tell my name directly. How can the gentleman give letters when he knows not who is asking for them?" Then I returned and told my master's name; so they told me there was one for him. I looked at it, being very small, and, asking the price of it, they told me it was sixpence. "Sixpence," said I; "will you take sixpence for that small thing, and selling bigger ones for twopence. Faith, I am not such a big fool. You think to cheat me now. This is not a conscionable way of dealing. I'll acquaint my master with it first." So I came and told my master how they would have sixpence for his letter, and was selling bigger ones for twopence. He took up my head and broke his cane with it, calling me a thousand fools, saying the man was more just than to take anything but the right for it; but I was sure there was none of them right, buying and selling such dear pennyworths. So I came again for my dear sixpence letter; and, as the fellow was shuffling through a parcel of them, seeking for it again, to make the best of a dear market, I picked up two, and home I comes to my master, thinking he would be pleased with what I had done. 'Now," said I, "master, I think I have put a trick upon them fellows for selling the letter to you." "What have you done." "I have only taken other two letters. Here's one for you, master, to help your dear pennyworth, and I'll send the other to my mother to see whether she be dead or alive, for she's always angry I don't write to her." I had not the word well spoken till he got up his stick and beat me heartily for it, and sent me back to the fellows again with the two. I had a very ill will to go, but nobody would buy them of me.

Tom. Well, Paddy, I think you was to blame, and your master, too, for he ought to have taught you how to go about these affairs, and not beat you so.

Teag. Arra, dear honey, I had too much wit of my own to be teached by him, or anybody else. He began to instruct me after that how I should serve the table, and such nasty things as those. One night I took ben a roasted fish in one hand and a piece of bread in the other. The old gentleman was so saucy he would not take it, and told me I should bring nothing to him without a trencher below it. The same night, as he was going to bed, he called for his slippers; so I clapt a trencher below the slippers, and ben I goes. No sooner did I enter the room than he threw the trencher at me, which broke both my head and the trencher at one blow. "Now," said I, "the evil one is in my master altogether, for what he commands at one time he countermands at another." Next day I went with him to the market to buy a sack of potatoes. I went to the potato-monger, and asked what he took for the full of a Scot's cog. He weighed them in. He asked no less than fourpence. "Fourpence!" said I; "if I were but in Dublin I could get the double of that for nothing, and in Cork and Linsale far cheaper. Them is but small things like pease," said I, "but the potatoes in my country is as big as your head—fine meat, all made up in blessed mouthfuls." The potato merchant called me a liar, and my master called me a fool; so the one fell a-kicking me and the other a-cuffing me. I was in such bad bread among them that I called myself both a liar and a fool to get off alive.

Tom. And how did you carry your potatoes home from the market?

Teag. Arra, dear shoy, I carried the horse and them both, besides a big loaf, and two bottles of wine; for I put the old horse on my back, and drove the potatoes before me; and when I tied the load to the loaf, I had nothing to do but to carry the bottle in my hand; but bad luck to the way as I came home, for a nail out of the heel of my foot sprung a leak in my brogue, which pricked the very bone, bruised the skin, and made my brogue itself to blood; and I having no hammer by me, but a hatchet I left at home, I had to beat down the nail with the bottom of the bottle; and by the book, dear shoy, it broke to pieces, and scattered the wine in my mouth.

Tom. And how did you recompense your master for the loss of the bottle of wine?

Teague. Arra, dear shoy, I had a mind to cheat him, and myself too, so I took the bottle to a blacksmith, and desired him to mend it, that I might go to the butcher and get it full of bloody water; but he told me he could not work in anything but steel and iron. "Arra," said I, "if I were in my own kingdom, I could get a blacksmith who would make a bottle out of a stone, and a stone out of nothing."

Tom. And how did you trick your master out of it?

Teag. Why, the old rogue began to chide me, asking me what way I broke it. Then I held up the other as high as my head, and let it fall to the ground on a stone, which broke it all to pieces likewise. "Now," said I, "master, that's the way," and he beat me very heartily until I had to shout out mercy and murder all at once.

Tom. Why did you not leave him when he used you so badly?

Teag. Arra, dear shoy, I could never think to leave him while I could eat; he gave me so many good victuals, and promised to prefer me to be his own bone-picker. But, by Shaint Patrick, I had to run away with my life or all was done, else I had lost my dear shoul and body too by him, and then come home much poorer than I went away. The great big bitch dog, which was my master's best beloved, put his head into a pitcher to lick out some milk, and when it was in he could not get it out; and I, to save the pitcher, got the hatchet and cut off the dog's head, and then I had to break the pitcher to get out the head. By this I lost both the dog and the pitcher. My master, hearing of this, swore he would cut the head off me, for the poor dog was made useless, and could not see to follow anybody for want of his eyes. And when I heard of this, I ran away with my own head, for, if I had wanted it, I had lost my eyes too, then I would not have seen the road to Port Patrick, through Glen-nap; but, by Shaint Patrick, I came home alive in spite of them.

Tom. O, rarely done, Paddy; you behaved like a man! But what is the reason that you Irish people swear always by Saint Patrick?

Teag. Arra, dear honey, he was the best shaint in the world, the father of all good people in the kingdom. He has a great kindness for an Irishman when he hears him calling on his name.

Tom. But, Paddy, is Saint Patrick yet alive?

Teag. Arra, dear honey, I don't know whether he be dead or alive, but it is a long time since they killed him. The people all turned heathens, but he would not change his profession, and was going to run the country with it, and for taking the gospel away to England, so the barbarous Tories of Dublin cutted off his head; and he swimmed over to England, and carried his head in his teeth.

PART II.

Tom. How did you get safe out of Scotland?

Teag. By the law, dear honey. When I came to Port Patrick, and saw my own kingdom, I knew I was safe at home, but I was clean dead, and almost drowned before I could get riding over the water; for I, with nine passengers more, leapt into a little young boat, having but four men dwelling in a little house in the one end of it, which was all thacked with deals; and, after they had pulled up her tether-stick, and laid her long halter over her mane, they pulled up a long sheet, like three pair of blankets, to the rigging of the house, and the wind blew in that, which made her gallop up one hill and down another, till I thought she would have run to the world's end.

Tom. Well, Paddy, and where did you go when you came to Ireland again?

Teag. Arra, dear honey, and where did I go but to my own dear cousin, who was now become very rich by the death of the old buck, his father, who died but a few weeks before I went over, and the parish had to bury him out of pity; it did not cost him a farthing.

Tom. And what entertainment did you get there?

Teag. O, my dear shoy, I was kindly used as another gentleman, and would have stayed there long enough, but when a man is poor his friends think little of him. I told him I was going to see my brother Harry. "Harry!" said he, "Harry is dead." "Dead!" said I, "and who killed him?" "Why," said he, "Death." "Allelieu, dear honey, and where did he kill him?" said I. "In his bed," says he. "Arra, dear honey," said I, "if he had been upon Newry mountains, with his brogues on, and his broad sword by his side, all the deaths in Ireland had not have killed him. O that impudent fellow Death. If he had let him alone till he died for want of butter milk and potatoes, I am sure he had lived all the days of his life."

Tom. In all your travels when abroad, did you never see none of your countrymen to inform you of what happened at home concerning your relations?

Teag. Arra, dear shoy, I saw none but Tom Jack, one day in the street; but when I came to him, it was not him, but one just like him.

Tom. On what account did you go a-travelling?

Teag. Why, a recruiting sergeant listed me to be a captain, and after all advanced me no higher than a soldier itself, but only he called me his dear countryman recruit, for I did not know what the regiment was when I saw them. I thought they were all gentlemen's sons and collegioners, when I saw a box like a Bible upon their bellies, until I saw G for King George upon it, and

R for God bless him. "Ho, ho," said I, "I shan't be long here."

Tom. O, then, Paddy, you deserted from them?

Teag. That's what I did, and ran to the mountains like a buck, and ever since when I see any soldiers I close my eyes, lest they should look and know me.

Tom. And what exploits did you when you was a soldier?

Teag. Arra, dear honey, I killed a man.

Tom. And how did you do that?

Teag. Arra, dear honey, when he dropt his sword I drew mine, and advanced boldly to him, and then cutted off his foot.

Tom. O, then, what a big fool was you, for you ought first to have cut off his head.

Teag. Arra, dear shoy, his head was cutted off before I engaged him, else I had not done it.

Tom. O, then, Paddy, you acted like a fool; but you are not such a big fool as many take you to be. You might pass for a philosopher.

Teag. A fulusipher. My father was a fulusipher; besides, he was a man under great authority by law, condemning the just and clearing the guilty. Do you know how they call the horse's mother?

Tom. Why, they call her a mare.

Teag. A mare, ay, very well minded. My father was a mare in Cork.

Tom. And what riches was left you by the death of your mother?

Teag. A bad luck to her own barren belly, for she lived in great plenty, and died in great poverty; devoured up all or she died, but two hens and a pockful of potatoes—a poor estate for an Irish gentleman, in faith.

Tom. And what did you make of the hens and potatoes? Did you sow them?

Teag. Arra, dear shoy, I sowed them in my belly, and sold the hens to a cadger.

Tom. What business did your mother follow after?

Teag. Greatly in the merchant way.

Tom. And what sort of goods did she deal in?

Teag. Dear honey, she went through the country and sold small fishes, onions, and apples; bought hens and eggs, and then hatched them herself. I remember of a long-necked cock she had, of an oversea brood, that stood on the midden and picked all the stars out of the north-west, so they were never so thick there since.

Tom. Now, Paddy, that's a bull surpasses all; but is there none of that cock's offspring alive now?

Teag. Arra, dear shoy, I don't think there are; but it is a pity but that they had, for they would fly with people above the sea, which would put the use of ships out of fashion, and nobody would be drowned at all.

Tom. Very well, Paddy, but in all your travels did you ever get a wife?

Teag. Ay, that's what I did, and a wicked wife, too; and, my dear shoy, I can't tell whether she is gone to Purgatory or the parish of Pig-trantrum, for she told me she should certainly die the first opportunity she could get, as this present evil world was not worth the waiting on, so she would go and see what good things is in the world to come; so when that old rover called the Fever came raging over the whole kingdom, she went away and died out of spite, leaving me nothing.

Tom. O, but, Paddy, you ought to have gone to a doctor, and got some pills and physic for her.

Teag. By Shaint Patrick, I had as good a pill of my own as any doctor in the kingdom could give her.

Tom. O, you fool, that is not what I mean. You ought to have brought the doctor to feel her pulse, and let blood off her if he thought it needful.

Teag. Yes, that's what I did, for I ran to the doctor whenever she died, and sought something for a dead or dying woman. The old foolish devil was at his dinner, and began to ask me some stupid questions, and then kicked me down stairs.

Tom. And in what good order did you bury your wife when she died?

Teag. O, my dear shoy, she was buried in all manner of pomp, pride, and splendour—a fine coffin, with cords in it; and within the coffin, along with herself, she got a pair of new brogues, a penny candle, a good, hard-headed old hammer, with an Irish sixpenny piece, to pay her passage at the gate, and what more could she look for?

Tom. I really think you gave her enough along with her, but you ought to have cried for her, if it was no more but to be in the fashion.

Teag. And why should I cry without sorrow, when we hired two criers to cry all the way before her to keep her in the fashion?

Tom. And what do they cry before a dead woman?

Teag. Why, they cry the common cry, or funeral lament, that is used in our Irish country.

Tom. And what manner of cry is that, Paddy?

Teag. Dear Tom, if you don't know I'll tell you. When any person dies there is a number of criers goes before, saying, "Luff, fuff, fou, allelieu, dear honey, what aileth thee to die? It was not for want of good butter milk and potatoes."

Part III.

Tom. Well, Paddy, and what did you do when your wife died?

Teag. Dear honey, what would I do? Do you think I was such a big fool as to die too? I am sure if I had I would not have got fair play, when I am not so old yet as my father was when he died.

Tom. No, Paddy, it is not that I mean. Was you sorry, or did you weep for her?

Teag. Weep for her! By Shaint Patrick, I would not weep, nor yet be sorry, suppose my own mother and all the women in Ireland had died seven years before I was born.

Tom. What did you do with your children when she died?

Teag. Do you imagine I was such a big fool as bury my children alive along with a dead woman? Arra, dear honey, we always commonly give nothing along with a dead person but an old shirt, a winding sheet, a big hammer, with a long candle, and an Irish silver threepenny piece.

Tom. Dear Paddy, and what do they make of all these things?

Teag. Then, Tom, since you are so inquisitive, you must go ask the priest.

Tom. What did you make of your children, Paddy?

Teag. And what should I make of them? Do you imagine that I should give them into the hands of the butchers, as they had been a parcel of young hogs. By Shaint Patrick, I had more unnaturality in me than to put them in an hospital as others do.

Tom. No; I suppose you would leave them with your friends?

Teag. Ay, ay, a poor man's friends is sometimes worse than a professed enemy. The best friend I ever had in the world was my own pocket while my money lasted; but I left two babes between the priest's door and the parish church, because I thought it was a place of mercy, and then set out for England in quest of another fortune.

Tom. I fancy, Paddy, you came off with what they call a moonshine flitting.

Teag. You lie like a thief now, for I did not see sun, moon, nor stars, all the night then, for I set out for Cork at the dawn of night, and I had travelled twenty miles all but twelve before gloaming in the morning.

Tom. And where did you go to take shipping?

Teag. Arra, dear honey, I came to a country village called Dublin, as big a city as any market town in all England, where I got myself aboard of a little young boat with a parcel of fellows and a long leather bag. I supposed them to be tinklers, until I asked what they carried in that leather sack. They told me it was the English mail they were going over with. "Then," said I, "is the milns so scant in England that they must send over their corn to Ireland to grind it?" The comical, cunning fellows persuaded me it was so. Then I went down to a little house below the water, hard by the rigg-back of the boat, and laid me down on their leather sack, where I slept myself almost to death with hunger. And, dear Tom, to tell you plainly, when I waked I did not know where I was, but thought I was dead and buried, for I found nothing all round me but wooden walls and timber above.

Tom. And how did you come to yourself to know where you was at last?

Teag. By the law, dear shoy, I scratched my head in a hundred parts, and then set me down to think upon it; so I minded it was my wife that was dead, and not me, and that I was alive in the young boat with the fellows that carries over the English meal from the Irish milns.

Tom. Oh, then, Paddy, I am sure you was glad when you found yourself alive?

Teag. Arra, dear shoy, I was very sure I was alive, but I did not think to live long, so I thought it was better for me to steal and be hanged than to live all my days and die directly with hunger at last.

Tom. Had you no meat nor money along with you?

Teag. Arra, dear shoy, I gave all the money to the captain of the house, or gudeman of the ship, to take me into the sea or over to England; and when I was like to eat my old brogues for want of victuals, I drew my hanger and cut the lock of the leather sack to get a lick of their meal; but, allelieu, dear shoy, I found neither meal nor seeds, but a parcel of papers and letters—a poor morsel for a hungry man.

Tom. Oh, then, Paddy, you laid down your honesty for nothing.

Teag. Ay, ay, I was a great thief, but got nothing to steal.

Tom. And how did you get victuals at last?

Teag. Allelieu, dear honey, the thoughts of meat and drink, death and life, and everything else, was out of mind. I had not a thought but one.

Tom. And what was that, Paddy?

Teag. To go down among the fishes and become a whale; then I would have lived at ease all my days, having nothing to do but to drink salt water and eat caller oysters.

Tom. What was you like to be drowned again?

Teag. Ay, ay, drowned, as cleanly drowned as a fish, for the sea blew very loud, and the wind ran so high, that we were all cast safe on shore, and not one of us drowned at all.

Tom. Where did you go when you came on shore?

Teag. Arra, dear honey, I was not able to go anywhere. You might cast a knot on my belly, I was so hollow in the middle, so I went into a gentleman's house and told him the bad fortune I had of being drowned between Ireland and the foot of his garden, where we came all safe ashore. But all the comfort I got from him was a word of truth.

Tom. And what was that, Paddy?

Teag. Why, he told me if I had been a good boy at home I needed not to have gone so far to push my fortune with an empty pocket, to which I answered, "And what magnifies that so long as I am a good workman at no trade at all?"

Tom. I suppose, Paddy, the gentleman would make you dine with him?

Teag. I really thought I was when I saw them roasting

and skinning so many black chickens, which was nothing but a few dead crows they were going to eat. "Ho ho," said I, "them is but dry meat at the best. Of all the fowls that flee commend me to the wing of an ox; but all that came to my share was a piece of boiled herring and a roasted potato. That was the first bit of bread I ever ate in England.

Tom. Well, Paddy, what business did you follow after in England when you was so poor?

Teag. What, sir, do you imagine I was poor when I came over on such an honourable occasion as to list, and bring myself to no preferment at all? As I was an able-bodied man in the face, I thought to be made a brigadeer, a grandedeer, or a fuzeleer, or even one of them blew-gowns that holds the flerry stick to the bung-hole of the big cannons when they let them off to fright away the French. I was as sure as no man alive ere I came from Cork, the least preferment I could get was to be riding master to a regiment of marines, or one of the black horse itself.

Tom. And where in England was it you listed?

Teag. Arra, dear shoy, I was going through a little country village. The streets were very sore by reason of the hardness of my feet and lameness of my brogues, so I went but very slowly across the streets. From port to port is a pretty long way; but I, being weary, thought nothing of it. Then the people came all crowding to me as I had been a world's wonder, or the wandering Jew, for the rain blew in my face and the wind wetted all my belly, which caused me to turn the back of my coat before and my buttons behind, which was a good safeguard to my body, and the starvation of my naked body, for I had not a good shirt.

Tom. I am sure, then, Paddy, they would take you for a fool?

Teag. No, no, sir; they admired me for my wisdom, for I always turned my buttons before when the wind blew

behind; but I wondered how the people knew my name and where I came from, for every one told another that was Paddy from Cork. I suppose they knew my face by seeing my name in the newspapers.

Tom. Well, Paddy, what business did you follow in the village?

Teag. To be sure I was not idle, working at nothing at all, till a decruiting sergeant came to town with two or three fellows along with him, one beating on a fiddle, and another playing on a drum, tossing their airs through the streets, as if they were going to be married. I saw them courting none but young men, so, to bring myself to no preferment at all, I listed for a soldier. I was too big for a grandedeer.

Tom. What listing money did you get, Paddy?

Teag. Arra, dear shoy, I got five thirteens and a pair of English brogues. The guinea, and the rest of the gold, was sent to London to the King, my master, to buy me new shirts, a cockade, and common treasing for my hat. They made me swear the malicious oath of devilry against the king, the colours, and my captain, telling me if ever I desert and not run away that I should be shot, and then whipt to death through the regiment.

Tom. No, Paddy; it is first whipt, and then shot, you mean.

Teag. Arra, dear shoy, it is all one thing at last; but it is best to be shot and then whipt—the cleverest way to die I'll warrant you.

Tom. How much pay did you get, Paddy?

Teag. Do you know the little tall fat sergeant that feed me to be a soldier?

Tom. And how should I know them I never saw, you fool?

Teag. Dear shoy, you may know him whether you see him or not. His face is all bored in holes with the smallpox, his nose is the colour of a lobster-toe, and his chin like a well washen potato. He's the biggest rogue in our kingdom. You'll know him when you meet him again. The rogue height me sixpence a day, kill or no kill; and when I laid Sunday and Saturday both together, and all the days in one day, I can't make a penny above fivepence of it.

Tom. You should have kept an account, and asked your arrears once a month.

Teag. That's what I did, but he reads a paternoster out of his prayer book, wherein all our names are written; so much for a stop-hold to my gun, to bucklers, to a pair of comical harn-hose, with leather buttons from top to toe; and, worst of all, he would have no less than a penny a week to a doctor. "Arra," said I, "I never had a sore finger, nor yet a sick toe, all the days of my life; then what have I to do with the doctor, or the doctor to do with me."

Tom. And did he make you pay all these things?

Teag. Ay, ay, pay and better pay: he took me before his captain, who made me pay all was in his book. "Arra, master captain," said I, "you are a comical sort of a fellow now; you might as well make me pay for my coffin before I be dead, as to pay for a doctor before I be sick:" to which he answered in a passion, "Sir," said he, "I have seen many a better man buried without a coffin;" "Sir," said I, "then I'll have a coffin, die when I will, if there be as much wood in all the world, or I shall not be buried at all." Then he called for the sergeant, saying, "You, sir, go and buy that man's coffin, and put it in the store till he die, and stop sixpence a week off his pay for it." "No, no, sir," said I, "I'll rather die without a coffin, and seek none when I'm dead, but if you are for clipping another sixpence off my pay, keep it all to yourself, and I'll swear all your oaths of agreement we had back again, and then seek soldiers where you will."

Tom. O then, Paddy, how did you end the matter?

Teag. Arra, dear shoy, by the nights of Shaint Patrick and help of my brogues, I both ended it and mended it, for the next night before that, I gave them leg bail for my fidelity, and went about the country a fortune-teller, dumb and deaf as I was not.

Tom. How old was you, Paddy, when you was a soldier last?

Teag. Arra, dear honey, I was three dozen all but two, and it is only two years since, so I want only four years of three dozen yet, and when I live six dozen more, I'll be older than I am, I warrant you.

Tom. O but, Paddy, by your account you are three dozen of years old already.

Teag. O what for a big fool are you now, Tom, when you count the years I lay sick; which time I count no time at all.

PADDY'S NEW CATECHISM.

Tom. Of all the opinions professed in religion tell me now, Paddy, of what profession art thou?

Teag. Arra, dear shoy, my religion was too weighty a matter to carry out of mine own country: I was afraid that you English Presbyterians should pluck it away from me.

Tom. What, Paddy, was your religion such a load that you could not carry it along with you?

Teag. Yes, that it was, but I carried it always about with me when at home, my sweet cross upon my dear breast, bound to my dear button hole.

Tom. And what manner of worship did you perform by that?

Teag. Why, I adored the cross, the pope, and the priest, cursed Oliver as black as crow, and swears myself a cut throat against all Protestants and church of Englandmen.

Tom. And what is the matter but you would be a church of Englandmen, or a Scotch Presbyterian yourself, Paddy?

Teag. Because it is unnatural for an Irishman: but had Shaint Patrick been a Presbyterian, I had been the same.

Tom. And for what reason would you be a Presbyterian then, Paddy?

Teag. Because they have liberty to eat flesh in lent, and everything that's fit for the belly.

Tom. What, Paddy, are you such a lover of flesh that you would change your profession for it?

Teag. O yes, that's what I would. I love flesh of all kinds, sheep's beef, swine's mutton, hare's flesh, and hen's venison; but our religion is one of the hungriest in all the world, ah! but it makes my teeth to weep, and my stomach to water, when I see the Scotch Presbyterians, and English churchmen, in time of lent, feeding upon bulls' and sheep's young children.

Tom. What reward will you get when you are dead, for punishing your stomach so while you are alive?

Teag. By Shaint Patrick I'll live like a king when I'm dead, for I will neither pay for meat nor drink.

Tom. What, Paddy, do you think that you are to come alive again when you are dead?

Teag. O yes, we that are true Roman Catholics will live a long time after we are dead; when we die in love with the priests, and the good people of our profession.

Tom. And what assurance can your priest give you of that?

Teag. Arra, dear shoy, our priest is a great shaint, a good shoal, who can repeat a paternoster and Ave Maria, which will fright the very horned devil himself, and make him run for it, until he be like to fall and break his neck.

Tom. And what does he give you when you are dying that makes you come alive again?

Teag. Why, he writes a letter upon our tongues, sealed with a wafer, gives us a sacrament in our mouth, with a pardon, and direction in our right hand, who to call for at the ports of Purgatory.

Tom. And what money design you to give the priest for your pardon?

Teag. Dear shoy, I wish I had first the money he would take for it, I would rather drink it myself, and then give him both my bill and my honest word, payable in the other world.

Tom. And how then are you to get a passage to the other world, or who is to carry you there?

Teag. O, my dear shoy, Tom, you know nothing of the matter: for when I die, they will bury my body, flesh, blood, dirt, and bones, only my skin will be blown up full of wind and spirit, my dear shoul I mean; and then I will be blown over to the other world on the wings of the wind; and after that I'll never be killed, hanged, nor drowned, nor yet die in my bed, for when any hits me a blow, my new body will play buff upon it like a bladder.

Tom. But what way will you go to the new world, or where is it?

Teag. Arra, dear shoy, the priest knows where it is, but I do not, but the Pope of Rome keeps the outer-port, Shaint Patrick the inner-port, and gives us a direction of the way to Shaint Patrick's palace, which stands on the head of the Stalian loch, where I'll have no more to do but chap at the gate.

Tom. What is the need for chapping at the gate, is it not always open?

Teag. Dear shoy, you know little about it, for there is none can enter but red hot Irishmen, for when I call Allelieu, dear honey, Shaint Patrick countenance your own dear countryman if you will, then the gates will be opened directly for me, for he knows and loves an Irishman's voice, as he loves his own heart.

Tom. And what entertainment will you get when you are in?

Teag. O, my dear, we are all kept there until a general

review, which is commonly once in the week; and then we are drawn up like as many young recruits, and all the blackguard scoundrels is picked out of the ranks, and one half of them is sent away to the Elysian fields, to curry the weeds from among the potatoes, the other half of them to the River sticks, to catch fishes for Shaint Patrick's table, and them that is owing the priests any money is put in the black hole, and then given to the hands of a great black bitch of a devil, which is keeped for a hangman, who whips them up and down the smoky dungeon every morning for six months.

Tom. Well, Paddy, are you to do as much justice to a Protestant as a Papist?

Teag. O, my dear shoy, the most justice we are commanded to do a Protestant, is to whip and torment them until they confess themselves in the Romish faith; and then cut their throats that they may die believers.

Tom. What business do you follow after at present?

Teag. Arra, dear shoy, I am a mountain sailor and my supplication is as follows—

PADDY'S HUMBLE PETITION, OR SUPPLICATION.

Good Christian people, behold me a man! who has com'd through a world of wonders, a hell full of hardships, dangers by sea, and dangers by land, and yet I am alive; you may see my hand crooked like a fowl's foot, and that is no wonder at all considering my sufferings and sorrows. Oh! oh! oh! good people. I was a man in my time who had plenty of the gold, plenty of the silver, plenty of the clothes, plenty of the butter, the beer, beef, and biscuit. And now I have nothing: being taken by the Turks and relieved by the Spaniards, lay sixty-six days at the siege of Gibraltar, and got nothing to eat but sea wreck and raw mussels; put to sea for our safety, cast upon the Barbarian coast, among the wicked Algerines, where we were taken and tied with tugs and tadders, horse locks, and cow chains: then cut and casteate yard and testicle quite away, put in your hand and feel how every female's made smooth by the sheer bone, where nothing is to be seen but what is natural. Then made our escape to the desart wild wilderness of Arabia; where we lived among the wild asses, upon wind, sand, and sapless ling. Afterwards put to sea in the hull of an old house, where we were tossed above and below the clouds, being driven through thickets and groves by fierce, coarse, calm, and contrary winds: at last, was cast upon Salisbury plains, where our vessel was dashed to pieces against a cabbage stock. And now my humble petition to you, good Christian people, is for one hundred of your beef, one hundred of your butter, another of your cheese, a cask of your biscuit, a tun of your beer, a keg of your rum, with a pipe of your wine, a lump of your gold, a piece of your silver, a few of your half-pence or farthings, a waught of your butter-milk, a pair of your old breeches, stockings, or shoes, even a chaw of tobacco for charity's sake.

THE HISTORY

of

DICK WHITTINGTON

and

HIS CAT.

In the reign of the famous King Edward the Third, there was a little boy called Dick Whittington, whose father and mother died when he was very young, so that he remembered nothing at all about them, and was left a dirty little fellow running about a country village. As poor Dick was not old enough to work, he was in a sorry plight. He got but little for his dinner, and sometimes nothing at all for his breakfast, for the people who lived in the village were very poor themselves, and could spare him little more than the parings of potatoes, and now and then a hard crust.

For all this, Dick Whittington was a very sharp boy, and was always listening to what every one talked about.

On Sundays he never failed to get near the farmers, as they sat talking on the tombstones in the churchyard before the parson was come; and once a week you might be sure to see little Dick leaning against the sign-post of the village ale-house, where people stopped to drink as they came from the next market town; and whenever the barber's shop-door was open Dick listened to all the news he told his customers.

In this manner Dick heard of the great city called London; how the people who lived there were all fine gentlemen and ladies; that there were singing and music in it all day long; and that the streets were paved all over with gold.

One day a waggoner, with a large waggon and eight horses, all with bells at their heads, drove through the village while Dick was lounging near his favourite sign-post. The thought immediately struck him that it must be going to the fine town of London; and taking courage he asked the waggoner to let him walk with him by the side of the waggon. The man, hearing from poor Dick that he had no parents, and seeing by his ragged condition that he could not be worse off, told him he might go if he would; so they set off together.

Dick got safe to London; and so eager was he to see the fine streets paved all over with gold that he ran as fast as his legs would carry him through several streets, expecting every moment to come to those that were all paved with gold, for Dick had three times seen a guinea in his own village, and observed what a great deal of money it brought in change; so he imagined he had only to take up some little bits of the pavement to have as much money as he desired.

Poor Dick ran till he was tired, and at last, finding it grow dark, and that whichever way he turned he saw nothing but dirt instead of gold, he sat down in a dark corner and cried himself asleep.

Little Dick remained all night in the streets; and next morning, finding himself very hungry, he got up and walked about, asking those he met to give him a halfpenny to keep him from starving; but nobody stayed to answer him, and only two or three gave him anything, so that the poor boy was soon in the most miserable condition. Being almost starved to death, he laid himself down at the door of one Mr. Fitzwarren, a great rich merchant. Here he was soon perceived by the cook-maid, who was an ill-tempered creature, and happened just then to be very busy dressing dinner for her master and mistress; so, seeing poor Dick, she called out, " What business have you there, you lazy rogue? There is nothing else but beggars; if you do not take yourself away, we will see how you will like a sousing of some dish water I have here that is hot enough to make you caper."

Just at this time Mr. Fitzwarren himself came home from the city to dinner, and, seeing a dirty, ragged boy lying at the door, said to him, " Why do you lie there, my lad? You seem old enough to work. I fear you must be somewhat idle." " No, indeed, sir," says Whittington, " that is not true, for I would work with all my heart, but I know nobody, and I believe I am very sick for want of food."

" Poor fellow!" answered Mr. Fitzwarren.

Dick now tried to rise, but was obliged to lie down again, being too weak to stand, for he had not eaten anything for three days, and was no longer able to run about and beg a halfpenny of people in the streets; so the kind merchant ordered that he should be taken into his house, and have a good dinner immediately, and that he should be kept to do what dirty work he was able for the cook.

Little Dick would have lived very happily in this worthy family had it not been for the crabbed cook, who was finding fault and scolding him from morning till night, and was withal so fond of roasting and basting that, when the spit was out of her hands, she would be at basting poor Dick's head and shoulders with a broom, or anything else that happened to fall in her way, till at last her ill-usage of him was told to Miss Alice, Mr. Fitzwarren's daughter, who asked the ill-tempered creature if she was not ashamed to use a little friendless boy so cruelly; and added she would certainly be turned away if she did not treat him with more kindness.

But though the cook was so ill-tempered, Mr. Fitzwarren's footman was quite the contrary. He had lived in the family many years, was rather elderly, and had once a little boy of his own, who died when about the age of Whittington, so he could not but feel compassion for the poor boy.

As the footman was very fond of reading, he used generally in the evening to entertain his fellow-servants, when they had done their work, with some amusing book. The pleasure our little hero took in hearing him made him very much desire to learn to read too; so the next time the good-natured footman gave him a halfpenny, he bought a horn-book with it; and, with a little of his help, Dick soon learned his letters, and afterwards to read.

About this time Miss Alice was going out one morning for a walk, and the footman happening to be out of the way, little Dick, who had received from Mr. Fitzwarren a neat suit of clothes to go to church on Sundays, was ordered to put them on, and walk behind her. As they walked along, Miss Alice, seeing a poor woman with one child in her arms and another at her back, pulled out her purse, and gave her some money; and, as she was putting it again into her pocket, she dropped it on the ground, and walked on. Luckily Dick, who was behind, saw what she had done, picked it up, and immediately presented it to her.

Besides the ill-humour of the cook, which now, however, was somewhat mended, Whittington had another hardship to get over. This was, that his bed, which was of flock, was placed in a garret, where there were so many holes in the floor and walls that he never went to bed without being awakened in his sleep by great numbers of rats and mice, which generally ran over his face, and made such a noise that he sometimes thought the walls were tumbling down about him.

One day a gentleman who paid a visit to Mr. Fitzwarren happened to have dirtied his shoes, and begged they might be cleaned. Dick took great pains to make them shine, and the gentleman gave him a penny. This he resolved to lay out in buying a cat, if possible; and the next day, seeing a little girl with a cat under her arm, he went up to her, and asked if she would let him have it for a penny, to which the girl replied she would with all her heart, for her mother had more cats than she could maintain, adding that the one she had was an excellent mouser.

This cat Whittington hid in the garret, always taking care to carry her a part of his dinner; and in a short time he had no further disturbance from the rats and mice, but slept as sound as a top.

Soon after this the merchant, who had a ship ready to sail, richly laden, and thinking it but just that all his servants should have some chance for good luck as well as himself, called them into the parlour, and asked them what commodity they chose to send.

All mentioned something they were willing to venture

but poor Whittington, who, having no money nor goods, could send nothing at all, for which reason he did not come in with the rest; but Miss Alice, guessing what was the matter, ordered him to be called, and offered to lay down some money for him from her own purse; but this, the merchant observed, would not do, for it must be something of his own.

Upon this, poor Dick said he had nothing but a cat, which he bought for a penny that was given him.

"Fetch thy cat, boy," says Mr. Fitzwarren, "and let her go."

Whittington brought poor puss, and delivered her to the captain with tears in his eyes, for he said, "He should now again be kept awake all night by the rats and mice."

All the company laughed at the oddity of Whittington's adventure; and Miss Alice, who felt the greatest pity for the poor boy, gave him some halfpence to buy another cat.

This, and several other marks of kindness shown him by Miss Alice, made the ill-tempered cook so jealous of the favours the poor boy received that she began to use him more cruelly than ever, and constantly made game of him for sending his cat to sea, asking him if he thought it would sell for as much money as would buy a halter.

At last the unhappy little fellow, being unable to bear this treatment any longer, determined to run away from his place. He accordingly packed up the few things that belonged to him, and set out very early in the morning on Allhallow Day, which is the first of November. He travelled as far as Holloway, and there sat down on a stone, which to this day is called Whittington's Stone, and began to consider what course he should take.

While he was thus thinking what he could do, Bow Bells, of which there were then only six, began to ring, and it seemed to him that their sounds addressed him in this manner—

"Turn again, Whittington,
Lord Mayor of London."

"Lord Mayor of London!" says he to himself. "Why, to be sure, I would bear anything to be Lord Mayor of London, and ride in a fine coach! Well, I will go back, and think nothing of all the cuffing and scolding of old Cicely if I am at last to be Lord Mayor of London."

So back went Dick, and got into the house, and set about his business before Cicely came down stairs.

The ship, with the cat on board, was long beaten about at sea, and was at last driven by contrary winds on a part of the coast of Barbary, inhabited by Moors that were unknown to the English.

The natives in this country came in great numbers, out of curiosity, to see the people on board, who were all of so different a colour from themselves, and treated them with great civility, and, as they became better acquainted, showed marks of eagerness to purchase the fine things with which the ship was laden.

The captain, seeing this, sent patterns of the choicest articles he had to the king of the country, who was so much pleased with them that he sent for the captain and his chief mate to the palace. Here they were placed, as is the custom of the country, on rich carpets flowered with gold and silver; and, the king and queen being seated at the upper end of the room, dinner was brought in, which consisted of the greatest rarities. No sooner, however, were the dishes set before the company than an amazing number of rats and mice rushed in, and helped themselves plentifully from every dish, scattering pieces of flesh and gravy all about the room.

The captain, extremely astonished, asked if these vermin were not very offensive.

"Oh, yes," said they, "very offensive; and the king would give half his treasure to be free of them, for they not only destroy his dinner, but they disturb him even in his chamber, so that he is obliged to be watched while he sleeps."

The captain, who was ready to jump for joy, remembering poor Whittington's hard case, and the cat he had entrusted to his care, told him he had a creature on board his ship that would kill them all.

The king was still more overjoyed than the captain. "Bring this creature to me," says he; "and if she can really perform what you say I will load your ship with wedges of gold in exchange for her."

Away flew the captain, while another dinner was providing, to the ship, and, taking puss under his arm, returned to the palace in time to see the table covered with rats and mice, and the second dinner in a fair way to meet with the same fate as the first.

The cat, at sight of them, did not wait for bidding, but sprang from the captain's arms, and in a few moments laid the greatest part of the rats and mice dead at her feet, while the rest, in the greatest fright imaginable, scampered away to their holes.

The king, having seen and considered of the wonderful exploits of Mrs. Puss, and being informed she would soon have young ones, which might in time destroy all the rats and mice in the country, bargained with the captain for his whole ship's cargo, and afterwards agreed to give a prodigious quantity of wedges of gold, of still greater value, for the cat, with which, after taking leave of their Majesties, and other great personages belonging to the court, he, with all his ship's company, set sail, with a fair wind, for England, and, after a happy voyage, arrived safely in the port of London.

One morning Mr. Fitzwarren had just entered his count-ing-house, and was going to seat himself at the desk, when who should arrive but the captain and mate of the merchant ship, the Unicorn, just arrived from the coast of Barbary, and followed by several men, bringing with them a prodigious quantity of wedges of gold that had been paid by the King of Barbary in exchange for the merchandise, and also in exchange for Mrs. Puss. Mr. Fitzwarren, the instant he heard the news, ordered Whittington to be called, and, having desired him to be seated, said, "Mr. Whittington, most heartily do I rejoice in the news these gentlemen have brought you, for the captain has sold your cat to the King of Barbary, and brought you in return more riches than I possess in the whole world; and may you long enjoy them!"

Mr. Fitzwarren then desired the men to open the immense treasures they had brought, and added that Mr. Whittington had now nothing to do but to put it in some place of safety.

Poor Dick could scarce contain himself for joy. He begged his master to take what part of it he pleased, since to his kindness he was indebted for the whole. "No, no, this wealth is all your own, and justly so, answered Mr. Fitzwarren; "and I have no doubt you will use it generously."

Whittington, however, was too kind-hearted to keep all himself; and accordingly made a handsome present to the captain, the mate, and every one of the ship's company, and afterwards to his excellent friend the footman, and the rest of Mr. Fitzwarren's servants, not even excepting crabbed old Cicely.

After this, Mr. Fitzwarren advised him to send for tradespeople, and get himself dressed as became a gentleman, and made him the offer of his house to live in till he could provide himself with a better.

When Mr. Whittington's face was washed, his hair curled,

his hat cocked, and he was dressed in a fashionable suit of clothes, he appeared as handsome and genteel as any young man who visited at Mr. Fitzwarren's; so that Miss Alice, who had formerly thought of him with compassion, now considered him as fit to be her lover; and the more so, no doubt, because Mr. Whittington was constantly thinking what he could do to oblige her, and making her the prettiest presents imaginable.

Mr. Fitzwarren, perceiving their affection for each other, proposed to unite them in marriage, to which, without difficulty, they each consented; and accordingly a day for the wedding was soon fixed, and they were attended to church by the lord mayor, the court of aldermen, the sheriffs, and a great number of the wealthiest merchants in London; and the ceremony was succeeded by a most elegant entertainment and splendid ball.

History tells us that the said Mr. Whittington and his lady lived in great splendour, and were very happy; that they had several children; that he was sheriff of London in the year 1340, and several times afterwards lord mayor; that in the last year of his mayoralty he entertained King Henry the Fifth on his return from the battle of Agincourt. And sometime afterwards, going with an address from the city on one of his Majesty's victories, he received the honour of knighthood.

Sir Richard Whittington constantly fed great numbers of the poor. He built a church and college to it, with a yearly allowance to poor scholars, and near it erected an hospital.

The effigy of Sir Richard Whittington was to be seen, with his cat in his arms, carved in stone, over the archway of the late prison of Newgate that went across Newgate Street.

THE MAD PRANKS OF
TOM TRAM,
SON IN LAW
TO
MOTHER WINTER.
TO WHICH ARE ADDED
HIS MERRY JESTS
AND
PLEASANT TALES.

CHAPTER I.
A merry Jest betwixt old Mother Winter and her Son-in-Law Tom.

THERE was an old woman named Mother Winter that had but one son-in-law, and his name was Tom; and though he was at man's estate, yet would do nothing but what he listed, which grieved his old mother to the heart. Upon a time being in the market, she heard a proclamation, "That those that would not work should be whipped." At which the old woman leapt, and with great joy home she comes meets with her son, and tells him the mayor of the town had made a decree, which was, "That all those that would not work should be whipped." "Has he so," says he, "marry, my blessing on his heart; for my part, I'll not break the decree." So the old woman left her son, and went again to the market; she was no sooner gone but her son looks into the stone pots, which she kept small beer in; and when he saw that the beer did not work, he takes the pot, strips off his doublet, and with a carter's whip he lays on them as hard as he could drive. The people who saw him do it, told his mother what he had done; which made the old woman cry out, "O! that young knave will be hanged." So in that tone home she goes. Her son seeing her, came running and foaming at the mouth to meet her, and told her, that he had broke both the pots; which made the old woman to say, "O thou villain! what hast thou done?" "O mother," quoth he, "you told me it was proclaimed, 'That all those that would not work must be whipped'; and I have often seen our pots work so hard, that they have foamed so much at the mouth, that they befouled all the house where they stood; but these two lazy knaves," said he, "told me, that they did never work, nor never meant to work; and therefore," quoth he, "I have whipped them to death, to teach the rest of their fellows to work, or never look me in the face again."

CHAPTER II.

Another Jest of old Mother Winter and her Son Tom.

UPON a time Mother Winter sent her son Tom into the market to buy her a penny-worth of soap, and gave him twelvepence, and charged him to bring it home safe. Tom told her it should be so; and to that end it should be safe brought home, according to his mother's charge, he goes and buys a penny-worth of soap, and hired two men with a handbarrow to carry the soap, and four men with brown bills to guard it along to her, giving them the elevenpence for their pains, which made his mother in great fury go to the mayor of the town, who committed him to prison. Now, the prison window joining close to the mayor's chamber window, Tom and some other merry prisoners like himself, getting a cup of good liquor in their heads, began to sing and roar and domineer, insomuch that the mayor heard them that night, and charged them they should leave off drinking and singing of loose songs, and sing good psalms. Tom told him that he should hear that he would amend his life if he would pardon his fault. The mayor said that for their misdemeanours, they should be that night in prison, and upon amendment, being neighbours, he would release them in the morning. They thanked the mayor, and Tom Tram prevailed so far with a friend of his that he borrowed three shillings; which three shillings he spent upon his fellow-prisoners, which made the poor men be ruled by him, and do what he enjoined them to do; so when the mayor was gone to bed, the prison window as before observed, being close to the chamber-window, they began to sing psalms so loud that the mayor could take no rest, which made him cause one of his servants forbid them leave off singing. Tom Tram said that it was the mayor's good counsel that they should sing psalms, and sing they would, as long as they lived three. Which made the mayor bid the jailer turn them out of prison, without paying their fees.

Chapter III.
How Tom served his Hostess and a Tobacco Seller—being another of his Jests.

It happened that Tom was sent on an errand forty miles from his abode, over heaths and plains, where having dispatched his business, he chanced to be lodged in a room that opened into a yard, where his hostess kept many turkeys, which Tom seeing he thrusts pins into two of their heads and in the night they died. The woman in the morning wondered how the fowls should come to die. Tom persuaded her that there was a great sickness where he dwelt amongst all manner of fowls, and wished his hostess to fling them away, which she did. Tom watched where she flung them, and when he took his leave of his hostess, it was at such a time when she was busy setting bread into the oven, so that he was sure she could not look after him. So he goes and wraps the turkeys in his coat, and away he runs; but finding his two turkeys heavy, he sees a man that sold tobacco up and down the country at the foot of a hill, when he alighted to lead his horse down the hill, at the bottom of which he falls down, and lies crying as if he had broken one of his legs, and makes to the man a most piteous lamentation; that he was six or seven miles from any town, there being no house near; and that he was like to perish for want of succour. The man asked where he dwelt. He said with a knight, to whom Tom did live as a jester. The man knowing the knight, and thinking Tom's leg had really been broken, with much ado lifted him upon the horse. When Tom was mounted, he prayed the man to give him his master's turkeys. Tom made the horse to gallop away, crying out, "I shall be killed! I shall be killed! O my leg! What shall I do! O my leg!" The man seeing him gone, stood in amaze, and knew not what to think; nevertheless, he durst not leave his turkeys behind him, for fear of displeasing the knight, but carried them lugging along fretting and swearing in his boots, till he came to the next town, where he hired a horse to overtake Tom, but could not, until he came to the knight's house, where Tom stood to attend his coming, looking out at the window. When the man alighted, Tom then called to him so loud, that most of the house heard him. "O," said e, " now I see thou art an honest man, I had thought you had set me upon your headstrong horse, on purpose to deceive me of my turkeys. The man replied, " A pox take you and your turkeys, for I never was played the knave with so in my life; I hope you will pay for the hire of the horse, which I was forced to borrow to follow you withal." "That I will," said Tom, " with all my heart."

CHAPTER IV.

How Tom paid the Man for his Horse Hire.

TOM asked the man what way he intended to travel. "Marry," said the man, "I must go back with the horse I have hired." Quoth Tom, "What did you give for the hire of him?" Said the man, "I gave five shillings." "Well," said Tom, "I will set you to the next public-house, and then we will eat one of the turkeys, and I will bring you in good silver the five shillings for the horse hire." The place appointed being two miles off, Tom appoints three or four of his companions to meet him, who did not fail, for they were there before Tom and his friend, who came riding upon the horses—Tom upon the hired horse, and the man upon his own. Tom alighted, and called the hostler to set up his horse, and to give him oats enough, and caused a turkey to be roasted with all possible haste, which, according as he commanded, was performed. But Tom whispered to his consorts, and wished them to ply the man with drink; while he, in the meantime, went to the host and told him they came to be merry, and money was short with him and desired he would lend him ten shillings upon his horse. The host having so good a pawn, lent it him, knowing it would be spent in his house. So Tom went and gave the man five shillings for the hire of the horse, and spends the other five shillings freely upon him. By that time the day was pretty nigh spent, so that the man could get no further that night, but Tom and his companions took their leaves and returned home, and the man went his way to bed little suspecting the trick Tom had put upon him. In the morning the man rising betimes, thinking to be gone, could have but one horse unless he paid ten shillings, for Tom had left word with his host, that paying the money he should have both horses. The man seeing himself cozened again by Tom, paid the ten shillings, and wished all such cheating knaves were hanged, away he went fretting and foaming to see see himself abused.

CHAPTER V.

How Tom served a Company of Gentlemen.

It happened that a company of gentlemen being disposed to create mirth, rode some miles from home to be merry. One of them would need have Tom to wait upon him, and Tom was as willing as he to be in that company, but as they were coming home, one of them cut the reins of Tom's bridle, so that when Tom mounted on his horse the reins broke, and the horse ran away with him in the midst of a great heath whereon stood a large gallows against which the horse stood, and rubbed his neck, so that the gentleman hooped and hallooed, and said, "Farewell, Tom, farewell." But Tom alighted from his horse, and made fast his reins, and with his sword cut three or four chips from off the gallows; and at the next tavern Tom met with them, where they jeer'd him not a little; but Tom very earnestly entreated them to forbear, yet the more he entreated them, the more they played upon him. But to be even with them, in the morning Tom calls the hostler, and sends him for nutmegs and ginger, and gets a grater, and when he had grated them he also grated the chips off the gallows, and mixed with the spice only a little nutmeg and ginger, he laid towards one end of the trencher for himself, and with a gallon of ale into the gentleman's chamber he goes, begging of them not to mock him any more with the gallows; and he would give them that ale and spice; and so, says he, "Gentlemen, I drink to you all." Now, as soon as he had drank, the hostler called him, as he gave him charge before so to do. Down stairs runs Tom as fast as he could. The gentlemen made all possible speed to drink up the ale and spice before he came up again, and that was what Tom desired. When he came again, seeing all the ale and spice gone, he says, "Gentlemen, will you know why my horse carried me to the gallows?" "Yes," says one of them. "Well," says Tom, "it was to fetch you some spice to your ale, and if you want, I have more for you"; and with that showed them the chips out of his pocket, and away he runs, leaving the gentlemen to look one upon another, studying how they should be revenged on him.

Chapter VI.
How Tom rode a-Gossiping.

Tom heard a company of women that would meet at the place a house-warming, to welcome one of the house. These women had formerly abused Tom, and now he thought to be even with them, so he goes to an apothecary's shop, buys a pound of purging comfits, and puts them in a cake with other spices, and dresses himself in women's apparel, and gets a horse and a pannel, and to the house he comes, knocks at the door, and asked the maid, whether there were any women come a house-warming? The maid said, "Not yet." "I pray," says Tom, "take this cake, and if I come not at the meeting, let them eat it and be merry, for I must go to a woman that is exceedingly unwell," and away he goes. The women came, and wondered what woman it should be that left the cake. Some of them supposed that it was some rich lady. They stayed a while and the person they expected to be with them not coming, they fell to their meat, and at last to the cake. But it was not long in their stomach before it began to work, so that all began vomiting, and were so sick, that they disordered the house. In which time Tom shifts himself into man's apparel, and with a staff in his hand came where his gossips were, and hearing them groaning all the house over, opened the door and asked them what was the matter? They answered they were all poisoned. "Marry," quoth Tom, "I hope not; if you please to let me have a horse, I will ride to Mr. Doctor's and fetch an antidote to deaden the poison." "Take my horse," quoth one; "Take my horse," said another; "Or mine," said a third. "Well, well," said Tom, "I will take one." And into the stable he goes and takes three horses, and to the doctor's he rides, and told him that all the people in such a house had eaten something that had poisoned them; and prayed him that he would, without delay, carry them some medicines, and that they had sent a horse for him and another for his man. The doctor, greedy of money, hastened thither with his medicine bottles as fast as the horses could carry him and his man. But the doctor no sooner came into the house, but he saw there was no need of medicines. In the meantime Tom told not only all he met with, that there were such women met to be merry at such a place; and not only they, but all the women of the house were poisoned, but went likewise to their husbands, and told them the like, so that all the people thereabouts repaired thither, which made the women so ashamed that they knew not which way to look, because all that saw them judged they were drunk; so that instead of comforting them which they expected, they fell a reviling them. The women also fell to scolding among themselves, and would have fought, had not their husbands parted them, by carrying them home.

CHAPTER VII.

How Tom served a Company of Gypsies.

IT happened on a day, towards night, that there came a company of gypsies into a town, and had not very long been there till Tom met them, and asked them, "What they made there?" They said they came to town to tell the people their fortunes, that thereby they might understand ensuing dangers. "Aye," says Tom, "and where do you lie to-night?" They told him they could not tell. "Nay," said Tom, "if you will be contented to lie in straw, I will bring you where you may lie dry and warm." They thanked him, and told him they would tell him his fortune in the morning for nothing. Tom thanked them, and therefore conveys them into a little thatched house which had a ditch round about it, very close to the wall thereof. That house Tom helped them to fill with straw, and saw them take their lodging; and then, it being dark, Tom bade them good-night, and as soon as he was over the bridge, which was a plank, he drew it after him; and in the dead time of the night Tom gets a long pole, with a wasp of straw at the end of it, and sets the straw on fire, calling out to the rest of the fellows to shift for themselves; who, thinking to run over the bridge, fell into the ditch, crying and calling out for help, while, by Tom's means, most part of the town stood to see the jest; and as the gypsies waded through the ditch, they took them and carried them into a house, where there was a good fire, for it was in the midst of winter; where Tom counsels them that they should never make him believe that they could tell him anything, that did not know what danger should befall themselves. "But," says he, "because you cannot tell me my fortune, I will tell you yours. For to-morrow in the forenoon you shall be whipped for deceivers, and in the afternoon be hanged for setting the house on fire." The gypsies hearing this so strict sentence, made haste to dry themselves, and next morning stole out of town, and never came any more there.

CHAPTER VIII.

How Tom sold his Mother's Trevet, and cozened an Acqua Vitæ Man that sold Hot Water.

IN a winter night, coming home very late, Tom Tram fell with his arms before him, and at the last run his nose against a post. "What," quoth Tom, "is my nose longer than my arms?" And afterwards he dropped into a well that was in the yard, and crying out, "Help, help." All is not well that is in the well. The neighbours came and pulled him out, and he dropped like a pig that had been roasted on a spit; but he was then in a cold condition, so he went to bed, and covered himself, but before morning Tom became unwell; and when some had discovered this, he told them that if he died of that sickness he should be buried by torchlight, because none should see him go to his grave. Just as he had said, in came a hot water man, of whom he requested to give him a sup, which having tasted, he feigned himself to be in a hot fever, and rose up in his clothes, ran away with the acqua vitæ man's bottle of hot water, and took his mother's trevet, and sold it for a long hawking pole, and a falconer's bag, which being tied to his side, and having drank up the poor man's hot water, he came reeling home with an owl upon his fist, saying, "It is gentlemanlike to be betwixt hawk and buzzard;" and he told the acqua vitæ man that he had sent the trevet, with three legs, to the next town to fill you bottles again.

Chapter IX.
How he Hired himself to the Justice, and what Pranks he played while with him.

THE justice at this time being without a man, and finding Tom to be a lively fellow, asked him if he would serve him. "Yes," quoth Tom, "for I am a great many miles from the country." As soon as they had agreed for wages, Tom was immediately entertained. But he had not lived long there before the justice and his family were obliged to go to London, leaving nobody at home but Tom. Now in the justice's absence, an officer brought a lusty young woman and a little man with a complaint. So they knocked at the door, and Tom let them in; then placing himself in his master's chair, he asked the woman what she had to say, who told him that the man whom she had brought before him ill-used her. "Adzooks," quoth Tom, "is it possible that such a little fellow as this could ill-use such a strapping dame as you." "Alas! sir," said she, "although he is little he is strong." "Well, little whipper-snapper," quoth Tom, "what do you say to this." He replied, "Like your worship it is false what she says. The truth is, I have been at sea, and coming ashore, where I received my pay, I met with this woman, and agreed with her for a pair of shoes for half a crown, and when they were put on, I pulled out my purse to pay her honestly what I had agreed for; but she seeing that I had a considerable sum of money, contrary to our bargain, would force me to give her ten shillings, and because I would not, but struck her as she deserved, she has brought me before your worship." "Have you got that purse of money?" quoth Tom. "Yes, sir," said the seaman. "Give it into my hand," said Tom. He receives it, and turning to the woman, said, "Here take it and get about your business." She replied, "I thank your worship, you are an honest good man, and have done me justice." The little seaman the meanwhile wrung his hands and bitterly cried out, "I am ruined, for it is every penny I had in the world." "Well," quoth Tom. "haste after her, and take it from her again." According to Tom's order he runs after her, and when he came after her, he said, "I must, and will have my purse again." Then she fell about his ears and cuffed him. Nay, this did not satisfy her, but she dragged him back again to Tom, who sat as justice, and told him that the fellow followed her for the purse, which he in justice gave her. "Well," said Tom, "and has he got it?" "No," said she, "I think not; before he should take it from me, I'd tear out both his eyes." "Let me see it again," says Tom. She gives it to him. "Is all the money in it?" quoth he. "Yes, sir," said she, "every penny." "Why then," said he, "here little whipper-snapper, take your purse again; and as for you Mrs. Impudence, had you kept your word as well as you did the money, I never had been troubled with this complaint. Here, Mr. Constable, give her a hundred lashes at the town's whipping post." Which was accordingly done, and Tom was applauded for his just proceedings.

CHAPTER X.
How Tom used a Singing Man of a Cathedral Church in the West.

ONCE there was a cathedral singing man that had very much angered Tom, and had made songs and jests upon him, whereupon Tom got on his back an ox-hide, with the horns set upon his head, and so lay in a hedge bottom, waiting till the singing man came by, who he was sure must pass that way. At last came the singing man. Up started Tom out of the hedge bottom in his ox-hide, and followed him, the singing man cried out, "The devil! the devil!" "No," quoth Tom, "I am the ghost of goodman Johnson, living hard by the Church stile, unto whose house ye came and sung catches, and owes me five pounds for ale, therefore appoint me a day when ye will bring me my money hither, or else I will haunt thee still. The singing man promised that day se'ennight, and accordingly he did; and Tom made himself brave clothes with the money, and sweethearts came about him as bees do about a honey pot. But Tom wore a rope in his pocket, and being asked if he would marry, he would pull it out, and laugh, saying, "I have broken my shins already, and will be wiser hereafter; for I am an old colt, and now may have as much wit as a horse."

Chapter XI.
Of Tom Tram's wooing Cicily Summers, the neat Wench of the West.

CICILY SUMMERS, whose nose was then as fair as the midnight sun, which shined as bright as Baconthine, was beloved of young Tom Tram; and a sad story to tell, he grew not worth the bread he ate, through pining away for her love. Tom was loath to speak but still whistled. At last, when Cicily made no answer, he burst out in thus:— "O Cicily Summers, if I Tom Tram, son of Mother Winter, and thou Cicily Summers be joined together what a quarter shall we keep, as big as three half years; besides Cicily Summers when thou scoldest, then Winter shall presently cool thy temper; and when we walk on the street they'll say yonder goes Summer and Winter; and our children, we shall call a generation of almanacks. So they went to the parson and were married; but they fell out so extremely that they scolded all the summer season; and Tom drank good ale, and told old tales all the winter time, and so they could never but thrive all the year through.

Tom lived by good ale, and his wife by eating oat-meal; and when Tom went to be drunk in the morning, she put oatmeal in the ale, and made caudle with mustard instead of eggs, which bit Tom so by the nose, that it would run water; but the next day he would be drunk again.

TOM TRAM'S
MERRY TALES.

Tale I.

Of a Scholar and a Tapster on a Winter Night.

The tapster said, "Sir, will you go to bed." "No," quoth the scholar, "There are thieves abroad, and would not willingly be caught napping." So the tapster left him, and being gone, in came a spirit into the chamber, with his head under his arm so that he durst not stir, but cried out, "Help! help! fire! thieves! thieves!" "Oh," quoth he, "the devil was here and spoke to me with his head under his arm; but now I will go to bed, and if he comes again I will send him to the tapster, to help him to make false reckonings. It being a cold night," quoth he, "I will first put fire to toe, that is, I will warm my toes by the fire, then I'll go to bed." And so he did, and a great reckoning put the scholar out of his jest saying, "That was in earnest made too large a reckoning," he being but poor Sir John, of Oxford.

Tale II.

Down in the west country a certain conceited fellow had a great nose; so a countryman by him with a sack of corn, jostled him, saying, "Your nose stands in my way," whereupon the other fellow with the great nose, took his nose in his hand, and held it to the other side, saying, "A pox on thee, go and be hanged."

Tale III.

Once there was a company of gypsies that came to a country fellow on the highway, and would needs tell Tom his fortune. Amongst other things, they bade him assure himself that his worst misfortunes were past, and that he would not be troubled with crosses as he had been. So coming home, and having sold the cow at the market, he looked into his purse for the money, thinking to have told it to his wife; but he found not so much as one cross in his purse; whereupon he remembered the words of the gypsies, and said that the gypsies had said true that he should not be troubled with crosses, and that they had picked his pocket, and left not a penny in his purse. Whereupon his wife basted and cudgelled him so soundly, that he began to perceive that a man that had a cursed wife should never be without a cross, though he had never a penny in his purse; and because it was winter-time, he sat a while by the fireside, and after went to bed supperless and penniless.

Tale IV.

A Farmer's wife in the west had three pigs, which she loved exceedingly well, and fed them with good butter milk and whey; but they would come running into the house and dirtied the rooms. Whereupon she resolved to sell them at the market, because they were better fed than taught, but afterwards they were stolen away from her; whereupon she supposed they were driven up to London to learn manners; "But," said she, "they were too old to learn to turn the spit in Bartholomew fair," and therefore believed some butchers had stolen them away.

Her cock had a piece of cloth sewn about him, and was left upon the porch, but afterwards stolen; whereupon she said, that her cock was turned scholar in a black gown, and so she went to Oxford to a conjurer, to know what was become of her pigs and her cock. The scholar smiled, and told her the three pigs were blown home, and the cock was made a bachelor of arts in one of the colleges. "I thought so," said the woman, "for sure bachelors of arts are very coxcombs."

A YORK DIALOGUE
BETWEEN
NED AND HARRY:
OR
Ned giving Harry an Account of his Courtship and Marriage State.

Ned.—Honest Harry, I am glad to see you. You're welcome to York. You're a great stranger. When came you to town?

Harry.—I came to your town last night, Ned, and am glad to see you. I inquired after you of my landlord, and he told me you was well, and had been married two or three years. I wish you much happiness; but how d'ye like matrimony?

Ned.—In good faith, Harry, scrubbing his shoulders, but so, so; however, I will not discourage you.

Harry.—But don't you remember, Ned, that you and I made an agreement that which of us two was married first, should tell one another of the way of courtship, and how he liked it and a married state.

Ned.—'Tis true we did so, Harry, but now I have not time to tell you, for it will take me more than two or three hours to give you a full account of both parts.

Harry.—What! are you in haste then, Ned? 'Tis a great while since I have seen you, and shan't we have one mug together?

Ned.—Faith, Harry, I'm loath to deny you; but if I go with you, I must send home to my wife, and let her know where I am.

Harry.—So you may Ned, and tell her you are with an old friend that would be glad to see her.

Ned.—Not a word of that, Harry, for if I go with you and stay any time, we shall have her company without sending for her.

Harry.—Say you so. Come then, let us go to Tom Swan's. Well, Ned, I am glad to see thee—ring the bell Jenny, bring us a pint of your best ale. Come, Ned, sit down. And how long was it before you got your wife into the mind to marry; for if I speak to any of the female sex they are so very coy, I can't tell what to make of them?

Ned.—That's very true. They are so, Harry, for when I spoke to my wife first, she was so very coy and huffish, and told me she did not know what I meant. She was not for marrying. She lived very well as she was, and if she should marry, she must then be confined to the humours of a husband.

Harry.—Well, but how then, Ned, tell me all.

Ned.—Faith I have not time now, Harry, for I must go home.

Harry.—Come, my service t'ye, Ned, I will have you be as good as your promise.

Ned.—Then if I must, I will stay a little longer and tell you. I told her I had as good a trade as any of my neighbours. Upon these words she was called away.

Harry.—How then, Ned?

Ned.—Faith I went home, but could not get her out of my mind. The next day I went again to see her, and took her by the hand, but she pulled it away with scorn, saying,

"Pray don't banter me, for I know you men love to banter us silly women." Upon my faith, madam, said I, I am in good earnest, for a man of my trade must have both journeymen and prentices, therefore I cannot well be without a wife, and you are the only person I always thought would make me happy. Then I took her by the hand again, and with much ado got a kiss off her. "Pray be quiet," said she, "Goodness! what do you mean? you are so troublesome!" and looked very angry, and so left me.

Harry.—Very well, Ned, go on, this is vastly pleasant.

Ned.—That very kiss made me think of her, and love her more than ever I did, for after that kiss I was always wishing myself in her company, and was never at rest. The Sunday after, I saw her in the minster at prayers, and thought everything handsome and pretty about her—her face, her eyes, her mouth, her breast, her shape. I watched her coming out of the choir, and walked with her in the minster, and asked her if she would please to take a walk into the Groves, but she told me she was engaged. Believe me, Harry; I was so daft with that answer that my heart was fit to break with fear that she should love another better than myself. However, I went home with her. She told me she was engaged, and I need not trouble myself any further. Madam, said I, the first that ever I saw you, I was struck with the thought that you was the woman that was to make me a happy wife. "You men," said she, "say so to all women you meet with." "Truly, madam," said I, "what I say is really true, from the bottom of my heart, and I hope you will find it so." "You men always promise fair," said she, "before you are married, but when the job is over you seldom or never perform your promise." "Pray, try me, madam," said I, "for upon my word, you will find me always as good as I have said, by this kiss." "Fye," said she, "I swear I will never come into your company any more, if you will not let me stand quietly by you." Then I asked her again the favour to take a walk, for it was a fine evening, and would do her a great deal of good. She told me at last, she was to meet two or three of her acquaintances at seven o'clock in the Groves, just to take a turn or two and so come home again, so bid me good night.

Harry.—Well, Ned, I hope you went to the Groves to meet her, did you not?

Ned.—Yes, you may be assured I did, and within a quarter of an hour after I was there, my mistress came, but her friends were not with her, as good luck would have it.

Harry.—Were not you glad of that, Ned, though I dare swear, she knew of nobody to meet her at that time.

Ned.—Yes, faith, I was very glad of it; and when we had taken a turn or two, I asked her if she would go to the cheese-cake house, and with much ado I got her to consent to go.

Harry.—Well, Ned, what discourse had you there?

Ned.—Why, faith, we were very merry. I called for some cheese-cakes, and a bottle of cider, and at last began to ask her about marrying me. She told me she heard I had a good trade, and did mind it now very well, but how I would mind it, if she should consent to marry me, was her fear. I told her she need never fear that, for marrying of her would be the only means to make me mind my business, if possible, more than I have done. I do assure you, Harry, that the servants which we call chamber-maids, stand as much upon their honour, as some of them will call it, in courting, as their mistress, nay, and more.

Harry.—Why, Ned, I have observed that all along you have called her madam whenever you named her, but I hope it is not a custom here at York, to call your chamber-maids madam at every word.

Ned.—Yes, faith we do, and they themselves call one another so, for if there be five or six of them together at the parting with one another, you shall hear them take leave of one another with, " Madam, good-night to you," says one; " Madam, your servant," says another; " Pray my service to you know who "——— 'Tis very true, Harry.

Harry.—How could you ever expect Ned, that such an one would make you a good wife that minded nothing but her pride.

Ned.—Well, Harry, but you are mistaken, for some of them do make very good wives and are very good housewives too.

Harry—How long were you a-courting her, before she gave consent to marry you?

Ned.—Why, about a year or more, and all that while I very little did mind myself for minding of her, for I was fain to watch her as a cat watcheth a mouse, for fear of a rival. At last I told her I hoped now she would consent to marry me, if not, to tell me so, for it was a great loss to me to lose my time so day after day. Upon these words she told me she thought I was in earnest, but she did not much like the house I lived in. I told her it was a very pretty house, and I should be glad to see her in it. Upon this she smiled and gave me her consent.

Harry.—Was you asked in the church, Ned, or had you a license?

Ned.—I went on purpose to ask her that question, and she told me she was a gentlewoman born, and did not care to be asked in the church, for, she said, there was nobody asked in the church but cook-maids and kitchen-maids, so it cost me about twenty shillings for a license. Well, married we were, and very merry were we that day.

Harry.—But now, Ned, in the second place, come tell me how you and your wife agree together, for I think it is said your York wives will be masters of their husbands in less than a year's time if possibly they can. Well then, Ned, I do suppose it is with you as with most of your neighbours, your wife is the master?

Ned.—Faith, Harry, not much matter (scratching his head), but I doubt she'll come and find us together, and then there will be ———

Harry.—What then, Ned, let her come, I have a mug or two at her service and shall be glad to see her.

Ned.—So shall not I, Harry.

Harry.—Why, Ned, how can she be angry with you when she sees you with an old acquaintance you have not seen for two or three years?

Ned.—That's nothing.

Harry.—What, Ned, do not you agree then really, and has been married but three years. Suppose she should come, what would or could she say to you?

Ned.—Dear Harry, do not desire me to tell you, for if I would, and if you should happen to tell it again, and it should come to her ears that it was I told you, I might as well run my country as stay at home.

Harry.—Ned, my service to you, upon my honour, as the gentleman says, I will never say anything of it to anybody.

Ned.—Well then, Harry, if I be out at any time, as now with you, when I go home, as soon as I get within doors' she'll begin with a pretty tone she has learned off her neighbours.

"Oh! brave sir! You are a fine husband, you mind your business and shop, as you promised me before we were married: do you not, you drunken dog? you rogue, you rascal, where have you been these six hours (though it were but three), sirrah, give me account where you have been."

Harry.—Well, Ned, do you give her an account where you were, or what answer do you make her?

Ned.—All that I say to her is, "Pray, my dear, be not in such a passion, for I was with an old friend that I have not seen two or three years." "A pox on your old friend," says she, "and you too must go and fill your belly with good meat and drink, and I and my poor children starve at home, with only a little bread and cheese. A curse on the first day I saw you.

Harry.—Why, Ned, I hope your circumstances are not so low in the world, but that you can afford your wife pretty well to keep house with.

Ned.—Why, Harry, there's hardly a day but we have a joint of meat, either boiled or roasted, and I am sure she never wants for good bread, cheese, eggs, and butter.

Harry.—Pray, Ned, what does she do towards maintaining your house, does she endeavour any ways to get a penny? What portion had you with her?

Ned.—Harry, never marry a chamber-maid, for they bring nothing with them but a few old clothes of their mistresses, and for house-keeping, few of them know anything of it; for they can hardly make a pudding or a pie, neither can they spin, nor knit, nor wash, except it be a few laces to make themselves fine withal.

Harry.—What would she be at?

Ned.—Why always a-gossiping, there is such a company of them in our street that there's never a day but some or other of them meet together.

Harry.—Where do they meet?

Ned.—Where the best country ale is.

Harry.—What, do they make a sitting of it when they meet?

Ned.—A sitting of it; yes, yes, they will sit from three till ten at night, and drink like fishes, and talk against their husbands.

Harry.—What do you say when she comes home? Do you not ask her where she has been that she stayed so late?

Ned.—I dare not say one word to her, but am glad she will let me go to bed and sleep quietly.

Harry.—What becomes of your children those days; who looks after them all this while?

Ned.—Nobody but a silly maid she hired who can do

nothing; I am fain as well as I can, to boil them their milk for their suppers and help to get them to bed.

Harry.—Does not she ask when she comes home how her children do, and who gave them their suppers and got them to bed?

Ned.—Never, never, Harry, but perhaps the next morning will get them up herself, and put them on, poor things, the same linen they had on three days before.

Harry.—How do you allow your wife? do you allow her so much a week? how gets she the money to spare for gossiping?

Ned.—Why, she watches me; and if I sell anything in the shop, then she comes to me and tells me, such a child wants this, and such a one that, so I am fain to give her money for quietness' sake.

Harry.—Why, Ned, she makes a mere fool of you.

Ned.—'Tis not my case alone, Harry, for most of my neighbours have not much better wives, for the better sort they say, love carding and gossiping and cold tea.

Harry.—Well, Ned, I think you have almost satisfied me, and I promise you for your sake I will never marry any one of that sort called chamber-maids.

Ned.—If ever you marry, Harry, marry one that's bred up in business, I mean one that knows how to look after her house? and as you endeavour to get a penny in your way she will endeavour to get another in hers, such a one will make both you and herself happy.

Harry.—Pray then, Ned, what can your wife or any other man's wife say against her husband if he takes all the pains, as you say you do, to maintain her and her children handsomely?

Ned.—I know not but I hear this is their way. If any new married wife come among them; first she must pay for her admittance, then presently after, some of them will begin, " Neighbour, your good health"; another, " Neighbour I wish you health and happiness"; another, "Pray neighbour, what kind of a humoured man is your husband?" another, "Is he kind to you?" another, "Does he allow you as he should do? If he does not, neighbour, let us know, and we will tell you how to manage him I warrant you."

Harry.—Well, Ned, I pity thee, with all my heart, and all them that have such wives; but now you must make the best of it, and live as quietly as you can.

Ned.—Harry, I must so. Well, come, let's know what's to pay. I have stayed too long, so I am sure of a lecture when I go home.

Harry.—Come, Ned, I treat you this time because I invited you, it may be you will find your wife in a better humour than you think of.

Ned.—I wish I may, Harry. I am sure of it that it shall make me stay at home and mind my business a great deal better than I have done of late.

Harry.—How many children have you, Ned?

Ned.—Two boys, and I believe another coming.

Harry.—Well, Ned, she cannot complain of the smallness of her family.

Ned.—Well, Harry, I must take my leave of you, and I thank you for me, and if you do not go out of town to-morrow, I hope I shall see you again; there is a great deal more in a married state than I have told you of, that is all charges to the husband, the sickening-day, the week-day, the christening-day, three-week-day, the churching-day; all these days they have their meetings and discourses, which would take half a day to tell the mall; and if the husband be not there to wait upon them on those days, some of them will say, "Neighbour, where is your husband? he should be here to wait on us." "If my husband should serve me so," says another, "when I lie in, odds had." A third will say, "Indeed, neighbour, you give your husband too much liberty, more than I would do." So, Harry, when I go home she falls a-telling me what such a one and such a one, and all the company said of me, for my not being there to wait upon them.

Harry.—Well, Ned, thou has satisfied me very well, and for thy sake will never marry a chamber-maid. Come, ring the bell, we'll see what there's to pay, and should be glad of your company longer, if it stand to your conveniency.

Ned.—Harry, I thank you, but home I must go now.

Harry.—Jenny, what's to pay ? " One shilling sir."—Ned, good-night to you, my service to your spouse ; and if I stay to-morrow, I'll come and see you and her.

Ned.—Harry, good night to you, I thank you for me, and I shall be glad to see you to-morrow ; but whether my wife will or no I cannot tell, for I doubt I will find her but so-and-so in her humour.

Harry.—Good-night to you, Ned, thank you for your good company ; it has been very pleasant, and I hope you will find all things easy and quiet at home.

DANIEL O'ROURKE'S

WONDERFUL

VOYAGE TO THE MOON.

PEOPLE may have heard of the renowned adventures of Daniel O'Rourke, but how few are there who know that the cause of all his perils, above and below, was neither more nor less than his having slept under the walls of the Phooka's tower.

"I am often axed to tell it, sir," said he, "so that this is not the first time. The master's son, you see, had come from beyond foreign parts in France and Spain, as young gentlemen used to go, before Buonaparte or any such was heard of; and, sure enough, there was a dinner given to all the people on the ground, gentle and simple, high and low, rich and poor. The ould gentlemen were the gentlemen after all, saving your honour's presence. They'd swear at a body a little, to be sure, and maybe give one a cut of a whip now and then, but we were no losers by it in the end;—and they were so easy and civil, and kept such rattling houses, and thousands of welcomes; and there was no grinding for rent, and few agents; and there was hardly a tenant on the estate that did not taste of his landlord's bounty often and often in the year;—but now it's another thing; no matter for that, sir, for I'd better be telling you my story.

"Well, we had everything of the best, and plenty of it; and we ate, and we drank, and we danced, and the young master, by the same token, danced with Peggy Barry from Bothereen—a lovely young couple they were, though they are both long enough now. To make a long story short, I got, as a body may say, the same thing as tipsy almost, for I can't remember ever at all, no ways, how I left the place; only I did leave it, that's certain. Well, I thought, for all that, in myself, I'd just step to Molly Cronohan's, the fairy woman, to speak a word about the bracket heifer that was bewitched; and so as I was crossing the stepping stones at the ford of Ballyashenogh, and was looking up at the stars, and blessing myself—for why? it was Lady-day—I missed my foot, and souse I fell into the water. 'Death alive!' thought I, 'I'll be drowned now!' However, I began swimming, swimming, swimming away for the dear life, till at last I got ashore, somehow or other, but never the one of me can tell how, upon a dissolute island.

"I wandered and wandered about there, without knowing where I wandered, until at last I got into a big bog. The moon was shining as bright as day, or your fair lady's eyes, sir (with your pardon for mentioning her), and I looked east and west, and north and south, and every way, and nothing did I see but bog, bog, bog. I could never find out how I got into it, and my heart grew cold with fear, for sure and certain I was that it would be my barrin place. So I sat down upon a stone which, as good luck would have it, was close by me, and I began to scratch my head and sing the Ullagon, when all of a sudden the moon grew black, and I looked up, and saw something for all the world as if it was moving down between me and it, and I could not tell what it was. Down it came with a pounce, and looked at me full in the face. And what was it but an eagle—as fine a one as ever flew from the kingdom of Kerry. So he looked at me in the face, and says he to me, 'Daniel O'Rourke,' says he, 'how do you do?' 'Very well, I thank you, sir,' says I; 'I hope you're well,' wondering out of my senses all the time how an eagle came to speak like a Christian. 'What brings you here, Dan?' says he. 'Nothing at all, sir,' says I; 'only I wish I was safe home again.' 'Is it out of the island you want to go, Dan?' says he. ''Tis, sir,' says I; so I up and told him how I had taken a drop too much, and fell into the water; how I swam to the island; and how I got into the bog and did not know my way out of it. 'Dan,' says he, after a minute's thought, 'though it is very improper for you to get drunk on Lady-day, yet, as you are a decent sober man, who tends mass well, and never flings stones at me or mine, nor cries out after us in the fields—my life for yours,' says he; 'so get up on my back, and grip me well for fear you'd fall off, and I'll fly you out of the bog.' 'I am afraid,' says I, 'your honour's making game of me; for who ever heard of riding a-horseback on an eagle before?' ''Pon the honour of a gentleman,' says he, putting his right foot on his breast, 'I am quite in earnest; and so, now, either take my offer or starve in the bog; besides, I see that your weight is sinking the stone.'

"It was true enough as he said, for I found the stone every minute going from under me. I had no choice; so thinks I to myself, faint heart never won fair lady, and this is fair persuadance. 'I thank your honour,' says I, 'for the load of your civility, and I'll take your kind offer.' I therefore mounted upon the back of the eagle, and held him tight enough by the throat, and up he flew in the air like a lark. Little I knew the trick he was going to serve me. Up—up —up—God knows how far up he flew. 'Why, then,' said I to him, thinking he did not know the right road home, very civilly—because why? I was in his power entirely—'sir,' says I, 'please your honour's glory, and with humble submission to your better judgment, if you'd fly down a bit, you're now just over my cabin, and I could be put down there, and many thanks to your worship.'

"'Arrah, Dan,' said he, 'do you think me a fool? Look down in the next field, and don't you see two men and a gun? By my word it would be no joke to be shot this way, to oblige a drunken blackguard that I picked up off a could stone in a bog.' 'Bother you,' said I to myself, but I did not speak out, for where was the use? Well, sir, up he kept flying, flying, and I asking him every minute to fly down, and all to no use. 'Where in the world are you going, sir?' says I to him. 'Hold your tongue, Dan,' says he; 'mind your own business, and don't be interfering with the business of other people.' 'Faith, this is my business, I think,' says I. 'Be quiet, Dan,' says he; so I said no more.

"At last, where should we come to but to the moon itself. Now, you can't see it from this; but there is, or there was in my time, a reaping-hook sticking out of the side of the moon, this way (drawing the figure on the ground with the end of his stick).

"'Dan,' said the eagle, 'I'm tired with this long fly; I had no notion 'twas so far.' 'And, my lord, sir,' said I, 'who in the world axed you to fly so far—was it I? Did not I beg, and pray, and beseech you to stop half an hour ago?' 'There's no use talking, Dan,' said he; 'I'm tired bad enough, so you must get off, and sit down on the moon until I rest myself.' 'Is it sit down on the moon?' said I. 'Is it upon that little round thing, then? Why, then, sure I'd fall off in a minute, and be kilt and split, and smashed all to bits; you are a vile deceiver, so you are.' 'Not at all, Dan,' said he; 'you can catch fast hold of the reaping-hook that's sticking out of the side of the moon, and 'twill keep you up.' 'I won't, then,' said I. 'Maybe not,' said he, quite quiet. 'If you don't, my man, I shall just give you a shake, and one slap of my wing, and send you down to the ground, where every bone of your body will be smashed as small as a drop of dew on a cabbage-leaf in the morning.' 'Why, then, I'm in a fine way,' said I to myself, 'ever to have come alone with the likes of you;' and so, giving him a hearty curse in Irish, for fear he'd know what I said, I got off his back with a heavy heart, took hold of the reaping-hook, and sat down upon the moon; and a mighty cold seat it was, I can tell you that.

"When he had me there fairly landed, he turned about on me, and said, 'Good morning to you, Daniel O'Rourke,' said he; 'I think I've nicked you fairly now. You robbed my nest last year ('twas true enough for him, but how he found it out is hard to say), and in return you are freely welcome to cool your heels dangling upon the moon like a cockthrow.'

"'Is that all, and is this the way you leave me, you brute, you?' says I. 'You ugly unnatural baste, and is this the way you serve me at last? Bad luck to yourself, with your hooked nose, and to all your breed, you blackguard.' 'Twas all to no manner of use; he spread out his great big wings, burst out a-laughing, and flew away like lightning. I bawled after him to stop, but I might have called and bawled for ever without his minding me. Away he went, and I never saw him from that day to this. Sorrow fly away with him! You may be sure I was in a disconsolate condition, and kept roaring out for the bare grief, when all at once a door opened right in the middle of the moon, creaking on its hinges as if it had not been opened for a month before. I suppose they never thought of greasing 'em; an I out there walks, who do you think, but the man in the moon himself. I knew him by his busk.

"'Good morrow to you, Daniel O'Rourke,' said he. 'How do you do?' 'Very well, thank your honour,' said I. 'I hope your honour's well.' 'What brought you here, Dan?' said he. So I told him how I was a little overtaken in liquor at the master's, and how I was cast on a dissolute island, and how I lost my way in the bog, and how the thief of an eagle promised to fly me out of it, and how, instead of that, he had fled me up to the moon.

"'Dan,' said the man in the moon, taking a pinch of snuff when I was done, 'you must not stay here.' 'Indeed, sir,' says I, ''tis much against my will I'm here at all; but how am I to go back?' 'That's your business,' said he, 'Dan; mine is to tell you that here you must not stay, so be off in less than no time.' 'I'm doing no harm,' says I, 'only holding on hard by the reaping-hook lest I fall off.' 'That's what you must not do, Dan,' says he. 'Pray, sir,' says I, 'may I ask how many you are in family, that you would not give a poor traveller lodgings? I'm sure 'tis not so often you're troubled with strangers coming to see you, for 'tis a long way.' 'I'm by myself, Dan,' says he; 'but you'd better let go the reaping-hook.' 'Faith, and with your leave,' says I, 'I'll not let go the grip; and the more you bids me, the more I won't let go, so I will.' 'You had better, Dan,' says he again. 'Why, then, my little fellow,' says I, taking the whole weight of him with my eye from head to foot, 'there are two words to that bargain; and I'll not budge, but you may if you like.' 'We'll see how that is to be,' says he; and back he went, giving the door such a great bang after him (for it was plain he was huffed) that I thought the moon and all would fall down with it.

"Well, I was preparing myself to try strength with him, when back again he comes with the kitchen cleaver in his hand, and, without saying a word, he gives two bangs to the handle of the reaping-hook that was keeping me up, and whap! it came in two. 'Good morning to you, Dan,' says the spiteful little old blackguard, when he saw me cleanly falling down with a bit of the handle in my hand, 'I thank you for your visit, and fair weather after you, Daniel.' I had no time to make any answer to him, for I was tumbling over and over, and rolling and rolling at the rate of a fox-hunt. 'God help me,' says I, 'but this is a pretty pickle for a decent man to be seen in at this time of night; I am now sold fairly.' The word was not out of my mouth when whiz! what should fly by close to my ear but a flock of wild geese, all the way from my own bog of Ballyashenogh, else how should they know me? The ould gander, who was their general, turning about his head, cried out to me, 'Is that you, Dan?' 'The same,' said I, not a bit daunted now at what he said, for I was by this time used to all kinds of bedevilment, and, besides, I knew him of ould. 'Good morrow to you,' says he, 'Daniel O'Rourke. How are you in health this morning?' 'Very well, sir,' says I; 'I thank you kindly,' drawing my breath, for I was mightily in want of some. 'I hope your honour's the same.' 'I think 'tis falling you are, Daniel,' says he. 'You may say that, sir,' says I. 'And where are you going all the way so fast?' said the gander. So I told him how I had taken the drop, and how I came on the island, and how I lost my way in the bog, and how the thief of an eagle flew me up to the moon, and how the man in the moon turned me out. 'Dan,' said he, 'I'll save you; put your hand out and catch me by the leg, and I'll fly you home.' 'Sweet is your hand in a pitcher of honey, my jewel,' says I, though all the time I thought in myself that I don't much trust you; but there was no help, so I caught the gander by the leg, and away I and the other geese flew after him as fast as hops.

"We flew, and we flew, and we flew, until we came right over the wide ocean. I knew it well, for I saw Cape Clear to my right hand, sticking up out of the water. 'Ah! my lord,' said I to the goose—for I thought it best to keep a civil tongue in my head any way—'fly to land, if you please.' 'It is impossible, you see, Dan,' said he, 'for a while, because, you see, we are going to Arabia.' 'To Arabia!' said I; 'that's surely some place in foreign parts, far away. Oh! Mr. Goose, why, then, to be sure, I'm a man to be pitied among you.' 'Whist, whist, you fool,' said he; 'hold your tongue. I tell you Arabia is a very decent sort of place, as like West Carbery as one egg is like another, only there is a little more sand there.'

Just as we were talking a ship hove in sight, scudding so beautiful before the wind. 'Ah! then, sir,' said I, 'will you drop me on the ship, if you please?' 'We are not fair over it,' said he. 'We are,' said I. 'We are not,' said he; 'if I dropped you now, you would go splash into the sea.' 'I would not,' says I; 'I know better than that, for it is just clean under us, so let me drop now at once.'

"'If you must, you must,' said he. 'There, take your own way;' and he opened his claw, and faith he was right, —sure enough, I came down plump into the very bottom of the salt sea! Down to the very bottom I went, and I gave myself up then for ever, when a whale walked up to me, scratching himself after his night's rest, and looked me full in the face, and never the word did he say; but lifting up his tail, he splashed me all over again with the cold salt water, till there wasn't a dry stitch upon my whole carcase; and I heard somebody saying—'twas a voice I knew too—'Get up, you drunken brute, out of that,' and with that I woke up, and there was Judy with a tub full of water, which she was splashing all over me; for, rest her soul! though she was a good wife, she never could bear to see me in drink, and had a bitter hand of her own.

"'Get up,' said she again; 'and of all places in the parish, would no place sarve your turn to lie down upon but under the ould walls of Carrigaphooka? An uneasy resting I am sure you had of it.' And sure enough I had; for I was fairly bothered out of my senses with eagles, and men of the moons, and flying ganders, and whales, driving me through bogs, and up to the moon, and down to the bottom of the great ocean. If I was in drink ten times over, long would it be before I'd lie down in the same spot again, I know that."

MOTHER BUNCH'S CLOSET
NEWLY BROKE OPEN;

CONTAINING

RARE SECRETS OF NATURE AND ART,

TRIED AND EXPERIENCED

BY LEARNED PHILOSOPHERS,

And recommended to all ingenious young men and maids, teaching them, in a natural way, how to get good wives and husbands.

Approved by several that have made trial of them; it being the product of forty-nine years' study.

By our loving Friend Poor Tom, for the King, a lover of Mirth, but a hater of Treason.

IN TWO PARTS.

PART I.

READING over many ancient Histories, it was my chance to meet with this story of an old woman who lived in the west, who took delight in studying her fortune. When she found herself full twenty years old, she thought her luck worse than some who were married at fifteen or sixteen, which much troubled her mind; but to prevent all doubts she resolved to try a story she had often heard her mother talk of, and, finding it true, she resolved to teach other maidens.

On a time, this old woman having newly buried her husband, was taking a walk in the fields, for the benefit of the air, sometimes thinking of the loss of her husbands, for she had had three, yet had a great desire for the fourth. So it happened, as she was walking alone, she espied a young maiden by the meadow-side. "Good morrow, maid," said the old woman, "how do you do? are not you well?" "Yes, mother, I am very well, but somewhat troubled in mind." "What is it troubles you so much? If I can, I will willingly relieve you, therefore be not ashamed to tell the truth. Is it anything of great concern?" "Indeed, mother, seeing you urge me so much, I will tell you the truth. We are three sisters, the youngest was married about a year ago, the middlemost last week, and I am the eldest, and no man heeds me." "Well, daughter, if this be all, I believe I can assist thee, for when I was young I was in the same condition, and with reading some histories, found out the art to know him that should be my husband, which, if you will keep my counsel, I am ready to teach thee." "I will, truly, and if you will do so much for me, I shall think myself much obliged to you; and, if my fortune proves right, I will make you amends."

"Why, then, I will tell you, in the first place, you must observe St. Agnes' day, which is the 21st of January, and on that day let no man speak to thee, and at night, when thou liest down lay thy right hand under thy head, and say these words, 'Now the God of hope let me dream of my love'; then go to sleep as soon as possible, and you shall be sure to dream of him who will be your husband, and see him stand before you, and may take notice of him and his complexion; and if he offer to salute thee honourably, do not deny him, but show him as much favour as thou canst; but if he offers to be uncivil, be sure to send him away. And now, daughter, the counsel I have given you, be sure to tell nobody. So, fare you well, till I see you again."

"I give you thanks for your advice; but one thing more I have to say, What is your name? and where do you live?" "I will tell you, daughter; my name is Mother Bunch, and I live at a place called Bonadventure, where, if you come, I will make you welcome."

Now Mother Bunch having departed from the maid, she met another pretty girl. "Good morrow, Mother Bunch." "Good morrow, pretty maid, whither are you going this morning? Methinks you are very fine to-day." "Fine! Mother Bunch, you do not think so." "Nay, I cannot discommend you; for such a brisk maid as you should go handsome, or you will never get a sweetheart, though you think the time long." "No, no, mother, I am too young." "How old are you?" "I am eighteen." "Eighteen! then I know thou thinkest thou hast stayed long enough, and wouldest as willingly have a husband as another." "Aye, Mother Bunch, but good husbands are hard to find, especially for me, who have no skill in choosing, or else it may be I would be glad of a good husband." "Be sure to take my advice: be wise in choosing, that is to say, take no one that has got a red head, for be sure he loveth a smock so well that he will scarce let his wife have a good one to her back; nor of yellow hair, as he is inclinable to be jealous; nor a black man, for he is dogged." "Aye, but mother, if I must not have yellow, black, nor red, what colour must I take?" "Why, daughter, I tell you, if he is jealous, you will be annoyed by his speeches, for how can a young woman forbear when she is always provoked? And be sure, if he is jealous of thee thou mayest well be so of him; for evil people and thieves think ill of each other. But hold a little, one thing more I have to say to you, and that is, to take notice of thy sweethearts when they come a-wooing to thee, I mean of their civil behaviour; for if they swear, vow, and make great protestations, then have a care of thyself, for many words breed dissimulation; therefore have a care of such: but if a man come to thee that is sober and civil behaved, there are hopes of his proving a good man." "Now, mother, I will take my leave of you, giving you many thanks for your good advice; and so, farewell, till I see you again, and I intend to take this counsel."

Another time Mother Bunch was in a little meadow, not far from her house, on the 30th of April, before sunrising. A handsome maid, seeing her alone, came to her, and said, "Mother Bunch, good morrow, how do you do? Pray, what makes you abroad so early in the morning? You seem to be in a deep study." "Daughter, you say very true; I am studying who shall be my next husband, and if thou wilt but please to stay a little while, thou shalt see a pretty art, which thou never saw before, to teach you how to know your sweetheart." "This is a pretty art indeed, and I should be glad to know it."

"Hark! hark! daughter, is not yonder the cuckoo singing?" "Yes, yes, and I have not heard her sing this year before now." "Then, daughter, sit down by me, but hold, Are you fasting?" "Yes." "But has no man kissed you?" "No." Then sit thee down by me. I think the cuckoo is mad, what a life she leads; I think she is a witch; but no matter: put off thy right shoe and stocking, and let me look between thy great toe and the next: Now, daughter, see, this hair is a long one; look well at it, and tell me what colour it is." "I think it is really yellow." "The same colour will thy husband's hair be." "But, Mother Bunch, I do not matter the colour so much as the condition." "I will tell you his condition: he may prove surly enough, and perhaps make you do as you did not imagine: you must give him good words, and give him good for evil." "Mother Bunch, you make me smile, you talk so merrily." "Come, daughter, it is no great matter; merry talk does no harm, but drives the time away. But hark! daughter, I have had three husbands myself, and I think to have another; and do you think I am so mad to tell him all I do? Then, my daughter, I have another way to tell you who must be your husband; I have proved it true; and it is the best time of the year to try it, therefore, observe what I say: Take a St. Thomas' onion, pare it, and lay it on a clean handkerchief under your pillow; and as you lie down, say these words—

> Good St. Thomas, do me right,
> And bring my love in dreams this night,
> That I may view him in the face.

Then go to sleep as soon as you can, and in your first sleep you shall dream of him who is to be your husband. This I have tried, and it has proved true. Yet I have another pretty way for a maid to know her sweetheart, which is as follows: Take a summer apple of the best fruit, stick pins close into the apple, to the head, and as you stick them take notice which of them is the middlemost, and give it what name you fancy; put it into thy left hand glove, and lay it under thy pillow on Saturday night; after thou gettest into bed, then clap thy hands together, and say these words—

> If thou be he that must have me
> To be thy wedded bride,
> Make no delay, but come away,
> In dream to my bedside.

And in thy sleep thou shalt see him, and be not afraid, for it is a sign he will prove a good husband. And this is a good way for a young man to know his sweetheart, giving the middlemost pin the name he fancies best, putting the apple in his right hand glove, and laying it under his pillow when he is in bed, saying—

> If thou be she that must have me
> In wedlock for to join,
> Make no delay, but come away
> So I may dream of mine.

"And that night he may see her, and if she come it is a sign she will prove a good wife. And now, daughter, the time passes away, and I must be gone, and so bid you farewell." "Mother Bunch, I give you many thanks for your good counsel, and intend to take your advice."

Upon a time, Mother Bunch, being at a wedding, where young men and maids were met, who had a mind for some discourse with her, one young man said, "Mother Bunch, we know you are a woman that has a judgment in many things, I pray, tell my fortune." "I cannot tell fortunes," said she, "but thou blinkest too much with one eye to be true to one woman." "Aye, but, mother," says another, "what think you of me?" "Thou mayest come to marry a lady, if thou canst but lay a great wager with her, three to one; and if she wagers with thee, thou wilt be very likely to win, for thou hast mettle in thee; but have a care she win not the odds, if she does thou art clean gone. So farewell."

Now Mother Bunch took her leave; and going home, she met a maid going to a wedding. "How do you do, mother?" "Thank you, daughter, whither are you going?" "To the wedding, I believe; but hark'you, mother, will you sit down a little, I have something to say to you." "What is it, daughter?" "When shall I be married?" "Would you fain be married?" "Yes, mother, if I could get a good husband." "Then, daughter, I will tell you the best I can, if you will take my advice. In the month of January are many dangerous days for thee to take notice of; these are the first, second, third, fourth, and fifth: there are a great many more; but if thou marriest on these days, thy husband will cuckold thee, or thou wilt make him one, or else you will soon be parted by one means or other; but for all there be so many bad days in this month I can tell you of one day which is lucky, and many young men and maids have a deal of heart's ease on that day, or the day after, as I shall let you understand; it is the 21st, called St. Agnes' day. This St. Agnes has a great favour for young men and maids, and will bring their sweethearts, if they follow my rules: Upon this day you must be sure to keep a fast, and neither eat nor drink all that day, nor at night; neither let man, woman, nor child kiss thee on that day; and thou must be sure, when thou goest to bed, to say—

> Now, St. Agnes, play thy part,
> And send to me my own sweetheart;
> And show me such a happy bliss,
> This night to dream of a sweet kiss.

And be sure to fall asleep as soon as you can, and before you awake out of your first sleep, you shall see him come before you, and shall perceive by his habit what tradesman he is; and be sure thou declare not thy dream unto any one in ten days, and by that time thou mayest see thy dream come to pass. All this I have proved three times; for I have had three husbands, and they all proved tradesmen. The first was a straw joiner, the second a louse-trap maker, and the third a gentle craft, and he came to me with his awl in his hand, and so I waked out of my dream; but I thought the time long till he came again; as all maids do that desire to be married. I know some maids would wait in order to have a husband with the best conditions, and endowed with the best qualifications; nay they would have impossibilities: but I am afraid they will make good the old proverb, that says—

> 'If you will not when you may,
> When you would you shall have nay.'

Therefore, take my advice, if a young man comes to you of a civil carriage, and you think you can love him, be not scornful to him, but give him a civil encouragement, according to his behaviour.

And as to young men, my advice is, they be wary in their choice, since there is as much danger in choosing of a wife as a husband: wherefore, all young men, take my advice: choose not one with a long nose, a scolding brow, and thin lips, for in such there is great danger. He who is tied to a scold is tied to sorrow; choose not one who is counted a slut, if she be a slut, she is idle also, and these two companions will bring thee to poverty; nay, besides this, the old saying is, 'A slut will poison the gout, and if you can't eat with her, you won't sleep with her.'

But this is the best way of choosing a wife: Take one for love, not for riches which fly away, for true love never varies; and where that is, the blessing of God is. If you desire to live a long life, be not overfond of riches, but choose a civil handsome maid, who is not given to pride: such a maid may make a fine wife. But she that brings a handsome fortune, will be always throwing it in your teeth, which often occasions great disturbances; therefore let this suffice for those who desire to get good wives; and take notice of what I have already said, and you may fare the better.

And as for young maids, this is my advice, if they will not try St. Agnes, let them be sure to choose a clever, honest man, who is able to support them in comfort."

Part II.

On Michaelmas Day, Mother Bunch, sitting on the bank of a river, joining to a neighbouring grove, beheld the late flourishing branches in their decay, whose sapless leaves were falling to the earth, from which she began seriously to consider her own mortality; and since time had hurried on the winter of her age, and covered her aged head with snowy locks, she might expect, ere long, to fall, like the enfeebled leaves. Therefore, she resolved, as she had been a kind friend to young men and maids, to give a further testimony of her regard before she left this world. For as her painful study and strict observation had made a large improvement in her stock of knowledge she would not have it buried in the grave with her, but leave it to posterity for the benefit of young men and maids, whereby they might learn to understand their good and bad fortunes, and by the directions of this book be thoroughly furnished with many secret rarities never before published to the world.

Accordingly, the next day she wrote letters of invitation to the young men and maids to repair to her house on St. Luke's Day. The maids she appointed to meet in the morning, to be first instructed, and that for two reasons. First, as she herself was a woman, she would teach them first, lest the bachelors should be too hard for them before they had learned their lessons. Secondly, that young women should be first served in this, it being Horn Fair Day, many of the bachelors would be employed in the morning, in handing old citizens' young wives to the fair; and in the afternoon they might be at liberty. This was the determination of old Mother Bunch.

Now against the time appointed, old Mother Bunch decked up her house, neat and fine, and, getting up early in the morning, placed herself in the closet, where her treasure lay.

Now the first that entered the room was one Margery Loveman, a maltster's maid, who, with a low curtsey, said, "Good morrow, Mother Bunch, I am come to partake of your bounty; for I hear you have a second time opened your Golden Closet of Curiosities for the benefit of young lovers." "Yes, daughter," quoth Mother Bunch, "so I have, and thou shalt partake of the same. Here is infallible rules and directions to guide you in all manner of love intrigues; also, how to know what sort of man you shall marry, and whither he will prove loving or not."

"Dear mother, these are things I fain would know; for, believe me, I have many sweethearts, and I willingly choose the best, lest I should marry in haste and repent at leisure. 'Tis true, I have near a hundred and fifty pounds to my portion, the great noise of which has brought many sweethearts, for I have no less than five or six at this time; and, mother, I would fain know which of them comes for love of me, and which of them for money." "Daughter," quoth Mother Bunch, "here is an experiment, if you will but try, it will make a clear discovery of the reality of their love. Let a report be spread that thou hast lately been robbed of all that thou hast, both money and apparel. Now, if after this, there is one of them that continues his love as before, you may be very certain that he is faithful; but, be sure that you keep this counsel to yourself, that the secret be not discovered." "I will take care of that, dear mother," quoth Margery, "and I heartily thank you for this kind and seasonable advice."

"Good morrow, daughter," she replied,
"Young men are false, and must be tried."

She was no sooner gone, but in comes Mrs. Susan, a young sempstress from Salisbury, with sorrowful lamentation, weeping and wringing her hands. "How now!" quoth good Mother Bunch; "what is the matter with you, daughter, that you go on at this rate?" "Alas! Mother Bunch," quoth Susan, "my—my—my—my—my—my!" "What my?" said Mother Bunch. Quoth sobbing Susan, "My sorrows are more than I am able to bear; for, mother, dear Frank the fiddler, my old love, and I are fallen out, and he swears he will not have me." "Come, daughter," quoth Mother Bunch, "be of good comfort, for I will put thee in an effectual way to find whither Frank the fiddler be really angry with thee or not; and if he be, I will teach thee infallibly how to obtain his favour again. 'She that is afraid of every grass, must not think to go in a meadow.' Let your angry love but alone for a season, and he will soon come to himself again; for I know that love is a puny darling, and wants very frequently to be humoured. Therefore, let him alone, in time he will forget his anger, and return to thee again, if he has any principle, good nature, or loyal love in him; and if not, you had better be without him than during your whole life to be tied to so sour an apple tree.

Remember the old proverb, 'Set thy stool in the sun; if a knave goes, an honest man may come.' I hope thou hast not been playing the wanton wagtail with him, hast thou?" "No, indeed, dear Mother Bunch; but yet, I must needs confess that he fain would have played a lesson on my lute last market day, but I would not let him; and that was the cause of our falling out." "Sayest thou so, daughter? Why, then, I will tell thee, that since he found thou withstood his temptations, with so much resolution, take my word for it he will never forget thee." "Well, dear mother," quoth young Susan, "your words have been comfortable to me; and when I find the good effects, I will return and give you an account of it. And so farewell, dear mother, for the present."

"Right happy, daughter, may you be,
In guarding your true purity."

The next that entered the room was Eliza, the miller's maid, who, after making a very low curtsey, and giving Mother Bunch the time of the day, desiring to know for what reason she sent her that letter? "Why," says the old woman, "to the end that I might reveal to you some secrets relating to love, which I have never discovered to the world." "But, dear Mother Bunch," quoth Margery, "I am a mere stranger to love, for I never in my life knew what it meant." "That may be," quoth Mother Bunch: "yet you know not how soon you may receive the arrows of Cupid, then you would be glad of some of my advice, for I know by myself, that the best woman of you all, at one time or other, has a desire to know what it is to be married." Quoth Margery, "You talk merrily, Mother Bunch." "Well, daughter," quoth Mother Bunch, "you may term it as you please: but I will appeal to your own conscience whether or no you would be glad, with all your heart, of a kind and loving husband."

"Dear Mother," quoth Margery, "you come quite close to the matter; and if I may be so free as to speak my own mind, I could willingly have such a one; for though housekeeping is said to be very chargeable often, yet, on the other hand, a married state is honourable." "Thou sayest well, daughter," quoth Mother Bunch, "and if thou hast a mind to see the man whom thou shalt marry, then follow strictly my directions, and you shall not fail of your desire. Let me see—this is St. Luke's Day, which I have found by long study to be of greater use to that purpose than that of the celebrated St. Agnes, which I formerly recommended you to; and the ingredients now to be used are of a quite different and finer quality, and far more excellent for performing the same.

Now I would have you take some marigold flowers, a large sprig of sweet marjoram, a sprig of fresh thyme, and a small quantity of wormwood; dry these together before the fire, till you may rub them to a powder; then sift the same through a piece of fine lawn. This being done, take a small quantity of virgin honey, and right white wine vinegar, and simmer them together in a new earthen porringer, over a mild and gentle fire; all which being done, anoint your forehead and cheeks, and lips, likewise, with the same, just the moment you are lying down in your bed; always remembering to repeat these words three times—

St. Luke, St. Luke, be kind to me,
And let me now my true love see.

This said, hasten to sleep with all speed; then in the soft slumber of your night's repose the very man you are to marry shall appear before you walking to and fro near to your bedside, very plain and visible to be seen: you shall perfectly behold the colour of his hair, his visage, stature, and deportment. And if he be one that will prove faithful, he will approach you with a smile, and offer to salute you; which, when he does, do not seem to be overfond or peevishly froward, but receive the same with a becoming mild and modest smile. Now, if he be one that will, after marriage, forsake his house to wander after strange women, then will he offer to be rude and uncivil with thee, at which time thou shalt lift up thy hand to smite him; so doing, it will go well with thee, and thy guardian angel will keep thee ever safe. Daughter, these are rarities which I never before divulged. Do but put this in execution, and I am certain it will answer the desired effect." "I must needs thank you for your love," quoth Margery; "and so farewell, Mother Bunch." "Good-bye, daughter," she replied.

"Let joy and pleasure crown your days,
And a kind man your fortune raise."

The next that appeared was Kate, the cloth-worker's daughter; then Doll, the dairymaid; Joan, Bridget, Nancy, and Phillis, in number about forty together, each of them crying out with a loud voice, "Dear Mother Bunch, remember me." "O remember me," quoth another; and so did they all, till they made the poor old woman's ears deaf with the clamorous noise. "My dear daughters," quoth Mother Bunch, "sit you all down and be quiet, for there is never a one amongst you but will partake of my bounty. Daughters, I will sit in the midst of you, where I shall read over a very interesting lecture. My real motive is to give you a full account of some rare and excellent curiosities, in my Golden Closet, newly broke open; declaring that it is my opinion that those things which are profitable to one maid may not be prejudicial, in any respect, to another, and this I shall begin.

First, if any of you here desire to know the name of the man whom you shall marry, let her seek in the summer time for a green peascod, in which there are nine pease; when you have done this, either write, or cause to be written, on a slip of paper, these words—

Come in, my dear,
And never fear.

Writing which, you must carefully close within the aforesaid peascod, and lay the same under the threshold of the door, and then observe the next man that comes into the house; for you shall certainly be married to one of the same name.

Secondly, she that desires to be satisfied whether she shall get the man desired or no, let her take two lemon-peels in the morning, and wear them all the day under her arm-pit, then at night let her not fail to take them, and rub the four posts of the bed with the same; which being done, in your first sleep, he will seem to come and present you with a couple of choice lemons, if not, there is no hope.

Thirdly, she that is desirous to know what manner of fortune she shall marry, whether a gentleman, a tradesman, or a traveller, the experiment is thus: Take a walnut, a hazel nut, and a nutmeg; crack the two nuts, and take off the scurf; peel them clear from the kernels, and grate part of the nutmeg to them; this being done, bruise the kernels of the nuts, and mix them with butter and sugar, making them up into peels, which are to be taken just when you are lying down in your bed. Then if your fortune be to marry a gentleman, your sleep will be filled with fine golden dreams, variety of sweet music, and many running footmen; if a tradesman, great noise and tumults; if a traveller (who is a seaman), then frightful visions of lightning and roaring thunder will disturb your sleep. This has been often tried, and as often approved.

Fourthly, St. Agnes' Day I have not wholly blotted out of my book; no, but I have found a more exact way of trial than before: You shall not need to abstain from kisses, nor be forced to keep a fast from a glance of your love in the night. If you can rise to be at the parish church door punctually between the hours of twelve and one in the morning, and then and there put only the fore-finger of your right hand into the keyhole of the said door, repeating the following words, three times over—

    O sweet St. Agnes, now draw near
    With my true love, let him appear.

Then he will straight approach to you with a cheerful and smiling countenance. This is a new and infallible way of making the trial.

Fifthly, my dear daughters, you all know the thirteenth day of February is Valentine's Day, at which time the fowls of the air couple together, and not only so, but the young men and maidens are for choosing mates at the same time. Now, that you may speed to your full satisfaction, follow this approved direction: Take five bay leaves, lay one under every corner of your pillow, and the fifth under the middle, then laying yourself down to rest, repeat the following words in the four lines, seven times over—

    Some guardian angel let me have
    What I most earnestly do crave,
    A valentine endowed with love,
    Which will both kind and constant prove.

Then to your great content, you shall either have the valentine of him you desire, or, at least, one much more excellent.

Sixthly, the experiment of the midsummer smock, found in a better manner than before, by my painful study in philosophy. And now, daughters," quoth she, "take particular notice, for it is thus: Let seven of you together, on a midsummer's eve, exactly at the sun's setting, go silently into some garden, and gather each of you a sprig of red sage, then return to some private room, prepared particularly for that purpose, with a stool placed in the middle, each one of you having a clean smock, turned the wrong side outwards, hanging upon a line across the room, then let every one lay her sprig of red sage on a clean plate of rosewater set on a stool; which done, place yourselves in a row, where continue till twelve or one o'clock, saying nothing, whatever you see, for after midnight, each one's sweetheart or husband, that shall be, will take each maid's sprig out of the rosewater, and sprinkle his love's smock, and those who are so unfortunate as never to be married, their sprigs shall not be moved; and in consequence hereof many sobs and heavy sighs will be heard. This has been very often tried in our own country, and never failed of the desired effect.

These things I have found out of late,
To make young lovers fortunate.

And now, my dear daughters, I have but a few more words to say at this time, and they are by way of caution: In the twelve months I find above one and thirty very unfortunate days; and therefore, as you regard the future happiness of your lives, take care that you do not enter into wedlock upon those days. Now, for your better instruction, I'll tell you which they be.

In January there are four; the 7th, 16th, 17th, and 18th.
February hath two; the 5th and 10th.
March hath three; the 9th, 10th, and 21st.
April hath two; the 6th and 7th.
May hath two; the 4th and 13th.
June hath three; the 7th, 9th, and 10th.
July hath two; the 9th and 17th.
August hath two; the 11th and 15th.
September hath three: the 2nd, 3rd, and 4th.
October hath three; the 4th, 14th, and 15th.
November hath two; the 5th and 24th.
December hath three; the 6th, 7th, and 9th.

Observe my rules for all these days,
And then you will your fortune raise."

This said, old Mother Bunch presented them with a cup of her fine cordial water, and so dismissed them; and the young damsels, with rapturous hearts, returned her their hearty thanks.

After Mother Bunch had done dinner, the young men came, to wit, Tom the miller, Ralph the thatcher, and Robin the ploughman, with a great number of other trades and callings, all whom Mother Bunch invited to sit down that she might deliver her wholesome counsels to them.

And first she begins with Tom the miller, saying, "Ah, Tom! thou art a sad wild young fellow; there is not a maid that can come to the mill but thou will be fooling with them, but take my word for it, if you do not leave off in time, you will certainly spoil all your fortune. What woman do you think, having a portion, will have such a one? She may justly conclude that you will still run a catterwauling after young wenches, and leave her to sigh and weep for want of domestic happiness,—you know what I mean, Tom."

"Yes, yes, mother," quoth Tom, "but sure you do not take me for such a one." "Yes, Tom, I do, and am seldom mistaken. It is you millers that fill the country so full of cracked-headed maidens, that when an honest husband comes to marry he finds the hearts already stolen away. But farewell, I'll have no more to say to such a fellow as you."

Then turning to Ralph the thatcher, she said, "I find you are very desirous of a wife, and your ambition is such that she must be rich, young, and beautiful: cannot you content yourself with honest Joan, to whom you gave promise of marriage? And now I find you have a mind to leave her, which if you do, and obtain such a one as you desire, I can tell you what will follow. She won't stand picking of straws with you, her fair face will find many friends in a corner, and you may chance to be a cuckold, and indeed but justly served in your kind; and, therefore, I advise you to return to your old love, for she is a very honest girl, and therefore far more fit for you than such a gay butterfly as you have lately followed."

Then she stretched forth her hand to Robin the ploughman, saying, "Thou art an honest fellow, and good fortune will always attend thee. I mean not bags of gold nor heaps of silver; but thou shalt have a careful and industrious wife, one that will ever be willing and ready to labour, a true and faithful yoke-mate, and one that will be a cheerful partner in thy weal and woe, to comfort and support thee under the greatest and most severe trials. For, as the poet has it—

'That burden may be borne
  By two with care,
Which is perhaps too much
  For one to bear.'

Honest Robin, this is thy happy fortune, and as thou art a downright honest fellow, I am glad to find it so."

    Thus Mother Bunch went round the room,
    And told them what would be their doom,
    If they her daughters did betray,
    And steal their maiden hearts away,
    Each would be punished with a bride,
    By whom he should be hornify'd;
    But if they were right honest men,
    Each of them should have fortune then.
    This said, she did her blessing give,
    In love and happiness to live;
    Which when they did the same receive,
    Of Mother Bunch they took their leave,
    Declaring she had told them more,
    Than e'er they understood before.

Now for these poor young creatures that have pined themselves to death, and have no cure, the worst of pretenders to physiognomy might prescribe them a remedy, and all those of what constitution soever that have hoped houses of their own, I will show you how you shall see the person that is to give you one, collected from Trismegistus and Cornelius Agrippa.

On midsummer Eve three or four of you must dip your dresses in fair water, then turn them wrong side outwards, and hang them on chairs before the fire, and lay some salt in another chair, and speak not a word. In a short time the likeness of him you are to marry will come and turn your dresses, and drink to you; but if there be any of you will never marry, they will hear a bell, but not the rest.

Another way, quickly tried.

TAKE hemp-seed, and go into what place you will by yourself, carry the seed in your apron, and with your right hand throw it over your shoulder saying,

> Hemp-seed I sow, hemp-seed I sow,
> And he that must be my true love,
> Come after me and mow.

And at the ninth time expect to see the figure of him you are to wed, or else hear a bell as before.

> Yet though you hear the sad and dismal bell
> It is your own fault if you hear the horrid knell.

Another way.

YOU that dare venture into a churchyard, just as it strikes twelve at night, take a naked sword in your hand, and go nine times about the church, saying,

> Here's the sword, but where's the scabbard?

Which continue the whole time you go round; and the ninth time the person you are to marry will meet you with a scabbard and so kiss you: if not, a bell as before.

Another, called the Dutch Cake.

THREE, four, or more of you must make a cake of flour and salt (no matter of what flour), and some of each of your own baking; make your cake broad, and each of you set the two first letters of your name with a pin, but leave such a distance that it may be cut; then set it before the fire, but speak not one word. Turn it each of you once; and the person to be your husband will cut out your name; then the next, unto the last.

Another way.

THE first change of the new moon on the New Year, the

first time you see it, hold your hands across, saying this three times—

New moon, new moon, I pray thee,
Tell me this night who my true love will be.

Then go to sleep without speaking a word, and you will certainly dream of the person you shall marry.

Another way experienced often.

YOUNG men and maids may take some rosemary flowers, bay leaves, a little thyme, sweet marjoram, and southernwood; make these into powder, and with barley flour make a cake, but do not bake it. Lay this under your head any Friday night; and if you dream of music, you will wed those you desire in a short time; if of the sea or ships, you will travel first; if of a church, you must be contented to die single.

THE COMICAL HISTORY
OF THE
COURTIER AND TINKER

CHAPTER I.

The Courtier finds the Tinker asleep; he has him carried in that posture to his house; lays him on a Bed in a stately Room with rich Clothes by him; feasts and entertains him with fine Music; makes him drunk, and then conveys him back again.

A COURTIER one day riding along with his retinue espied a Tinker who had been taking a very early draught to quench the spark in his throat, lying fast asleep, and snoring under a sunny bank, having made his budget into his pillow, to rest his drowsy head upon; and the Courtier's country house not being far off, he immediately caused his servants to take him up very softly, and carry him thither, then to put him in a stately bed in the next chamber, pull off his foul shirt, and put on him a clean one, then convey away his old clothes, and lay rich ones by him. This was punctually observed. The Tinker being thus laid, slept soundly till evening; when rousing up between sleeping and waking, and being dry, as drunkards usually are, he began to call for some drink, but was greatly frighted to find himself in such a palace, furnished with lights and attendants about him, that bowed to him, and harmonious music, accompanied with most charming voices, but none of them to be seen. Whereupon looking for his old clothes and budget, he found a muff and rich attire glistening with gold by him, which made him fancy himself metamorphosed from a Tinker to a Prince. He asked many questions, but in vain, yet being willing to rise, the attendants arrayed him in the richest attire; so then he looked on all sides admiring the sudden change of fortune, and as proud as a peacock when he spreads his tail against the glittering beams of the sun. And being arrayed, they had him into another room, where was a costly banquet prepared, and placed him in a chair, under a fine canopy, fringed with gold, being attended with wine in gilded cups. At first he strained courtesy, but being entreated to sit down, the banquet being solely at his disposal, he fell to most heartily. Then after supper they plied him with so much wine, as to make him dead drunk, then stripped him, and put on his old clothes; they carried him as they had brought him, and laid him in the same posture they found him, being all this time asleep; and when he awoke he took all that had happened before for a vision, telling it wherever he came, that he had really and verily dreamed he had been a prince, telling them as well as he could all that had happened, but plainly he saw now again his fortune would raise him no higher than to mend old kettles; yet he made the following song for the fraternity to sing at their leisure :—

> All you that jovial Tinkers are,
>   Come listen unto me:
> I dreamed a dream that was so rare,
> That none to it I can compare,
>   No Tinker such did see.
>
> I thought I was a King indeed,
>   Attired gay and fine;
> In a stately palace I did tread,
> Was to a princely banquet led,
>   And had good cheer of wine.
>
> But soon I found me in a ditch,
>   That did no comfort lend;
> This shows a Tinker, though he itch
> To be a Prince, or to grow rich,
>   Must still old kettles mend.

CHAPTER II.

The Courtier's Trick upon the Tinker for complaining that he could get no drink at his house.

THE Tinker I have before mentioned, not knowing the house where he had been so nobly entertained, and which he only took for a vision, and often walking that road and crying old brass to mend, had been called in to work, and was often asked various questions by the servants, and as often told them his imaginary vision; but they giving him no strong liquor, he often complained of it in the town, saying, "Though some had praised Sir John's liberality, and how free he was of his liquor, yet for his own part, he could say no such thing, as having ever found him so stingy and niggardly, that not so much as one sup of his famed March or October beer could he get." This being babbled about came to the Courtier's ears, who was resolved to punish his sauciness, though in a comical way. So one day as he was passing by, he ordered him to be called in to do some work; and after he had done it to come to him (as having laid all his schemes with his servants beforehand). "Come, old fellow," said he, "you look as if you were as dry as Vulcan. What say you if I should order you where you may have your fill of good drink? Would not you be glad of it?" "Ay, master," said he, making a nod and a scrape, "God's blessing on your heart for it, and I thank you too."

Upon this he ordered his butler to have him down, and be sure not to stint him, and let him have his full swill. They instantly went, and the Tinker followed them very joyfully. But they had no sooner gotten him down, but shutting to the door close, they ordered him to strip immediately; at the which he much wondered, and began to make excuses on account of the blackness of his hide, which would be very undecent and unseemly. But they pretended it was the way of the cellar, when a new comer was to be made free of it, but never after, how oft soever he came. He being willing to comply, that he might have his skin full of good liquor, that might prove both as meat and cloth to him, off went his leathern doublet, breeches, shoes, stockings, and hat; as for shirt he had none, having pawned it to his hostess that morning for three noggins of brandy. Then taking a frisk or two in a merry vein, they surprisingly whipped him up by the heels, and put him into a full butt of strong beer, the upper head being taken up for that purpose. So he dipped over head and ears like a duck that dives. Yet after he had recovered his legs, it was but just shoulder deep, for when upon winding of the horn, whilst he would have been scrambling out, down came Sir John, demanding what was the matter. They told him "the Tinker was not content to drink full horns at the cock, but would needs go in to drink all at a draught." "Aye," said he, "this is a thirsty soul indeed; but since he undertakes to drink it, he shall do it, for none of my servants shall drink it now, he has washed his dirty hide in it;" crying to him with an angry voice, "Sirrah, you rogue, drink it as you proposed, or it shall be worse for you," and while he stood shivering up to his neck, and was endeavouring to lay the blame upon others, the Courtier seemed impatient to be dallied with, drew a broad sword that was two-edged, protesting his head should go off for abusing his good liquor, was there no more Tinkers in the world, and with that, making a full blow at him, as the Tinker believed. And seeing him in such a passion, he to avoid the coming stroke dropped down over head and ears, staying under as long as he could, and peeping up, and seeing the threatening danger, he dropped down again for six or seven times. Till fearing to carry the jest too far, he gave him a short respite, telling him, "Now he could not report abroad he was so very niggardly of his drink, for he had or might have enough of it." Then bidding his servants to take him out, and ordered him to depart, or drink it up, which he thought fit. And thus he went away laughing. The Tinker, who was at first very angry, but being cheered up with a cordial dram, and so made sensible that all this was but a frolic, and that for the future their master would be his good friend if he behaved civilly, he was pacified, and so putting on his clothes, he beat the road for a gang of merry fellows of his acquaintance, informing them, there was a hogshead of March beer at Sir John's, which they all might be partakers of if they choosed; they came joyfully, and had it brought into the court-yard, in black jacks. After they had drunk it, the Tinker told them the cause of its being given away, was because there was a swine that had unexpectedly fallen into it; but on further inquiry he told them all the circumstances, which set them a-laughing till their sides were almost cracked. Afterwards they had plenty of victuals sent them, and the Tinker being thus made free of the cellar, was ordered to call at the house, and have victuals and drink as often as he came that way.

And so they departed, spreading the fame of Sir John in every place they came, as a bountiful benefactor; singing as they went, the following song:—

>Good house-keeping, they say, is fled,
>>Or hawks or hounds, and whores have rid her;
>But we say she's not fled nor dead,
>>Who have so plentiful beheld her.

>Long may he flourish in this nation,
>>And get it praised as of old,
>That we by following the French fashion,
>>May not make charity grow cold.

Chapter III.

A Comical Trick he made the Tinker serve an old Farmer, who used to ride sleeping, making him think that his horse was the Devil.

THE Tinker being better pleased with his treatment, often frequented the house, making the Knight merry with his pleasant songs, etc., so that he was much pleased with his conversation, and often gave him money, and one day put him upon a frolic, seeing him an apt fellow. He had seen an old curmudgeon farmer, sleeping and nodding on his horse, as he came from market, and giving the Tinker directions what to do, when he should come by, knowing his hour, and delivering him a parcel of crackers and other fireworks, he caused him to be dressed in a raw hide with horns, when the Tinker, according to order, with the help of a servant, having stopped the farmer's horse, while the rider was sleeping, pitched four stakes, one at each corner of the pannel, and ungirting, he drew the horse from under, when taking off the bridle, he put his own head into the headstal; so then after he placed the fireworks under the pannel, he put a fuse lighted to them, and so kept motion as the horse used to do with the nodding farmer, who having the reins about his wrist, by his kicking he awaked, and seeing himself on a frightful beast, which he took for Beelzebub, he cried out, when the fire-work taking, blew up him and the pannel, and made him to fall quash to the ground, so that the Tinker made off with the stakes and pannel. The old man no sooner got up, but he fell to running, crying out, "The Devil, the Devil," and never durst come that way again but in company, rather choosing to go five miles about.

CHAPTER IV.
The Tinker complains to the Courtier of a Butcher's Dog that often assaulted him. The Courtier, in the Tinker's habit, fights and kills him; and of his Examination before a Justice.

THE Tinker being awarded with a crown for his dexterity, went away; but one day being in merry talk with our Courtier, he changed his tone sadly, and told him that a butcher, on such a road, kept a lion-like mastiff dog; that he was not so much afraid to encounter him, as that if he would kill him, the butcher as he told him, would send him to jail, and punish him at the next sessions, having one Justice Clodpole on his side, who was his landlord, and whose house he served with meat, and doubted not would hearken to anything he said against him although ever so false and unjust.

Sir John having listened to his complaint, and laughed, bid him be of good cheer, for himself would try the dog adventure. Upon this he ordered some clothes to be brought, which the Tinker stripping, put on, and the Knight put on his, except his shirt, and taking his budget, pikestaff, kettle, and hammer, away he went, beating his kettle, and crying, "Work for a Tinker," till he came near the butcher's house. The dog soon heard the tink, tink, and away he runs open-mouthed to meet the Tinker, they laughing to see how he would fright him; but Sir John having now thrown down his budget, was ready to receive him with the pike end of the staff, and after the dog wheeled, he returned and advanced eagerly to fly at his throat, but he thrust the pike of his staff into his breast; upon which he ran away howling, and tracing the ground with his blood, till he came to his master's, where he died. At this he was so much enraged, that he carried a constable, and seized the Knight, who purposely made no resistance. So taking him before a Justice, he made very great complaints against him.

The Justice very gravely demanded what the fellow was brought before him for? The butcher said, "An't please your Worship, for killing my servant." "Aye," said the Justice, "he looks like a bloody-minded villain, therefore write his mittimus, and see he be well-ironed, lest he make his escape."

"I beseech your good Worship not to be so rash and hasty," said the Knight, "as to pass sentence upon me so hard. Pray ask this butcher what servant of his I killed?" "Ay," said the Justice, "let him speak." "Then in truth," said the Butcher, "I ought in conscience to speak the truth; it was but a dog, but such a dog, as I say I would not have taken the best five guineas in the country for. Do you see me, sir, he had rare qualities over other dogs; he would not only fetch home my sheep out of the field when I wanted them, and save me that trouble, but do you see, Mr. Justice, he would go a sheep-hunting, and drive me home a couple, and sometimes half a dozen of wild sheep, which nobody owned or I did not think fit to inquire after, or they after me; so that he made me a thriving man: besides he was the safeguard of my house, and I believe that he killed him on purpose that he might rob me."

"Ay, ay," said the Justice; "all this is true, and you speak like an honest man, and he looks indeed like a rogue, and I believe you; but, however, we can't, indeed hang men for a dog, but I'll send him to jail, and there he shall lie and rot in his lousy linen, and drink kennel-water, and not one bit of meat, unless now and then a roasted turnip, cooled on a burdock leaf." "This is a very hard sentence, indeed, Mr. Justice," said our counterfeit Tinker. "No, no," replied the Justice, "it is too mild a one for such a villain as you are." But added, "I had like to have forgot a material point in his examination. Tell me, sirrah, how you came to kill this honest man's dog?" "Why, sir," said he, "with the pike end of my staff for running at me to bite me." "Aye, aye," said the Justice, "that was villainous in you; could you not have turned the other end, and given him a rap upon the pate?" "Yes," replied he, "if he had come to me with his tail foremost."

"Prithee, show me," said the Justice, "how he came at thee?"—"I will show your worship; he came open mouthed, as I do to you now, crying, bow, wow, wow." And here running against the Justice, overthrew him in his chair to the ground; so that he most loudly cried out, "Murder!" and being got up he ordered his mittimus to be made, reviling him at a desperate rate. But all on a sudden the tables were turned; for no sooner being asked, but he told his name. When up starts the Justice, and coming unto him with a low reverence, "Oh! Sir John," said he, "Is it you! who could ever have thought it! I am heartily sorry for what I have said." Then turning to the butcher, who stood wondering, said, "Sirrah, you rascal, do you keep dogs to assault gentlemen? but I will teach you better manners; come bind him over to the sessions directly, and if he has no bail, take him to jail. This is a pretty thing indeed, that people cannot pass the road peaceably for such rogues as you keeping dogs." But Sir John interposing, all was pacified, and the butcher went home with a flea in his ear.

THE HISTORY OF THE FOUR KINGS

OF

Canterbury, Colchester, Cornwall, and Cumberland,

Their Queens and Daughters;

BEING

The Merry Tales of TOM HODGE and his School-Fellows.

THE PREFACE.

Not to detain the reader with many words to little purpose, I shall only here observe that Tom Hodge, with the rest of his old companions, belonging to the school of Cockermouth, were walking on a very pleasant morning in May, and having tired themselves with pranks and intrigues, towards evening they sat themselves down on a green bank, beneath a lovely oak, where they agreed amongst themselves that everyone should tell a tale, or pay a fine; and because Tom was the eldest scholar, it was concluded and agreed upon that he should begin first.

Says Tom, "With all my heart,
So I'll begin my part."

TALE I.

ONCE upon a time, when the opinion was common in England that those whose age and experience enabled them to determine the consequences of certain actions were wizards and witches, there was a queen in this realm, whose name was Elizabeth; and by reason that the famous town of Lancaster was strangely pestered with witches, the queen sent some judges down to arraign and try them in order to bring them to justice.

Now the news of this court being to be kept in Lancaster, spread through all the country, so that a husbandman living near forty miles from that place, hearing of this news, and believing they were come to tell the folks whether they were witches or not, resolved to go to be satisfied in himself, for he was possessed with a fear that he was a witch, because he had a wart grew on his neck, which he imagined to be a dug.

His wife, who had a friend in a corner, and was therefore glad of his absence, did not only give her consent, but also dressed him in his best leathern suit and broad-brimmed hat. So taking leave of his good wife Joan, he trudged on day and night until he came to the place where the court was kept; so rushing on and pressing through the crowd, the crier of the court believing him to be some evidence, gave orders that they should let him in, which was soon done, and he was required to speak what he had to say. "Why," says the countryman, "d'ye see, I've a dug upon my neck, which makes me afraid I am a witch, and volks tell me that these vine gentlemen (pointing to the judges) can tell a body whether one is a witch or no." The crier of the court seeing the simplicity of the man, said, "No, no, my friend, I can assure thee thou art no witch; thou lookest more like a cuckold than a witch or a conjurer." "I thank you, zur; and zo zays these vine gentlemen." Then having given three or four scrapes and half a dozen congees, he came back as wise as Waltham's calf. The next day he was met by his wife, who waited for his return at the town's end, to whom she said, "Well, husband, what do the gentlemen say? are you a witch or no?" "A witch, sweet wife, no; they tells a body one looks more like a cuckold than a witch or a conjurer." "Why say you so?" replied she; "I prithee go back and have them taken up for witches; for except they had been so, they would not have known you were a cuckold."

This merry tale so pleased them that they set up a hearty laugh, which, being ended, the second boy began his tale in the following manner.

Tale II.

In the days of yore, when this land was governed by many kings, among the rest the king of Canterbury had an only daughter, and she was wise, fair, and beautiful. Her father sent forth a decree that whoever would watch one night with his daughter, and neither sleep nor slumber, he should have her the next day in marriage; but if he did either, he should lose his head. Many knights and squires attempted it, but lost their heads.

Now it happened a young shepherd, grazing his flock near the road, said to his master, "Zur, I zee many gentlemen ride to the court at Canterbury, but ne'er see 'em return again." "O, shepherd!" said his master, "I know not how they should; for they attempt to watch with the king's daughter, according to the decree, and not performing it, they are all beheaded." "Well," said the shepherd, "I'll try my vorton; zo now vor a king's daughter or a headless shepherd." And taking his bottle and bag, he trudged to court. Now, in his way, he was to cross a river, over which lay a plank; down he sits, and pulls off his shoes and stockings to wash his feet, lest the smell of his toes might be the means of keeping her awake. While he was washing his feet a fish came smelling and biting his toes; he caught it and put it into his bag: after which came a second, a third, and a fourth, which he caught and put in his bag likewise. This done, and dried his feet, he put on his stockings and shoes, and pursued his journey till he came to the palace, where he knocked loudly with his crook. He was no sooner let in, and having told his business, but he was conducted to a hall, prepared for that purpose, where the king's daughter sat ready to receive him; and the better to lull his senses, he was placed in a rich easy chair, having delicious wines for his supper, with many fine dishes of fruit, etc., of which the shepherd ate and drank plentifully, insomuch that he began to slumber before midnight. "O shepherd," said the lady, "I have caught you napping?" "Not, zweet ally, I was busy." "At what?" said she. "Why a feeshing." "Nay, shepherd, there is no fish-pond in the hall." "No matter vor that, I have been feeshing." Says the lady, "Where do you fish?" "O," quoth he, "in my bag." "O me, have you catched e'er a one?" "Ay, lady," said he. "I'd willingly see it," replied she. "Ay, an't please you, you shall with all my heart." This said, he slyly drew one of the fishes out of his bag, at the sight of which she was greatly pleased, and praised it for a pretty fish: and withal said, "Dear shepherd, do you think you could catch one in mine too?" "Ay, ay, doubtless I can." Then he fell to fishing, and in a short time drew a second fish out of the bag pretending he drew it from her. The king's daughter was so pleased with it that she kissed it, declaring it was the finest she ever saw. And about half an hour after she said, "Shepherd, do you think you could get me one more?" He answered, "Mayhap I may, when I have baited my hook." "Then make haste, for I am impatient till I have another." Then the shepherd acted as before, and so presented her with another fish, which she also extolled and praised, saying, "It was ten times finer than the other;" and then gave him leave to sleep, promising to excuse him to her father.

In the morning the king came into the hall as usual, followed by the headsman with a hatchet; but the lady cried out, "You may return with your hatchet, here is no work for you." "How so," said the king, "has he neither slumbered nor slept?" "No, royal father, he has not." "How has he employed himself?" "In fishing." "Why, there is never a fish-pond; where did he catch them?" "One in his own bag, and two in this one of mine." "Say you so? Well, friend, dost thou think thou can'st catch one in mine?" "An't please you, my liege, I believe I can." Then directing the king to lie down, he poked him with a packing needle, which made him cry out exceedingly; at which time he drew the other fish out of the bag, and showed it to the king. His majesty said, "He never knew such sort of fishing before; however, take my daughter, according to my royal decree." And so they were married, and the wedding kept in great triumph, and the shepherd became a king's son.

"O that was mighty well," said the third boy, "he had wonderful good fortune. This puts me in mind of a story, which I will now tell in my turn."

Tale III.

If I may believe my old grandmother, there lived in the county of Cumberland a nobleman, who had three sons. Two of them were comely and tall youths, wise and learned; the third a merry fool, and went often in a party-coloured coat and steeple crowned hat, at the top of which was a tassel. In this dress he made a comical figure. At this time the king of Canterbury had a fine daughter, adorned with all the gifts of nature, joined to an ingenious education, she being very ripe-witted, as appeared by her ready answers and the comical questions she put forth. The king, her father, published a decree, that whoever should come to the court, and answer his daughter three questions, without study or stumbling, should have her in marriage, and also be heir to the crown at his decease. On publishing this decree, the said gentleman's two sons agreed between themselves to go and try how favourable fortune might be to them in this undertaking; but all their care was what they should do with their silly brother Jack; for, as they said, if he follows us, he will out with some foolish bolt, and so spoil our business. At length it was agreed on going to the court, to go out of the back door, which led to the road over several fields, about a mile from the house. They did so, but were no sooner got into the highway, but looking behind, they saw their brother Jack coming capering and dancing after them, saying, with a loud laughter, "So you are going to get a king's daughter, but I will pursue you." They saw there was no way to get rid of him, but by walking fast and leaving him behind, hoping thereby to get entrance before Jack, and then have the gates shut against him. They had not gone half a mile before Jack set up a great fit of laughter, at which one of his brothers said, "What's the fool found out now?" "Why, I've found an egg." "Put it in thy pocket," said his brothers. "Adad, and so I will," says Jack. Presently after he was taken with another fit of laughter. "What's the fool found now?" "What have I found?" says Jack, "why a crooked stick." They bid him put that in his pocket also. "Ay, marry, will I." They had not walked much farther before Jack burst into a greater fit of laughter than before. His brothers said, "What's the fool found now?" "Found! why an orange." "Put that in your pocket likewise." "I intend it," says Jack. Now, by this time they were come near the palace gate, at which they no sooner knocked but they were admitted. But Jack never stood for ceremonies, but ran through the midst of the court, and as the wise brothers were making their addresses, Jack was laughing at the ladies, unto whom he said, "What a troop of fair ladies are got here!" "O yes, yes," said the king's daughter, who was among them, "we are fair ladies, for we carry fire in our bosom." Do you?" said Jack; "then roast me an egg."

"How will you get it out again?" "By a crooked stick which I have." "Ay, you will?" said she. "I have it in my pocket," says Jack." In this Jack answered the three questions proposed. Then he was preferred to that honour which was mentioned in the decree. His two wise brothers then went home like two fools, and left foolish Jack to be reverenced at court with the king's fair daughter.

Said the fourth boy, "This verifies the old proverb, 'Fools have fortune'; besides, it has put me in mind of a story that was told me by my aunt."

Tale IV.

Long before Arthur and the Knights of the Round Table, here reigned, in the easterly part of this land, a king who kept his court at Colchester. He was witty, strong and valiant, by which means he subdued his enemies abroad and planted peace among his subjects at home.

Nevertheless, in the midst of all his earthly glory, his queen died, leaving behind her an only daughter, about fifteen years of age, under the care of her royal husband. This lady, from her courtly carriage, beauty, and affability, was the wonder of all that knew her; but, as covetousness is the root of all evil, so it happened here.

The king hearing of a lady who had likewise an only daughter, for the sake of her riches had a mind to marry her, though she was old, ugly, hook-nosed, and hump-backed, yet all could not deter him from marrying her. The daughter of the said piece of deformity was a yellow dowdy, full of envy and ill-nature; and, in short, was much of the same mould as her mother. This signified nothing, for in a few weeks the king, attended by the nobility and gentry, brought the said piece of deformity to his palace, where the marriage rites were performed. Long they had not been in the court before they set the king against his own beautiful daughter, which was done by false reports and accusations.

The young princess, having lost her father's love, grew weary of the court, and on a certain day meeting with her father in the garden, she desired him, with tears in her eyes, to give her a small subsistence and she would go and seek her fortune, to which the king consented, and ordered her mother-in-law to make up a small sum according to her discretion. To her she went, who gave her a canvas bag of brown bread, a hard cheese, with a bottle of beer. Though this was but a very pitiful dowry for a king's daughter, she took it, returned thanks, and so proceeded, passing through groves, woods, and valleys, till at length she saw an old man sitting on a stone at the mouth of a cave, who said, "Good morning, fair maiden, whither away so fast?" "Aged father," says she, "I am going to seek my fortune." "What hast thou in thy bag and bottle?" "In my bag I have got bread and cheese, and in my bottle good small beer; will you please to partake of either?" "Yes," said he, "with all my heart." With that the lady pulled out her provision, and bid him eat and welcome. He did, and gave her many thanks, telling her there was a thick thorny hedge before her, which will appear to you impassable, but take this wand in your hand, strike three times, and say, "Pray hedge, let me come through;" and it will open immediately. Then a little further you will find a well, sit down on the brink of it, and there will come up three golden heads which will speak; and what they require, that do. Then promising she would, she took her leave of him. Coming to the hedge, and following the old man's direction, the hedge divided and gave her a passage. Then coming to the well, she had no sooner sitten down, but a golden head came up with a singing note, "Wash me, comb me, lay me down softly." "Yes," said the young lady; then putting forth her hand, with a silver comb performed the office, placing it upon a primrose bank. Then came up a second, and a third, saying as the former, which she complied with: and then pulling out her provision, ate her dinner. Then said the heads one to another, "What shall we do for this lady, who hath used us so very kindly?" The first said, "I will cause such addition to her beauty as shall charm the most powerful prince in the world." The second said, "I will endow her with such perfume, both in body and breath, as shall far exceed the sweetest flowers." The third said, "My gift shall be none of the least, for as she is a king's daughter, I'll make her so fortunate that she shall become queen to the greatest prince that reigns." This done, at their request she let them down into the well again, and so proceeded on her journey. She had not travelled long before she saw a king hunting in the park with his nobles. She would have shunned him, but the king having a sight of her, made towards her, and between her beauty and perfumed breath, was so powerfully smitten that he was not able to subdue his passion, but proceeded on his courtship, where, after some compliments and kind embraces, he gained her love. And bringing her to his palace, he caused her to be clothed in the most magnificent manner.

This being ended, and the king finding that she was the king of Colchester's daughter, ordered some chariots to be got ready that he might pay him a visit. The chariot in which the king and queen rode was beautified with rich ornamental gems of gold. The king, her father, was at first astonished that his daughter had been so fortunate as she was till the young king made him sensible of all that happened. Great was the joy at court among the nobility, except the queen and her club-footed daughter, who were ready to burst with malice, and envied her happiness; and the greater was their madness because she was now above them all. Great rejoicings, with feasting and dancing, continued many days. Then at length, with the dowry that her father gave her, they returned home.

"Well," said the fifth boy, "had she not been kind and

beautiful, such good fortune had never come to her lot. And pray what became of her hump-backed sister-in-law?" "Indeed I know not." "Why, then," said the fifth boy, "I can tell you something of her."

Tale V.

SHE, perceiving that her sister was so happy in seeking her fortune, would needs do the same; so disclosing her mind to her mother, all preparations were made; not only rich apparel, but sweetmeats, sugar, almonds, etc., in great quantities, and a large bottle of Malaga sack. Thus furnished she went the same road as her sister, and coming near the cave, there sat the old man, who said, "Young woman, whither so fast?" "What is that to you?" said she. Then said he, "What have you in your bag and bottle?" She answered, "Good things, what you shall not be troubled with." "Won't you give me some?" said he. "No, not a bit nor a drop, unless it would choke you." The old man frowned, saying, "Evil fortune attend thee." Going on, she came to the hedge, through which she espied a gap, where she thought to pass, but going in the hedge closed, and the thorns run into her flesh, so that with great difficulty she got out. Being now in a bloody condition, she looks for water to wash herself, and looking round she saw a well, and sitting down, one of the heads came up to her, saying, "Wash me, comb me, lay me down softly." But she banged it with her bottle, saying, "Hang you, take this for your washing." So the second and third heads came up, and met with no better welcome than the first. Whereupon the heads consulted among themselves what evils to plague her with for such usage. The first said, "Let her be struck with leprosy in her face." The second said, "Let an additional stink be added to her breath." The third bestowed on her a husband, though but a poor country cobbler. This done, she goes on till she came to a market town, and it being market day, the people smelt a stink, and seeing such a mangy face, all fled but a poor cobbler, who not long before had mended the shoes of an old hermit, who, having no money, gave him a box of ointment for the cure of the leprosy, and a bottle of spirits for a stinking breath. Now the cobbler having a mind to do an act of charity, was minded to try an experiment; so going up to her, asked her who she was? "I am," said she, "the king of Colchester's daughter-in-law." "Well," said the cobbler, "if I restore you to your natural complexion, and make a sound cure both in face and breath, will you in reward take me for a husband?" "Yes, friend," replied she, "with all my heart." With this the cobbler applied the remedies, and they worked the effect in a few weeks, which being done, they were married. After some few days spent in town, they set forward for the court at Colchester. At length coming there, and the queen understanding she had married nothing but a poor cobbler, fell into distraction, and in wrath hanged herself. The death of the queen pleased the king much, who was glad he had got rid of her so soon. Having buried her, he gave the cobbler one hundred pounds, on condition that he and his lady would quit the court. The cobbler received it, and promised he would. Then setting up his trade in a remote part of the kingdom, they lived many years, he mending shoes, and she spinning thread.

Quoth the sixth boy, "I think for a king's daughter she hath spun a very fine thread, but now for my story."

Tale VI.

A tinker in our town had but one daughter, whose name was Tib, and because her father would not let her marry a miller's man named Jobson, nothing would serve her but she must go and seek her fortune, so over hills and mountains, through groves and lonesome woods she passed, till at length she met with an old woman, who said unto Tib, "Where are you going?" "To seek service," says Tib. "Will you live with me?" replied the old woman; "my family is small, myself, my cat, and my dog." Tib answered, "With all my heart." So home they went to her cottage, which stood by the side of a grove on the bank of a pleasant river. She no sooner entered in at the door than she beheld the shelves furnished with abundance of earthen ware and glasses. She had not lived long with her before Tib had committed a fault, for which the old woman was resolved to break every bone in her skin. For that end she put her into a sack, and having tied the mouth of the same, she went to the grove to cut a stick; but while she was gone, Tib with a penknife opened the sack and got out; and put the dog and cat into it, filling it up with pans, pipkins, etc., then dragged it to the door, that the old woman might not come in to miss them, who, on her return, thinking that Tib had rolled thither, began to lay on like fury, when the dog howled, the cat mewed, and the pipkins cracked; while the old woman cries out, "Ah! howl if you will and be poxed, for before you come out of this sack I'll thrash your bones to chaff." Now Tib stood at a distance laughing to see how busy she was in destroying her own furniture, then fled for it, and never after returned.

"It was well she did," replied the seventh boy, "or else the old woman would certainly have been revenged on Tib at last. But now for my story, which shall be the last at this meeting."

TALE VII.

A YOUNG man having found a purse in which was five pounds, he made a proclamation that if anyone would lay any just claim to it to come to such a tavern, and they would have it again. To the tavern he went, where, in meat and drink, he spent a crown. At last when the young man was ready to go the owner came and demanded the purse, which he was ready to surrender; but the owner, on knowing a crown was spent, would not receive it, unless he made up the whole sum. The young man told him he could not; so an officer was sent for, but before he came the youth took to his heels, and ran for it with that swiftness, that, an ass standing in his way, he took hold of his tail to swing himself by, and twitched it off. A little farther he overthrew a woman with a child and caused her to fall. At length he was taken and brought before a justice by the three sufferers. Having heard their complaints he turned to the young man, and said, "Young man, several complaints are here laid against you, which I shall clear up. First, keep the money you have found, and trade with it till you have improved it so far as to make him satisfaction, and then let him have it. You take the ass, and work him till a new tail grows, then give him to his owner. And you take the woman home, till she is as quite recovered as she was before, and then send her home to her husband. So with these determinations he dismissed them.

TALE VIII.

In the reign of King Arthur, near the Land's End of England, namely the county of Cornwall, there lived a wealthy farmer, who had one only son, commonly known by the name Jack Hornby. He was brisk and of a ready wit, so that whatever he could not perform by strength, he completed by ingenious wit and policy.

For instance, when he was no more than seven years of age, his father sent him into the field to look after his oxen. The laird, by chance coming across the field, asked Jack many questions, particularly, "How many commands there were?" Jack told him there were nine. The laird replied there were ten. "Nay," quoth Jack, "sir, you are out of that; it is true there were ten, but you broke one of them when you coveted my father's bull." The landlord replied, "Thou art an arch wag, Jack."

"But, sir," says Jack, "can you tell me how many sticks goes to build a crow's nest?" "Why," says the landlord, "there are as many goes as are sufficient for the size of the nest." "Oho, you are out again, sir," quoth Jack, "there is none goes, they are all carried."

The landlord finding himself so fooled, trudged away, leaving Jack in a fit of laughter.

THE PENNY BUDGET OF WIT AND PACKAGE OF DROLLERY.

Scottish Prudence.

A PARISH clerk in the north of England, not long ago, hired a Scotchman for his servant, who was to go to the cart and plough, and do other occasional jobs when wanted. In the course of conversation at hiring, the clerk asked him, if he could submit to the unpleasant business of digging graves; to which he exclaimed, "I'll warrant ye, maister, I could dig doon the kirk for that matter; but let me see, I hasn't been put to that wark yet; aye, our auld bellman at Jedburgh used to say, he never had better pay nor better jobs than howking holes for fowk—faith he was aye merry when folk dee'd." It happened soon after entering on his service, that there was a severe storm of snow, which impeded all outdoor work. One morning he came to his master, and asked him what employment he was to go to that day. The employer hesitated for some moments, and at last told him, he could find nothing for him to do. Sawney, with great gravity, replied, "I think, maister, I'll awa up to the kirk-yard an' howk some graves; we may as weel hae a wheen ready, for they may come faster in when they ken we are prepared for them."

Scottish Atmosphere.

An English gentleman on a tour through Scotland, was unfortunately accompanied by wet weather most of the time. When he set out from Glasgow to Greenock, the morning was very fine. However, before he had proceeded half way, he was overtaken by a heavy shower. "Boy," says he to a little fellow herding near the road-side, "does it always rain in this country?" "Na," replied the boy, "it sometimes snaws."

Liberty of the Press.

A master tailor in Glasgow, lately reading the newspapers to his family, and when expressing the title "Liberty of the Press in France," one of his daughters interrupted him by asking what the liberty of the press meant? "I'll soon answer that question," said he: "You know when your mother goes out, and leaves the key in the cupboard door, where the bread, butter, and sugar lies, then you have access—That's the liberty o' the press."

Donald and the Laird.

A Scottish Laird and his man Donald, travelling southward; at the first English Inn, the room in where they were to sleep contained a bed for the master and a truckle for the man, which drew forth from beneath the larger couch. Such furniture being new to the Highlanders, they mistook the four-posted pavilion for the two beds, and the Laird mounted the tester, while the man occupied the comfortable lodging below. Finding himself wretchedly cold in the night, the Laird called to Donald to know how he was accommodated. "Ne'er sae weel a' my life," quoth the gilly. "Ha, mon," exclaimed the Laird, "if it wasna for the honour of the thing, I could find in my heart to come down."

How to read a Sign-Board.

A HIGHLAND DROVER passing through a certain town, noticed a sign-board above an entry, with the following inscription :—

  Green Teas, Raw Sugars, Marmalades, Jellies,
   Capped Biscuits, and all sorts of
    Confectionery Goods
    sold down this entry,

read it as follows :—

  Green Trees, Raw Sodgers, Mermaids, Jades.
   Scabbed Bitches, and all sorts of
    Confusionery Goods,
    sold down this entry.

How to Escape Robbery.

A PERSON extremely hard of hearing, travelling between Paisley and Greenock on horseback, some time since, had occasion to come off his horse, when the reins slipped from among his fingers: the horse finding himself at liberty immediately ran off. The deaf man quickly followed, determined to inquire at all he met if they had seen his horse. The night was very dark; however, he had not gone far till he met with two men, whom he accosted with, "Did you see a horse without a rider?" when he was immediately collared. He thought it diversion; says he, "That's no a way to use a man in the dark"; and endeavouring to shake himself clear, when instead of slackening their hold they took fresh and firmer holds, and no doubt used violent language, of which his deafness deprived him of hearing; seeing all attempts to get clear fruitless, and dreading they had nothing in view but an intention to rob him, it instantly occurred to him his having an ear trumpet sticking in the top of his boot, which he used in conversation. He immediately pulled it up, laid the muzzle of it across the fellow's arm, and exclaimed, "If you don't let go your grups I'll blaw your brains out in a moment!" They jumped over a hedge, and were out of sight in an instant, the deaf man called after them, "Set aff, set aff, my lads or I'll be the death o' baith o' you, learn never to meddle wi' a man i' the dark, for ye dinna ken what deadly weapons he carries."

Daft Will Speirs.

WILL, one day, upon his journey to Eglinton Castle to pay his regular daily visit, met his Lordship, who seemed not to notice him. The Earl being only on a walk of pleasure through his policies, soon came in contact with Will again sitting at the bottom of a tree, picking a huge bone. "Ay, ay;" says the Earl, "what this you've got noo, Will." "Ay, ay," says Will, "anew o' frien's whan folk has ocht: ye gaed by me awee sin' an' ne'er loot on ye saw me."

How to find Work.

A SLATER being employed by a gentleman to repair his house in the country, took along with him a prentice, when they set to work, and continued to work for some days. The gentleman having no conception the job was to be of such duration, came out one morning, and found the apprentice at work alone, when he expressed himself as surprised at the continuation of them working so long, and inquired what had become of his master, to which the boy replied, "He's awa to Glasgow to look for a job, and if he got ane, this ane would be done the morn, and if he didna get ane, he didna ken when it would be done."

Will Scott.

A CELEBRATED attendant upon the sheriff, well known for his activity in the execution of his orders, as well as for taking a bit comfortable guzzle when finances would afford it, was one Sabbath day snugly seated in a pew behind the bailies at church. Will had not been there long till he was soon lulled into a sweet slumber, and found himself seated along with his companions over a good imperial half-mutchkin; and in a short time the reckoning came a-paying when some of the party insisted it was already paid. However, Will happened not to be of that opinion, and true to his integrity, bawled out with all his might in the midst of the sermon, "No, no, by my faith it's no pay't, we have had just ae half-mutchkin, an' twa bottles o' ale, an' there's no a fardin o't pay't."

Grave-Digger of Sorn.

THE grave-digger of Sorn, Ayrshire, was as selfish and as mean a sinner as ever handled mattock or carried mortcloth. He was a very querulous and discontented old man, with a voice like the whistle of the wind through a key-hole. On a bleak Sunday afternoon in the country, an acquaintance from a neighbouring parish accosted him one day, and asked how the world was moving with him. "Oh, very puirly, sir, very puirly indeed," was the answer, "the yard has done nothing ava for us this summer,—if you like to believe me I havena buriet a leevin' soul this sax weeks."

Scottish Parrot.

A PARROT perched upon a pole at a cottage door, beaking itself in the sun, was observed by a rapacious hawk, which happened to be passing over it, suddenly dived down and seized poor Poll by the back; away the hawk flew with his prey. When passing over a garden Poll observed his old friend the gardener, and exclaimed, "I'm ridin' noo, John Laurie." Hawky alarmed at hearing a voice so near, darted into a tree for safety, when after recovering a little, commenced to devour poor Poll, when it roared out with all its might, "Will you bite, you rascal." The hawk terrified out of its wits, flew off with a birr, leaving Poll to proceed homewards at pleasure.

The Restless Haggis.

DAFT Will Callander lived with his sister Babie, in Port-Glasgow. Babie kept a lodging-house for sailors. One Saturday night Babie was making a Haggis for Sunday's dinner, when one of her lodgers put four ounces of quicksilver into the haggis unknown to Babie. On Sunday Will was left at home to cook the dinner; but when the pot began to boil, the haggis would be out of the pot. Will, faithful to his charge, held the lid on the pot until his patience was exhausted; at last Will ran off to the church for Babie. She sat in one of the back pews. Will beckoned to her two or three times; Babie as often nodded and winked to Will to be quiet. At last he bawled out, "Babie, come hame, for I believe the de'il's got into the haggis, it'll no bide in the pat; it's out dancing on the floor, and if I had not locked the door, I think it would have been at the kirk as soon's mysel."

Expense of a Wife.

AN old bachelor who lived in a very economical style, both as regards food and clothing, and not altogether so very trig as some bachelors sometimes appear, was frequently attacked by his acquaintances on the propriety of taking a wife. He was very smartly set upon one day, and told how snod a wife would keep him, and many other fine things to induce him to take a wife, and among the rest, what a comfort it would be to him, if it was for naething else but to make his parritch in the morning. Says he, "I dinna doubt but she wad mak my parritch, but the plague is, she wad be fair to sup the hauf o' them."

An Honest M'Gregor.

DONALD M'GREGOR, a notorious sheep-lifter (alias sheep-stealer), in the north Highlands, being at last overtaken by the grim tyrant of the human race, was visited by the minister of the parish, whose appearance, however, was by no means agreeable to Donald. The holy man warmly exhorted the dying Highlander to reflect upon the long and black catalogue of his sins, before it was too late, otherwise he would have a tremendous account to give at the great day of retribution, when all the crimes he had committed in this world would appear in dreadful array, as evidence of his guilt. "Och! sir," cries the dying man, "an' will a' the sheeps an' the cows, an' ilka thing Tonal has helped hersel to, be there?" "Undoubtedly," replied the parson. "Then let ilka shentleman tak her nain, an' Tonal will be an honest man again."

Negro and the Musquito.

A WEST Indian who had a remarkably fiery nose, having fallen asleep in his chair, a negro boy who was waiting, observed a musquito hovering round his face. Quasi eyed the insect very attentively; at last he saw him alight on his master's nose, and immediately fly off. "Ah! bless your heart," exclaimed the negro, "me right glad see you burn your foot."

A Brush for the Barber.

A HIGHLANDER who sold brooms, went into a barber's shop in Glasgow a few days since to get shaved. The barber bought one of his brooms, and after having shaved him, asked the price of it. "Twopence," said the Highlander. "No, no," said the barber, "I'll give you a penny, if that does not satisfy you take your broom again." The Highlander took it, and asked what he had got to pay? "A penny," said strap. "I'll gie you a bawbee," said Duncan, "an' if that dinna satisfy ye, put on my beard again."

The Kellochsyde Grace.

THE following is preserved traditionally as the grace of the farmer of Kellochsyde, or Killocsyde, in Clydesdale:—"O Lord, we'r ay gaugan, an we'r ay gettan. We soud ay be coman to thee, but we'r ay forgettan. We leive in the gude mailen o' Kellochsyde, suppan thy gude peisie kale, puir sinfou sons of evil that we are. Monie mercies we receive gude trowth; and we're little thankfou for them, gude feth Janet, rax by the spunes, and a' praise and glory sall be thine. Amen."

New Method of Teaching Music.

A HIGHLAND piper having a scholar to teach, disdained to crack his mind with the names of semibreves, minims, crotchets, and quivers—"Here, Donald," said he, "tak your pipies, lad, and gi's a blast—so, very weel blaun indeed; but what is sound Donald without sense?—ye may blaw for ever without makin' a tune o't, if I dinna tell you how thae queer things on the paper maun help you—you see that big fellow wi' a round open face (pointing to a semibreve between the two lines of the bar), he moves slowly, slowly, from that line to this, while you beat ane wi' your fit, and gi'e a blast: if now ye put a leg to him, ye mak' twa o' him and he'll move twice as fast; gif ye black his face, he'll rin four times faster than the fallow wi' the white face; but if, after blackin' his face, ye'll bend his knee, or tie his legs, he'll trop eight times faster than the white faced chap that I showed you first. Now, whene'er you blaw your pipes, Donald, remember this, the tighter the fallow's legs are tied, the faster they will rin, and the quicker they are sure to dance."

Long-Winded Preacher.

A PARSON in the country taking his text in St. Matthew, chapter viii. verse 14, "And Peter's wife's mother lay sick of a fever," preached for three Sundays together on the same subject. Soon after two fellows going across the churchyard, and hearing the bell toll, one asked the other who it was for. "Nay I can't tell; perhaps," replied he, "it's for Peter's wife's mother, for she has been sick of a fever these three weeks."

Distinction of Sons and Daughters.

ABOUT the year thretty-sax, a company differed "Whether it was better for a man to ha'e sons or dochters." They could not 'gree, but disputed it *pro* and *con*. At last one of them said to Graham of Kinross (wha hadna yoked wi' them in the argument), "Laird, what's your opinion?" Quo' he, "I had three lads and three lassies; I watna whilk o' them I liked best say lang as they sucket their mither; but de'll ha'e my share o' the callants when they cam to suck their father."

Patrimony and Matrimony.

AT an examination of a school in Edinburgh, a gentleman asked one of the scholars by what name they called property that descended from a father? "Patrimony," answered the scholar; "And what do you call it when descended from a mother?" "Matrimony," was the reply.

An Officer's Wife.

ONE of the town's officers of Ayr was struck severely by accident on the head by his wife. After the fray was adjusted, the wife said to her husband, "Henry, had I killed you, and I been hanged for it, would you marry Kate M'Lauchlan?"

Highlander and Parrot.

AN honest Highlander walking along Holborn, heard a cry, "Rogue Scot, Rogue Scot." His northern blood fired at the insult, drew his broad sword, looking round him on every side to discover the object of indignation. At last he found it came from a parrot, perched on a balcony within his reach, but the generous Scot disdaining to stain his trusty blade with such ignoble blood, put up his sword again, with a sour smile, saying, "Gin ye were a man, as ye're a green goose, I would split your weem."

An Irishman.

AN Irishman one day was walking on the streets of Belfast, found a light guinea, and got 18s. for it. Next day he was walking, and sees another, and says, "Allelieu, dear honey, I'll have nothing to do with you, for I lost 3s. by your brother yesterday."

Captain Silk.

IN a party of ladies, on it being reported that a Captain Silk had arrived in town, they exclaimed, with one exception, "What a name for a soldier!" "The fittest name in the world," replied a witty female, "for Silk can never be Worsted."

A Clever Son.

A FARMER'S son, who had been some time at the university, came home to visit his father and mother; and being one night with the old folks at supper on a couple of fowls, he told them, that by the rules of logic and arithmetic, he could prove these two fowls to be three. "Well, let us hear," said the old man. "Why, this," said the scholar, "is one and this," continued he, "is two; two and one, you know, make three." "Since you ha'e made it out sae weel," answered the old man, "your mother shall ha'e the first fowl, I'll ha'e the second, and the third you may keep to yoursel."

Breaking the Commandments.

A CLERGYMAN who wished to know whether the children of the parishioners understood their Bibles, asked a lad that he one day found reading the Old Testament, who was the wickedest man? "Moses, to be sure," said the boy. "Moses!" exclaimed the parson, "how can that be?" "Why," said the lad, "because he broke all the commandments at once."

Not Lost but Drowned.

A LEITH merchant being on his usual ride to the south, came to the ford of a dark river, at the side of which a boy was diverting himself. The traveller addressed him as follows :—"Is this water deep?" "Ay, gaen deep," answered the boy. "Is there ever any person lost here?" "No," replied the boy, "there was never any lost; there has been some drowned, but we aye get them again."

A Just Remark.

A CERTAIN son of St. Crispian, who resides in Paisley, lifting up his four cornered hat the other morning in a hurry, found it filled with his wife's fal-de-ral-lals; in a fit of wrath he exclaimed "Gudesake, Janet, what the de'il gars you stap a' the trash in the house intil a body's hat." "Trash, indeed!" exclaimed the indignant spouse, "stap it on your ain head, and the biggest trash in the house'll be in't."

Scotchman and Irishman.

A SCOTCHMAN and an Irishman were sleeping at an inn together. The weather being rather warm, the Scotchman in his sleep put his leg out of the bed. A traveller, in passing the room door, saw him in this situation, and having a mind for a frolic, gently fixed a spur upon Sawney's heel; who drawing his leg into the bed, so disturbed his companion, that he exclaimed, "Arrah, honey, have a care of your great toe, for you have forgot to cut your nails I belaiv." The Scotchman being sound asleep, and sometimes, perhaps, not a little disturbed by other companies, still kept scratching poor Pat, till his patience being quite spent, he succeeded in rousing Sawney, who, not a little surprised at finding the spur on his heel, loudly exclaimed, "De'il tak' the daft chiel of a hostler, he's ta'en my boots aff last night and left on the spur."

Charity.

A PERSON who resides in the ancient town of Kilwinning, was proverbial for his liberality in meat and drink to friends and acquaintances. Strangers, too, seldom passed without experiencing a due share of kindness. Lately while feasting nearly a dozen of random visitors on "Pat Luck," a beggar called at the door soliciting charity, when he very good humouredly called out, "I canna help you the day, I ha'e plenty o' your kin' here already."

Shooting the Devil.

A Scotch parson preaching upon these words, "Resist the devil, and he will fly from you," began thus:—" My beloved, you are all here to-day, but wot ye who is among ye, even the meikle horned devil. You cannot see him, but by the eye of faith I see him. But some of you say, what will we do with him now we have him here? How shall we destroy him? We will hang him. Alas, my beloved, there are not so many tows in the parish as will hang him, he is as light as a feather. Then some of you will say we will drown him. Humph, my beloved, there is owre muckle cork in his leg, he's as souple as an eel, he will not sink. Others of you will say, we will burn him. Na, na, sirs, you may scald yourselves, but you canna burn him, for a' the fire in Hades could never yet singe a hair o' his tail. Now, sirs, ye canna find a way among you all to kill him, but I will find it. What way will this be, sirs? We will even shoot him. Wherewith shall we shoot him? We shall shoot him with the Bible. Now, sirs, I shall shoot him presently. So, presenting the Bible, as soldiers do their muskets, he cries out, "Toot! toot! toot! Now he is shot. There lies the foul thief as dead as a herring."

Long Credit.

Soon after the battle of Preston, two Highlanders, in roaming through the south of Mid-Lothian, entered the farm house of Swanston, near the Pentland Hills, where they found no one at home but an old woman. They immediately proceeded to search the house, and soon finding a web of coarse home-spun cloth, made no scruple to unroll and cut off as much as they thought would make a coat to each. The woman was exceedingly incensed at their rapacity, roared and cried, and even had the hardihood to invoke divine vengeance upon their heads. "Ye villains!" she cried, "ye'll ha'e to account for this yet." "And when will we pe account for't?" asked one of the Highlanders. "At the last day, ye blackguards!" exclaimed the woman. "Ta last day," replied the Highlander; "Tat be coot lang chredit —we'll e'en pe tak a waistcoat too!" at the same time cutting off a few additional yards of the cloth.

Bird's Nest.

THE mother of a respectable grocer in a town in the west, called her son to her, while on her death bed, and declared to him that his reputed father was not really his father; but that such a one (naming him) really was his father; and that the deed was done one night when travelling from Greenock, when at the Clun-Brae-Head. This story got wing, and ran through the town like wildfire, and was a fine source of amusement for some time. One day a boy vulgarly named the "Linty," went into the said grocer's shop to purchase some article, when he was assailed with "Weel Linty, whar is'tu gaun to big thy nest the year?" The boy replied, "I was thinkin' to big it doon about the Clun-Brae-Head."

Elder's Hours.

A CUNNING carle invested with the semi-sacred office of "Ruling Elder," or practically seemingly identified with that office, in order to gratify an inclination, scratched wi' the neb o' a fork the figure 10 on the one side of his outer door, and figure 11 on the other; by which plan he was able to say wi' "a good conscience," at a' times, and on a' occasions, that he came aye hame atween ten and eleven.

The Thistle.

A FEW Scotch and English travellers being met together, an Englishman took it upon him to run down the Thistle, exclaimed against the empty boast of its motto, "Nemo me impune lacessit," when a Scotchman present observed,

"The Thistle, sir, is the pride of the Scotish nation, but it is nothing in the mouth of an ass."

Cold Gentleman.

In the west of Scotland, some time ago, there happened to be an auction of books. A book-buyer who attended the sale, was summoned by his son to supper, according to the directions of his mother. The boy flurried by the presence of the audience, and in his attempt to be as explicit as possible, thus cried out, "Fayther, yer parritch is ready." "Very well, my dear," said the father, and at the door gave him a salute *a posteriori*, which was repeated with the following injunction—"Recollect rascal, when you come again, to say *a gentleman* wants me." Next evening up comes the boy according to direction. "Is my Fayther here?" "Yes," said the father. "*A gentleman* wants ye." "Very well, my man," was repeated by the boy's parent; but little time elapsed when the boy returned; "What now, my man," said the old book worm. "Oh naething," said his son, "but gin ye dinna rin fast *the gentleman* will be quite cauld."

Dougal Graham.

Dougal Graham, author of the well-known metrical history of the rebellion in 1745, being candidate for the place of town bell-man in the City of Glasgow, was desired to call "Gude fresh herrings new come in at the Broomielaw." It not being the season for herrings, Dougal added,

"But, indeed, my friends, it's a blaeflum,
For the herrings no catch'd, and the boats no come,"

which procured for Dougal the situation.

Dougal was a kind of Scotch Æsop, he had a large humph on one of his shoulders, and like his patrotype had wit. Calling in the street of the Gallowgate, opposite the Saracen's Head Inn, where several officers of the gallant 42d regiment were dining, at the close of the American war, some of whom knew Dougal before they went abroad, opening the window, called out, " What's that you've got on your back, Dougal?" Knowing what the regiment suffered at Bunker's Hill, Dougal replied, " It's *Bunker's Hill;* do you choose to mount?"

A New Way to Wauken Sleepers in Church.

Mr. OGILVIE, minister of the parish of Lunan in the county of Forfar, had a great deal of eccentricity in his composition. One Sunday an old woman, who kept a public-house in the parish, with whom Mr. Ogilvie was well acquainted, fell asleep in the church during sermon—not an uncommon occurrence. Her neighbour kept jogging in order to awake her. Mr. Ogilvie observing this, cried out, " Let her alane, I'll wauken her mysel', I'll warrant ye." " Phew! Phew! (*whistling*) a bottle o' ale and a dram, Janet." " Comin', sir," was instantly replied. " There now," says the minister, " I tald ye it wadna be lang afore I waken'd her."

Sage Instruction.

A LABOURING Highlandman, who lived in the upper parts of Perthshire, whose wife was taken in labour, wished him to retire out of the house. Janet says to him—" Oh! you be gang awa', Duncan, gang awa'!" The man, however, kept loitering about the door, seemingly impressed with something of great importance. At last he cries to his wife, " You speak a me, Shanet! you speak a me." The wife asks, " What you say, Duncan?" ." Gie the cummer (the midwife) a dram, Shanet, gie the cummer a dram!" " What for Duncan?" " Gie the cummer a dram, Shanet, an' tell him to *make her a laddie*."

The Purse and the Penny Siller.

THREE young Highlanders, some years ago, set out from their native hills, to seek a livelihood amongst their countrymen in the Lowlands. They had hardly learned any English. One of them could say, " We three Highlandmen;" the second, " For the purse and the penny siller ; " and the third had properly learned, " And our just right too ;" intending thus to explain the motives o' their journey. They trudged along, when, in a lonely glen, they saw the body of a man who had been recently murdered. The Highlanders stopped to deplore the fate of the unhappy mortal, when a gentleman with his servant came up to the spot. " Who murdered this poor man ? " said the gentleman, " We three Highlandmen," answered the eldest of the brothers (thinking the gentleman inquired who they were). " What could induce you to commit so horrid a crime ?" continued the gentleman. " The Purse and the Penny Siller," replied the second of the travellers. " You shall be hanged, you miscreants!" " And our just right too," returned the third. The poor men were thus brought to the gallows on their own evidence, and presumption of guilt.

Lump of Old Wood.

An aged man, named Thomas Wood, sitting on a high three-footed stool in the gallery of the old Church of Falkirk, during divine service happened to fall asleep, tumbled on the floor with a great noise. The preacher stopped and demanded the reason of the noise. " Nothing, sir," cries a wag, " but a lump of Old Wood fallen down."

The Great Want.

A female pauper lately made a very strong and forcible appeal to the elders and heritors of a certain parish, for an advance of 4s. 6d. Some one of the grave quorum inquired what made her so urgent on this occasion, when she had lately got a supply of coals, shoes, etc. To this she replied, " Why, deed, sirs, it's just to buy a pair o' corsets to my daughter Tibbie, ilk lass that's ocht respectable has them but hersel', so ye see she canna do wantin them, an' ye maun e'en let me ha't sirs."

The Devil Defined.

The Rev. Mr. Shirra, burgher minister in Kirkcaldy, once

gave the following curious definition of the devil:—"The devil, my brethren, is ill ony way ye'll tak him. Tak' the D from his name, he's *evil*; tak' the E from his name, he's *vil*; tak' the V from his name, he's *il*;" then shrugging up his shoulders, and lengthening his sanctified snout, he said with peculiar emphasis, "He's naething but an *il*, *vil*, *evil*, Devil, ony way ye'll tak' him!"

Mark me Well.

A GENTLEMAN having missed his way, fortunately met a boy going with a pot of tar to mark his master's sheep, asked the road to Banff, but was directing by so many turnings, right and left, that he agreed to take the boy behind him on the horse as he was going near to the same place. Finding the boy pert and docile, he gave him some wholesome advice relative to his future conduct, adding occasionally, "Mark me well, my boy." "Yes, sir, I do." He repeated the injunction so often, that the boy at last cried out, "Sir, I have no more tar!"

Death of a Watch.

AFTER the battle of Falkirk, in 1746, a Highlandman was observed extracting a gold watch from the fob of an English officer, who had been killed. His comrade viewed him with a greedy eye, which the man taking notice of said to him, "Tamn you gapin' greedy bitch, gang and shoot a shentleman for hersel', an' no envie me o' my pit watch."

Next morning finding his watch motionless, and meeting his comrade, says to him, "Och! she no be care muckle about a watch, an' you be like mine, what will ye gi'e me for her?" The other replied, "I be venture a kinny." "Weel then," said the other, "Shust tak her, an' welcome, for she be die yester night."

Our Lawful Sovereign.

AN English officer dining with Lord Saltoon some years after the Battle of Culloden, his Lordship was adverting to the strong attachment manifested by the generality of Buchan to the unfortunate house of Stuart, and particularly remarked the devoted loyalty of his gardener, whom no bribe or entreaty could in the smallest degree influence. "I'll let 50 guineas," said the Englishman, "that I shall make him drink the health of King George. "Done!" replied his Lordship. The honest gardener was called in. The officer began by praising his fidelity and loyalty to his prince; pressed him to drink some glasses of wine; and when he thought him a little off his guard from the effects of the generous liquor, he began thus:—"Now, my friend, I know you are a good Christian and wish well to every human being; you can certainly have no objection to drink the health of King George? Come, my worthy fellow, a bumper to the health of his Majesty." "Here's to the health of our *lawful* Sovereign," said the gardener. "Bless you, sir," cried the officer, "That's not King George!" "I am very much of your opinion," replied the man, making a profound bow and retiring.

Down the Rotten Row.

A FEW years ago, when resurrectionists throughout the country were become very common, a person of respectability was interred in the High Church burying ground of Glasgow. The relatives who were persons of property, hired a few hungry weavers, who generally at that time were *atomies* ready made, to watch the grave of their deceased relative: these, as they were one night on duty, perceived some persons enter the churchyard; they kept snug till such time as they could learn the object of their visit. It was not long before the intruders opened a grave, took out the corpse, put it into a sack and left it at the grave, and went in search of something else. One of the weavers, a droll fellow, said to his comrade, "Take out the corpse, and I'll go into the sack, but do you observe the proceedings." In a little time the resurrection men returned, and one of them getting the sack upon his back marched off. When they got to the street, the one says to the other, "Which way will we take?" When the weaver putting out his hand and gripping the fellow who was carrying him, by the hair, bawled out, "Down the Rotten Raw, ye beggar." He was soon set down, and the man who carried him went mad of the fright.

Resurrection Men.

Some years ago, a poor boy, whose mother was buried in the churchyard of Falkirk, used frequently to sit on her grave, and when destitute of other accommodation, would crawl in below one of the gravestones, and slept there for the night. On one of these occasions, the boy was roused from his sleep by the noise of some voices in the churchyard. This was nothing more than a couple of resurrection men who had come on purpose to begin that great work rather prematurely; and as those who are raised before their due time cannot be supposed capable of standing on their legs, they had provided themselves with a horse to gi'e them a lift. They were then disputing about how they could secure the beast, while they were raising the corpse. The lad hearing this, and creeping out of his hole, cries, "I'll haud him," expecting some remuneration no doubt. The fellows seeing a resurrection commencing from under a stone, and hearing the offer of holding the horse, scampered off and left the animal, with a couple of sacks; and although the horse and sacks were advertised, they were never claimed, but sold for the benefit of the boy, which procured him better lodging than beneath a grave stone.

March of Intellect.

Two country carters, passing the entrance to the Arcade, Argyle Street, Glasgow, observed painted on the wall, "No dogs to enter here." "No dogs to enter here!" exclaimed one of them, "I'm sure there's no use for that there." "What way, Jock," replied the other. "'Cause dogs canna read signs," said he. "Ha, ha, Jock, ye're maybe wrang, I'se warran ye gentle folks' dogs 'ill ken't brawly, for there's schools, noo, whar they learn the dumb baith to read and speak."

THE MERRY CONCEITS
OF
TOM LONG
THE CARRIER

Being many Pleasant Passages and Mad Pranks which he observed in his Travels.

Full of Honest Mirth and Delight.

Of all the Toms that ever yet was named,
Was ever any Tom like Tom Long framed?
Tom Tram, who now as many mad pranks shows,
Unto Tom Long will prove a mere goose.

Tom Thumb is dumb, until the pudding creep,
In which he was entomb'd, then out doth peep;
Tom Fool may go to school, but ne'er be taught,
Such rare conceits with which Tom Long is fraught.

Tom Ass may pass, but only for his ears,
No such rich jewels as our Tom Long he wears;
Tom Tell-truth is but froth, but truth to tell,
From all these Toms, Tom Long doth bear the bell.

Chapter I.

How Tom Long at first set up the trade of being a Carrier, and where he took up his Lodging.

Tom Long, the subject of this discourse, having spent some few years like a wandering Jew, oft visiting the coasts of Essex and Kent, where he did many notable exploits, sometimes cheating the calves-heads of their money, by the virtue of hocus pocus, having learned the art of legerdemain. Other times he used, as opportunity served, to rob the henroost. At last, his cheating tricks were so well known, that the country kicked him out like a knave as he was, and he was willing to be gone as they to be rid of him, soon gave them three slips for a teaster, and travelled towards Gotham, where he, well knowing what wit those wise men had in their noddles, took up his abode near the place where the men made a hedge to keep in the cuckoo all the year. Not long after, he set up his trade of being a carrier; under pretence of which he with ease played his pranks, and the wisdom of these men was such, that he cheated them of all, and yet the fools had no mistrust of him. And having set him up, he found great store of small doings, and above all others, the men of Gotham and Dunstable would employ him; who, being more knave than fool, ever advised some cheating trick or other to gull those idiots; for let him go out ever so full, he would be sure to come home empty, telling them one mischance or other had befallen him. He took up his lodging at the sign of the Whip and Egg-Shell in Thieving Lane, not far from Charing Cross, where Dunstable men are sure to find him; if not, they may go into Turnagain Lane, and come back again as wise as they went in.

Chapter II.

How Tom Long the Carrier met with a Young Man upon the way, with what happened to them, and how they were entertained by an Hostess.

Tom Long being newly set up a carrier, as he was travelling he happened to take up a young lad, who had straggled from his parents to play the truant, which Tom perceiving, entertained him into his service; but they had not gone far before their stomachs were up, so they resolved at the next place to take a bit, where, as soon as they came, they demanded what was for to eat. The hostess, being one of Seldom Cleanly's daughters, said there was nothing but eggs, of which, she said, she would make them a froize; and seeing them to come in, in a full breast and an empty stomach, she (like a slut as she was) resolved to give them their bellies full before they went; and so, with some three or four good eggs, she mixed as many bad ones, some addle and rotten, and others ready for to hatch; and having set them down at a certain wash block, which served instead of a table, she set before them as good a froize as any woman possibly could make of coarse materials, making her sauce alike suitable, being nothing else but kitchen stuff melted a little—oil as good as ever was burned. Tom and the young man fell presently to it, with stomachs as greedy as hogs, swallowing down all by wholesale, tag-rag and long-tail, without any chewing, although they conceited something cracking in their teeth like young bones. Yet hunger, which is the best sauce, made every morsel sweet, although it had but an ill going down with it, and worse troubled their patience afterwards, for they had no sooner eaten of it, but like squeezy stomachs they began to cast backwards and forwards; and being in this pitiful pickle, they called for their hostess, who, thinking to receive her reckoning, was paid in her own coin; for, having some of their froize left, Tom furiously cast it on her face, which stuck as fast as a plaister to the wall, insomuch that for a while she lost her eyesight; which being done, Tom departed without paying anything for his dinner.

Chapter III.
How Tom and his Young Man discoursed of their Dinner, and how they resolved to mend the matter at night, but met with as bad Entertainment.

Tom and his man being now on their way, began to discourse of their dinner, and how prettily they served their hostess; but still conceited that they heard these young chickens which they had eaten in their froize cry, "Peep, peep, peep," and having cast up all again, their bellies began to cry "Cupboard," whereupon Tom, to comfort his young man, told him they would be sure to have a good host at night, and good fare to. But "like to like," quoth the devil to the collier, out of the frying-pan into the fire; for their new host proved not only a knave, but a thief, and instead of dainty veal, provided for them part of a young colt, which, being foaled before its time, ate very tenderly; and going to supper, the host, like a flattering knave, told them he would feast them bravely; and they, not mistrusting anything, fed most courageously, having for to please their pallets several kinds of dishes made thereof, the host still crying, "You are welcome, gentlemen,"—all which they swallowed down as greedily as the lawyer his fee. And having filled their ungodly guts with this supposed good cheer, they hastened to bed, where the fleas fed as fast on their corpse as they had done upon this new found veal, insomuch that they looked as if they had the smallpox. In the morning (thinking to have breakfast of the same) they missed their coats and other things, which their host had thievishly deprived them of. So, searching the house about, they found hanging in a corner some pieces of flesh, which they supposed to be part of the veal they had eaten of; but by the ears of the skin which hanged by, they saw plainly it was an ass, and that they were once more made fools of; whereupon Tom caused his host to be apprehended, who was committed to prison about their goods, where Tom left him and departed.

Chapter IV.

Tom relates how a certain counterfeit Merchant cheated divers Gentlemen of very great sums of Money.

In the North of England arrived a pretended merchant, but, indeed, a very cheating knave, who, residing there a while, came to be greatly acquainted with divers gentlemen, who, looking on him as one of great account, at last he received several great sums of money which he was to pay at London, upon the receipt of which he gave every man a bill of exchange, receiving of some twenty pounds, some thirty, some forty, fifty, some a hundred pounds; and, having pretty well feathered his nest, leaving those gentlemen to receive their money where they could get it, he departed beyond sea; and when the gentlemen came to receive their money, they could neither find nor hear of their merchant: whereat they were very much vexed, as well as they might be, to see how they were cheated of their money. But their hopes are that they shall have it brought them again by Tom Long the Carrier.

Chapter V.

Of the great request that Tom Long was in, and how the wise Mayor of Huntingdon seized on Tom's ragged Colt for a Sturgeon.

Tom Long having been a carrier for many years, grew in great request, and though he was not very well beloved, yet he was sure to have many customers that he got carriage of, especially the country farmers, who often used to send tokens by him to their friends, as gammons of bacon, collars of brawn, pies, and other good things, and now and then small pieces of silver from Dunstable men: all which Tom ever made use of himself, though they perceived it not: for by reason they sent by Tom Long the Carrier, they could never receive any answer about what he brought. Also, all the broken shopkeepers and decayed gentlemen sent their creditors' debts by Tom Long the Carrier.

But it happened that, as Tom was going to London, he chanced to be at Huntingdon, where, putting his horses to grass, amongst which he had a young ragged colt,—this colt having straggled down into the river, certain wise men of the town coming by, that had been at Gotham, thought it had been a sturgeon, and thereupon acquainted the Right Wisdom-Fool the Mayor of it, who assembled together his wise brethren, made a very wise speech to them, and acquainted them therewith, who very unanimously accompanied his foolship; and, after a deep consultation, they all agreed to seize the poor colt for a sturgeon; but carrying it with great triumph into the town, the inhabitants, who were wiser than the rest, exceedingly laughed them to scorn for their great folly. And so Tom, promising the Mayor to bring him a piece of sturgeon at his return, he had his colt again.

CHAPTER VI.
A Story of the Seven Sleepers, who slept above three hundred years, and not yet awakened.

IN a great city there lived several men who for their religion were forced to fly for their lives, and not far from the city was an ancient cave under a hill, in which these men entered to secure and refresh themselves; but their persecutors, hearing where they were, stopped up the mouth of the cave, intending to famish them therein; and they, not knowing what was done, so soon as they had refreshed their bodies with victuals, laid themselves down to sleep, and so continued sleeping very sound a long season, until such time as in after ages a shepherd, intending to make himself a harbour, set divers masons to work to dig in this cave, who, with the noise, awakened the men who had been asleep so long therein. The cave being opened, they, thinking it to be day, and had slept but one night, sent one of their company privately into the city for food, for in all this time they had eaten nothing, and well they might be hungry; so, coming to the town, he found all things altered, the inhabitants being other kind of people, as he supposed, than he left the night before. So going to buy some bread, the people refused to take his money, saying they knew not the coin, at which he greatly marvelled. But inquiring further, he found that since their being there three generations had been dead and gone, and a fourth in being; and by computation of time, it appeared they had slept above three hundred years, and lay all this time in their clothes, which were no whit decayed, whereat the people all wondered; and Tom Long the Carrier, staying all the time they slept to see when they would awake, at last brought the news with him.

Chapter VII.

How Tom Long the Carrier sold his Horse for the Skin, supposing him to be dead; and how a crafty fellow coming by knew what the Horse ailed, and so bought him.

Tom Long the Carrier, travelling on the road, chances to put his horse in a field that was overgrown with hemlock, which Tom's horse, having had no meat all day, ate so greedily on, that it cast him into so sound a sleep that Tom thought he had been dead. Being thus sorely crossed, as he supposed, he began to flay his skin off to sell, whereupon a crafty fellow coming by that way, well knew what the horse ailed, bought him for the price of the skin, and paid Tom the money. He departed, appointing to fetch the horse the very next morning. And when he came on the morrow, the horse was awakened out of his sleep, and got upon his legs again; which, when Tom perceived, he was sorely vexed at his foolish bargain; but his chapman laughed him to scorn for his folly, and so departed with his horse.

Chapter VIII.

How Tom Long the Carrier converted all his Carriage to his own use, and thereby recruited himself with another Horse, and of a sad mischance that befel his Horse.

Tom Long the Carrier, seeing himself thus fooled out of his horse, resolved not to bear all the loss himself, and so converted all his carriage into money, and returning home, pretended he had been robbed of his horse and all his carriage. Not long after, Tom being willing to set up again, purchased with his money a new horse; but ill-gotten goods seldom thrive. So Tom, having a horse again, received divers things to carry from divers places, especially from the wise men of Gotam, who were the best customers Tom Long the Carrier had. But being on his way not far from his inn, he chanced to spy a fine plot of grass under a hedge in a corn field, under which Tom, to save charges, secretly conveyed his mare, tying her to the hedge with a cord, and so left her. But the mare, like an unruly jade, not being willing to be confined in so narrow a compass, was minded to see what fare was on the other side of the hedge, and foolishly venturing to leap over, very unfortunately hanged herself, whose untimely death had then nigh broke the heart of poor Tom Long; and his grief was the more by reason she died without any visitation.

> Tom nine ways looks, and needs must vexed be;
> Now bought wit's best, Tom Long doth plainly see.
> Tom tells he's robbed, and counteth all his losses,
> And is in hopes he shall have no more crosses.
> "Come, lads, all's gone," Tom takes his comfort then;
> He will be repaid by other men.
> Now many men do Tom Long dispraise,
> Saying, "He has small conscience in his ways,
> But sure I'll lay no such fault to his charge;
> I rather think his conscience was too large."

Chapter IX.

How Tom Long the Carrier was assaulted by a Dog, and how valiantly he defended himself, and killed him.

As Tom Long the Carrier was travelling between Dover and Westchester, he fortuned to pass something near a house, where was kept a great mastiff dog, who, as soon as he had espied Tom, came running open mouthed at him, and so furiously assaulted him, as if he meant to devour him at a bite. But Tom, having in his hand a good pikestaff, most valiantly defended himself like a man, and to withstand the danger, he thrust the pike-end of his staff into his throat, and so killed him. Whereupon the owner thereof, seeing his dog lost, comes earnestly unto Tom, and between threatening and chiding, asking him why he struck him not with the great end of the staff? "Marry," quoth he, "because your dog runs not at me with his tail."

Chapter X.

Of a merry conceited Jest brought to Town by Tom.

A CERTAIN king kept a fool to be his jester, whose manner was to set down in a note-book, which he kept for that purpose, all the follies that he saw committed in or about the court, or at least write so many as he discovered. So, upon a time, a certain Italian horse-courser arrived at the court who professed great skill in horsemanship, and it being declared unto the king, he presently sent him with three thousand pounds to buy horses in a far country, which this fool hearing of, put down in his note-book among the rest. When the king heard that, he was much offended, and would needs know of Jack Lackwit why he had set him down in his note. "Because," quoth the fool, "I think he will come no more to you." "But what if he does come again?" said the king. "Why, then," said the fool, "I will take you out and put him in."

Chapter XI.

Of the Hard Lodging which Tom Long the Carrier found on the Ground, having under him but one Poor Feather.

Tom Long, by reason of the great loss of his horses, became very poor, and so turned foot-post; and being in a wearisome condition, he was forced, having not coin to pay for better, to take up his lodging on the ground, where, tumbling and tossing, he could hardly rest all night; and stirring himself betimes in the morning, he espied under him one feather. "Now," quoth Tom, "I see what was the cause of my trouble that I could not sleep all the night. I wonder, seeing I found such hard lodging upon one feather, how they do that lie upon thousands."

Chapter XII.

How Tom Long cozened two Shoemakers out of a pair of Shoes.

Tom Long being now a foot-post, with hard travelling had worn his shoes so very thin that he was in great danger to lose soles and all; whereupon Tom came to refresh himself, after which he sent for a shoemaker to bring him a pair of shoes.

Now Tom, having no coin left, resolved to try his wits; so drawing on one of the shoes, he said it fitted well; but drawing on the other, he complained that it pinched his foot and was too low in the instep; whereupon he desired the shoemaker to take that shoe home and let it stand in the last for an hour or two, and he would stay so long. As soon as he was gone Tom pulled off the other shoe, and sent for another shoemaker to bring him a pair of shoes, which he did; so, drawing on one of them on the other foot, he said it pinched him likewise, and so wished him also to take that shoe home, and let it stand for an hour on the last, and then come again. But the shoemakers saw the last of their shoes, for when they came again Tom Long was gone, leaving these verses behind them:—

"Whom seek ye, sirs—Tom Long? Oh, fie upon
Your tediousness, he's long since gone;
He went a good while since, no question store
Are glad, who vex'd he did not go before;
And some are griev'd he went so soon away,
The reason was, he could no longer stay;
Nor is it a wonder that he thus is gone,
Since all men know he long was drawing on."

CHAPTER XIII.
Witty Conceits of Tom Long the Carrier.

TOM LONG the Carrier, upon a time, asked a merry conceited fellow which was the best husband for a young wench to marry. "Marry," quoth the fellow, "an old man, for then he shall be sure to be proud of her." Another standing by asked Tom Long the Carrier what trade he thought to be best? "Marry," quoth Tom, "a cut-purse; for he hath no sooner done his work but he hath his money in his hand."

CHAPTER XIV.
The Conclusion of the Merry Conceits of Tom Long the Carrier.

TOM LONG the Carrier coming to an inn,
Asked the maid what meat there was within?
"Cow-heels," said she, "and a fine breast of mutton."
"Then," said Tom, "since that I am no glutton,
Either or both shall serve—to-night the breast,
The heels in the morning, when light meat is best."
At night he took the breast, and did not pay,
And in the morning took his heels and ran away.
When the worst is past, all things begin to mend,
And here the brave story of Tom Long doth end.

THE STORY OF BLUE BEARD

OR THE
EFFECTS OF FEMALE CURIOSITY.

THERE was, some time ago, a gentleman who was extremely rich. He had elegant town and country houses; his dishes and plates were of gold and silver; his rooms were hung with damask; his chairs and sofas were covered with the richest silks, and his carriages were all magnificently gilt with gold.

But, unfortunately, this gentleman had a blue beard, which made him so very frightful and ugly that none of the ladies in the neighbourhood would venture to go into his company.

It happened that a lady of quality, who lived very near him, had two daughters, who were both extremely beautiful. Blue Beard asked her to bestow one of them upon him in marriage, leaving to herself the choice which of the two it should be.

They both, however, again and again refused to marry Blue Beard: but, to be as civil as possible, they each pretended that they refused because she would not deprive her sister of the opportunity of marrying so much to her advantage. But the truth was they could not bear the thoughts of having a husband with a blue beard, and, besides, they had heard of his having already been married to several wives, and nobody could tell what had afterwards become of them.

As Blue Beard wished very much to gain their favour, he invited the lady and her daughters, and some ladies who were on a visit at their house, to accompany him to one of his country seats, where they spent a whole week, during which nothing was thought of but parties for hunting and fishing, music, dancing, collations, and the most delightful entertainments. No one thought of going to bed, and the nights were passed in merriment of every kind.

In short, the time had passed so agreeably that the youngest of the two sisters began to think that the beard which had so much terrified her was not so very blue, and that the gentleman to whom it belonged was vastly civil and pleasing.

Soon after they returned home she told her mother that she had no longer any objection to accept of Blue Beard for her husband, and, accordingly, in a short time they were married.

About a month after the marriage had taken place, Blue Beard told his wife that he should be obliged to leave her for a few weeks, as he had some business to do in the country. He desired her to be sure to procure herself every kind of amusement, to invite as many of her friends as she liked, and to treat them with all sorts of delicacies that the time might pass agreeably during his absence. "Here," said he, "are the keys of the two large wardrobes. This is the key of the great box that contains the best plate, which we use for company; this belongs to my strong box, where I keep my money; and this to the casket in which are all my jewels. Here also is a master key to all the apartments in my house, but this small key belongs to the closet at the end of the long gallery on the ground floor. I give you leave," continued he, "to open or do what you like with all the rest excepting this closet: this, my dear, you must not enter, nor even put the key into the lock, for all the world. Should you disobey me, expect the most dreadful of punishments."

She promised to obey his orders in the most faithful manner; and Blue Beard, after tenderly embracing her, stepped into his carriage and drove away.

The friends of the bride did not, on this occasion, wait to be invited, so impatient were they to see all the riches and magnificence she had gained by marriage; for they had been prevented from paying their wedding visit by their aversion to the blue beard of the bridegroom.

No sooner were they arrived than they impatiently ran from room to room, from cabinet to cabinet, and then from wardrobe to wardrobe, examining each with the utmost curiosity, and declaring that the last was still richer and more beautiful than what they had seen the moment before. At length they came to the drawing-rooms, where their admiration and astonishment were still increased by the costly splendour of the hangings, of the sofas, the chairs, carpets, tables, girandoles, and looking-glasses, the frames of which were silver gilt, most richly ornamented, and in which they saw themselves from head to foot.

In short, nothing could exceed the magnificence of what they saw; and the visitors did not cease to extol and envy the good fortune of their friend, who all this time was far from being amused by the fine compliments they paid her, so eagerly did she desire to see what was in the closet her husband had forbidden her to open. So great indeed was her curiosity that, without recollecting how uncivil it would be to leave her guests, she descended a private staircase that led to it, and in such a hurry that she was two or three times in danger of breaking her neck.

When she reached the door of the closet she stopped for a few moments to think of the charge her husband had given her, and that he would not fail to keep his word in punishing her very severely should she disobey him. But she was so very curious to know what was in the inside that she determined to venture in spite of everything.

She accordingly, with a trembling hand, put the key into the lock, and the door immediately opened. The window shutters being closed, she at first saw nothing; but in a short time she perceived that the floor was covered with clotted blood, on which the bodies of several dead women were lying. These were all the wives whom Blue Beard had married and murdered, one after another. She was ready to sink with fear, and the key of the closet door, which she held in her hand, fell on the floor. When she had somewhat recovered from her fright she took it up, locked the door, and hastened to her own room that she might have a little time to get into humour for amusing her visitors; but this she found impossible, so greatly was she terrified by what she had seen.

As she observed that the key of the closet had got stained with blood in falling on the floor, she wiped it two or three times over to clean it; still, however, the blood remained the same as before. She next washed it, but the blood did not stir at all; she then scoured it with brickdust, and afterwards with sand, but notwithstanding all she could do, the blood was still there; for the key was a fairy, who was Blue Beard's friend, so that as fast as she got it off on one side it appeared again on the other.

Early in the evening Blue Beard returned home, saying he had not proceeded far on his journey before he was met by a messenger who was coming to tell him that his business was happily concluded without his being present, upon which his wife said everything she could think of to make him believe she was transported with joy at his unexpected return.

The next morning he asked her for the keys. She gave them to him; but as she could not help showing her fright, BlueBeard easily guessed what had happened. "How is it," said he, "that the key of the closet upon the ground floor is not here?" "Is it not? then I must have left it on my dressing-table," said she, and left the room in tears. "Be sure you give it me by-and-bye," cried Blue Beard.

After going several times backwards and forwards, pretending to look for the key, she was at last obliged to give it to Blue Beard. He looked at it attentively, and then said—"How came the blood upon the key?" "I am sure I do not know," replied the lady, turning at the same time as pale as death. "You do not know," said Blue Beard sternly; "but I know well enough. You have been in the closet on the ground floor. Vastly well, madam; since you are so mightily fond of this closet, you shall certainly take your place among the ladies you saw there."

His wife, almost dead with fear, fell upon her knees, asked his pardon a thousand times for her disobedience, and entreated him to forgive her—looking all the time so very sorrowful and lovely that she would have melted any heart that was not harder than a rock.

But Blue Beard answered, "No, no, madam; you shall die this very minute!"

"Alas!" said the poor trembling creature, "if I must die, allow me, at least, a little time to say my prayers."

"I give you," replied the cruel Blue Beard, "half a quarter of an hour; not one moment longer."

When Blue Beard had left her to herself, she called her sister, and after telling her, as well as she could for sobbing, that she had but half a quarter of an hour to live, "Prithee," said she, "sister Ann" (this was her sister's name), "run up to the top of the tower, and see if my brothers are yet in sight, for they promised to come and visit me to-day; and if you see them, make a sign for them to gallop as fast as possible."

Her sister instantly did as she was desired, and the terrified lady every minute called out to her, "Ann! sister Ann! do you see any one coming?" and her sister answered, "I see nothing but the sun, which makes a dust, and the grass, which looks green."

In the meanwhile Blue Beard, with a great scimitar in his hand, bawled as loud as he could to his wife, "Come down instantly, or I will fetch you."

"One moment longer, I beseech you," replied she; and again called softly to her sister—"Sister Ann, do you see any one coming?" To which she answered, "I see nothing but the sun, which makes a dust, and the grass, which looks green."

Blue Beard now again bawled out, "Come down, I say, this very moment, or I shall come and fetch you."

"I am coming; indeed I will come in one minute," sobbed his unhappy wife. Then she once more cried out—"Ann! sister Ann! do you see any one coming?" "I see," said her sister, "a cloud of dust a little to the left." "Do you think it is my brothers?" continued the wife. "Alas! no, dear sister," replied she; "it is only a flock of sheep."

"Will you come down or not, madam?" said Blue Beard, in the greatest rage imaginable.

"Only one single moment more," answered she. And then she called out for the last time—"Sister Ann! do you see any one coming?"

"I see," replied her sister, "two men on horseback coming to the house, but they are still at a great distance."

"God be praised!" cried she; it is my brothers; give them a sign to make what haste they can.

At the same moment Blue Beard cried out so loud for her to come down that his voice shook the whole house.

The poor lady with her hair loose, and her eyes swimming in tears, instantly came down, and fell on her knees to Blue Beard, and was going to beg him to spare her life; but he interrupted her saying—"All this is of no use at all, for you shall die." Then, seizing her with one hand by the hair, and raising the scimitar he held in the other, was going with one blow to strike off her head.

The unfortunate creature turning towards him, desired to have a single moment allowed her to recollect herself.

"No, no," said Blue Beard, "I will give you no more time, I am determined—you have had too much already;" and again raising his arm. Just at this instant a loud knocking was heard at the gates, which made Blue Beard wait for a moment to see who it was. The gates were opened, and two officers, dressed in their regimentals, entered, and, with their swords in their hands, ran instantly to Blue Beard, who, seeing they were his wife's brothers, endeavoured to escape from their presence; but they pursued and seized him before he had gone twenty steps, and, plunging their swords into his body, he immediately fell down dead at their feet.

The poor wife, who was almost as dead as her husband, was unable at first to rise and embrace her brothers. She soon, however, recovered; and as Blue Beard had no heirs, she found herself the lawful possessor of his great riches.

She employed a portion of her vast fortune in giving a marriage dowry to her sister Ann, who soon after became the wife of a young gentleman by whom she had long been beloved. Another part she employed in buying captains' commissions for her two brothers, and the rest she presented to a most worthy gentleman, whom she married soon after, and whose kind treatment soon made her forget Blue Beard's cruelty.

THE
LIFE OF
MANSIE WAUCH
TAILOR IN DALKEITH.

I was born during the night of the 15th of October, 1765, in that little house, standing by itself, not many yards from the eastmost side of the Flesh Market Gate, Dalkeith. Long

was it spoken about that something mysterious would happen on that dreary night, as the cat, after washing her face, gaed mewing about with her tail sweeing behind her like a ramrod; and a corbie, from the Duke's woods, tumbled down Jamie Elder's lum when he had set the little still a-going—giving them a terrible fright, as they took it for the deevil and then for an exciseman—and fell with a great cloud of soot and a loud skraigh into the empty kail-pot.

The first thing that I have any clear memory of was my being carried out on my auntie's shoulder, with a leather cap tied under my chin, to see the Fair Race. Oh! but it was a grand sight! I have read since then the story of Aladdin's Wonderful Lamp, but this beat it all to sticks. There was a long row of tables, covered with carpets of bonny patterns, heaped from one end to the other with shoes of every kind and size, some with polished soles and some glittering with sparables and cuddyheels, and little red worsted boots for bairns with blue and white edgings, hinging like strings of flowers up the posts at each end; and then what a collection of luggies! The whole meal in the market sacks on a Thursday did not seem able to fill them, and horn spoons, green and black freckled, with shanks clear as amber, and timber caups, and ivory egg cups of every pattern. Have a care of us! all the eggs in Smeaton dairy might have found resting places for their seats in a row. As for the gingerbread, I shall not attempt a description. Sixpenny and shilling cakes, in paper tied with skinie, and roundabouts, and snaps, brown and white quality, and parliaments on stands covered with calendered linen clean from the fold. To pass it was just impossible; it set my teeth a-watering, and I skirled like mad until I had a gilded lady thrust into my little nieve—the which, after admiring for a minute, I applied my teeth to and of the head I made no bones, so that in less than no time she had vanished, petticoats and all, no trace of her being to the fore save and except long treacly daubs extending east and west from ear to ear, and north and south from cape nep of the nose to the extremity of beardyland.

But what of all things attracted my attention on that memorable day was the show of cows, sheep, and horses, mooing, baaing, and neighering; and the race—that was the best! Od, what a sight! We were jammed in the crowd of auld wives with their toys and shining ribbons, and canter lads with their blue bonnets, and young wenches carrying home their fairings in napkins as muckle as would hold their teeth going for a month. There scarcely could be muckle for love when there was so much for the stomach, and men with wooden legs and brass virls at the end of them playing on the fiddle, and a bear that roared and danced on its hind feet with a muzzled mouth, and Punch and Polly, and puppie shows, and mair than I can tell, when up came the horses to the starting-post. I shall never forget the bonny dresses of the riders. One had a napkin tied round his head, another had on a black velvet hunting cap and his coat stripped—oh, but he was a brave lad—and sorrow was the folks for him when he fell off in taking ower sharp a turn, by which auld Pullen, the bell-ringer, wha was holding the post, was made to coup the creels. And the last was all life, as gleg as an eel. Up and down he went, and up and down gaed the beast on its hind legs and its fore legs, funking like mad. Yet though he was not aboon thirteen, or fourteen at most, he did not cry out for help more than five or six times, but grippit at the mane with one hand and at the back of the saddle with the other, till daft Robie, the hostler at the stables, caught hold of the beast by the head, and off they set. The young birkie had neither hat nor shoon, but he did not spare the stick; round and round they flew like daft. Ye would have thought their een would have loupen out, and loudly all the crowd were hurrahing when young hatless came up foremost, standing in the stirrups, the long stick between his teeth, and his white hair fleeing behind him in the wind like streamers on a frosty night.

CALF-LOVE.

Just after I was put to my apprenticeship, having made free choice of the tailoring trade, I had a terrible stound of calf-love. Never shall I forget it. I was growing up long and lank as a willow-wand, brawns to my legs there were none, as my trousers of other years too visibly effected to show. The long yellow hair hung down, like a flax-wig, the length of my lantern jaws, which looked, notwithstanding my yapness and stiff appetite, as if eating and they had broken up acquaintanceship. My blue jacket seemed in the sleeves to have picket a quarrel with the wrists and had retreated to a tait below the elbows. The haunch-buttons, on the contrary, appeared to have taken a strong liking to the shoulders, a little below which they showed their tarnished brightness. At the middle of the back the tails terminated, leaving the well-worn rear of my corduroys like a full moon seen through a dark haze. Oh! but I must have been a bonny lad.

My first flame was the minister's lassie, Jess, a buxom and forward queen, two or three years older than myself. I used to sit looking at her in the kirk, and felt a droll confusion when our een met. It dirled through my heart like a dart, and I looked down at my psalm-book sheepish and blushing. Fain would I have spoken to her, but it would not do; my courage aye failed me at the pinch, though she whiles gave me a smile when she passed me. She used to go to the well every night with her twa stoups to draw water after the manner of the Israelites at gloaming, so I thought of watching to give her the two apples which I had carried in my pouch for more than a week for that purpose. How she laughed when I stappit them into her hand and brushed by without speaking. I stood at the bottom of the close listening, and heard her laughing till she was like to split. My heart flap flappit in my breast like a pair of fanners. It was a moment of heavenly hope; but I saw Jamie Coom, the blacksmith, who I aye jaloused was my rival, coming down to the well. I saw her give him one of the apples, and hearing him say with a loud gaffaw, "Where is the tailor?" I took to my heels, and never stopped till I found myself on the little stool by the fireside, and the hamely sound of my mother's wheel bum-bumming in my lug like a gentle lullaby.

Every noise I heard flustered me, but I calmed in time, though I went to my bed without my supper. When I was driving out the gaislings to the grass on the next morn who was it my ill fate to meet but the blacksmith. "Oh, Mansie," said Jamie Coom, "are ye gaun to take me for your best man? I hear you are to be cried in the kirk on Sunday."

"Me!" answered I, shaking and staring.

"Yes," said he; "Jess, the minister's maid, told me last night that you had been giving up your name at the manse. Ay, it's ower true, for she showed me the apples ye gied her in a present. This is a bonny story, Mansie, my man, and you only at your apprenticeship yet."

Terror and despair had struck me dumb. I stood as still and as stiff as a web of buckram. My tongue was tied, and I couldna contradict him. Jamie faulded his arms and gaed away whistling, turning every now and then his sooty face over his shoulder and mostly sticking his tune, as he could not keep his mouth screwed for laughing. What would I not have given to have laughed too!

There was no time to be lost; this was the Saturday. The next rising sun would shine on the Sabbath. Ah, what a case I was in; I could mostly have drowned myself had I not been frighted. What could I do? My love had vanished like lightning; but oh, I was in a terrible gliff!

Instead of gundy, I sold my thrums to Mrs. Walnut for a penny, with which I bought at the counter a sheet of paper and a pen, so that in the afternoon I wrote out a letter to the minister telling him what I had been given to hear, and begging him, for the sake of mercy, not to believe Jess's word, as I was not able to keep a wife, and as she was a leeing gipsy.

PUSHING MY FORTUNE.

The days of the years of my apprenticeship having glided cannily over on the working board of my respected maister, James Hosey, where I sat working cross-legged like a busy bee in the true spirit of industrious contentment, I found myself at the end of the seven year so well instructed in the tailoring trade, to which I had paid a near-sighted attention, that, without more ado, I girt myself round about with a proud determination of at once cutting my mother's apron string and venturing to go without a hold. Thinks I to myself "faint heart never won fair lady," so, taking my stick in my hand, I set out towards Edinburgh as brave as a Hielander in search of a journeyman's place. I may set it down to an especial providence that I found one, on the very first day, to my heart's content in by at the Grassmarket where I stayed for the space of six calendar months.

Had it not been from a real sense of the duty I owed to my future employers, whomsoever they might be, in making myself a first-rate hand in the cutting, shaping, and sewing line, I would not have found courage in my breast to have helped me out through such a long and dreary time.

Never let us repine, howsomever, but consider that all is ordered for the best. The sons of the patriarch Jacob found out their brother Joseph in a foreign land, and where they least expected it, so it was here—even here where my heart was sickening unto death, from my daily and nightly thoughts being as bitter as gall—that I fell in with the greatest blessing of my life, Nanse Cromie!

In the flat below our workshop lived Mrs. Whitterraick, the wife of Mr. Whitterraick, a dealer in hens and hams in the poultry market, who, coming from the Lauder neighbourhood, had hired a bit wench of a lassie that was to follow them come the term. And who think ye should this lassie be but Nanse Cromie, afterwards, in the course of a kind providence, the honoured wife of my bosom, and the mother of bonny Benjie.

In going up and down the stairs—it being a common entry, ye observe—me may be going down with my every-day hat on to my dinner, and she coming up carrying a stoup of water or half-a-pound of pouthered butter on a plate, with a piece of paper thrown over it—we frequently met half-way, and had to stand still to let one another pass. Nothing came of these forgetherings, howsomever, for a month or two, she being as shy and modest as she was bonny, with her clean demity short gown and snow-white morning mutch, to say nothing of her cherry mou, and me unco douffie in making up to strangers. We could not help, nevertheless, to take aye a stoun look of each other in passing, and I was a gone man, bewitched out of my seven senses, falling from my claes, losing my stomach, and over the lugs in love, three weeks and some odd days before ever a single syllable passed between us.

If ever a man loved, and loved like mad, it was me, Mansie Wauch, and I take no shame in the confession; but, kenning it all in the course of nature, declared it openly and courageously in the face of the wide world. Let them laugh who like; honest folk, I pity them. Such know not the pleasures of virtuous affection. It is not in corrupted, sinful hearts that the fire of true love can ever burn clear. Alas, and ohon orie! They lose the sweetest, completest, dearest, truest pleasure that this world has in store for its children. They know not the bliss to meet that makes the embrace of separation bitter. They never dreamed the dreams that make awakening to the morning light unpleasant. They never felt the raptures that can dirl like darts through a man's soul from a woman's e'e. They never tasted the honey that dwells on a woman's lip, sweeter than yellow marigolds to the bee; or fretted under the fever of bliss that glows through the frame on pressing the hand of a suddenly met and fluttering sweetheart. But tuts-tuts—hech-how! my day has long since passed; and this is stuff to drop from the lips of an auld fool. Nevertheless, forgive me, friends; I cannot help all-powerful nature.

Nanse's taste being like my own, we amused one another in abusing great cities, and it is curious how soon I learned to be up to trap—I mean in an honest way; for when she said she was wearying the very heart out of her to be home again to Lauder, which, she said, was her native and the true land of Goshen, I spoke back to her by way of answer—"Nancy, my dear," says I, "believe me that the real land of Goshen is out at Dalkeith, and if ye'll take up house wi' me, and enter into a way of doing, I daursay in a while ye'll come to think so too."

What will you say there? Matters were by-and-bye settled full tosh between us, and though the means of both parties were small, we were young and able and willing to help one another. For two three days, I must confess, after Nanse and me found ourselves in the comfortable situation of man and wife I was a dowie and desponding, thinking we were to have a numerous small family and where work was to come from; but no sooner was my sign nailed up with four iron handfasts by Johnny Hammer, painted in black letters on a blue ground, with a picture of a jacket on one side and a pair of shears on the other, and my shop door opened to the public with a wheen ready-made waistcoats, gallowses, leather caps, and Kilmarnock cowls, hung up at the window, than business flowed in upon us in a perfect torrent. First one came in for his measure and then another.

A wife came in for a pair of red worsted boots for her bairn, but would not take them for they had not blue fringes. A bare-headed lassie, hoping to be hansel, threw down twopence and asked tape at three yards a halfpenny. The minister sent an old black coat beneath his maid's arm, preened up in a towel, to get docked in the tails down into a jacket, which I trust I did to his entire satisfaction, making it fit to a hair. The duke's butler himself patronized me by sending me a coat which was all hair powder and pomate to get a new neck put to it.

No wonder than we attracted customers, for our sign was the prettiest ye ever saw, though the jacket was not just so neatly painted as for some sand-blind creatures not to take it for a goose. I daresay there were fifty half-naked bairns glowering their een out of their heads at it from morning till night, and after they all were gone to their beds both Nanse and me found ourselves so proud of our new situation in life that we slipped out in the dark by ourselves and had a prime look at it with a lantern.

MANSIE WAUCH'S FIRST AND LAST PLAY.

Mony a time and often had I heard of play-acting and of players making themselves kings and queens, and saying a great many wonderful things, but I had never before an opportunity of making myself a witness to the truth of these hearsays. So Maister Glen, being as fu' of nonsense and as fain to have his curiosity gratified, we took upon us the stout resolution to gang ower thegither, he offering to treat me and I determined to run the risk of Maister Wiggie, our minister's rebuke, for the transgression, hoping it would make na lasting impression on his mind, being for the first and only time. Folks shouldna at a' times be ower scrupulous.

After paying our money at the door, never, while I live and breathe, will I forget what we saw and heard that night. It just looks to me by a' the world, when I think on't, like a fairy dream. The place was crowded to the e'e, Maister

Glen and me having nearly got our ribs dung in before we fand a seat, and them behint were obliged to mount the back benches to get a sight. Right to the fore hand of us was a large green curtain some five or six ells wide, a guid deal the waur of the wear, having seen service through two or three simmers, and just in the front of it were eight or ten penny candles stuck in a board fastened to the ground to let us see the players' feet like when they came on the stage, and even before they came on the stage, for the curtain being scrimpit in length we saw legs and feet moving behind the scenes very neatly, while twa blind fiddlers they had brought with them played the bonniest ye ever heard. Od, the very music was worth a sixpence of itsel'.

The place, as I said before, was choke full, just to excess, so that ane could scarcely breathe. Indeed I never saw ony pairt sae crowded, not even at a tent preaching when Mr. Roarer was giving his discourses on the building of Solomon's Temple. We were obligated to have the windows opened for a mouthful of fresh air, the barn being as close as a baker's oven, my neighbour and me fanning our red faces with our hats to keep us cool; and, though all were half stewed, we had the worst o't, the toddy we had ta'en having fomented the blood of our bodies into a perfect fever.

Just at the time that the twa blind fiddlers were playing the "Downfall of Paris" a hand bell rang, and up goes the green curtain, being hauled to the ceiling, as I observed wi' the tail o' my e'e, by a birkie at the side that had haud o' a rope. So, on the music stopping and all becoming as still as that you might have heard a pin fall, in comes a decent old gentleman at his leesure, weel powdered, wi' an auld-fashioned coat and waistcoat wi' flap pockets, brown breeches with buckles at the knees, and silk stockings with red gushets on a blue ground. I never saw a man in sic distress. He stampit about, and better stampit about, dadding the end of his staff on the ground, and imploring all the powers of heaven and yearth to help him to find out his runawa' daughter that had decampit wi' some ne'er-do-well loon of a half-pay captain that keppit her in his arms frae her bed-room window up twa pair o' stairs. Every father and head of a family maun ha'e felt for a man in his situation thus to be rubbit of his dear bairn, and an only daughter, too, as he telt us ower and ower again, as the saut, saut tears ran gushing down his withered face, and he aye blew his nose on his clean calendered pocket napkin. But, ye ken, the thing was absurd to suppose that we should ken onything about the matter, having never seen either him or his daughter between the een afore, and no kenning them by head mark; so, though we sympathized with him, as folks ought to do with a fellow-creature in affliction, we thought it best to haud our tongues to see what might cast up better than he expected. So out he gaed stamping at the ither side, determined, he said, to find them out though he should follow them to the world's end, Johnny Groat's House, or something to that effect.

Hardly was his back turned, and amaist before ye could cry Jack Robison, in comes the birkie and the very young leddy the auld gentleman described arm and arm thegither, smoodging and lauching like daft. Dog on it, it was a shameless piece of business. As true as death, before all the crowd of folk he pat his arm round her waist and ca'ed her his sweetheart, and love, and dearie, and darling, and everything that is sweet. If they had been courting in a close thegither on a Friday night they couldna ha'e said mair to ane anither, or gaen greater lengths. I thought sic shame to be an e'e-witness to sic ongoings that I was obliged at last to haud up my hat afore my face and look down, though, for a' that, the young lad, to be sic a blackguard as his conduct showed, was weel enough faured and had a guid coat on his back wi' double gilt buttons and fashionable lapels, to say little o' a very weel-made pair of buckskins a little the waur o' the wear, to be sure, but which, if they had been cleaned, would ha'e looked amaist as good as new. How they had come we never could learn, as we neither saw chaise nor gig; but, from his having spurs on his boots, it is mair than likely that they had lighted at the back door of the barn frae a horse, she riding on a pad behint him, maybe with her hand round his waist.

The faither lookit to be a rich auld bool, baith from his manner of speaking and the rewards he seemed to offer for the apprehension of his daughter; but, to be sure, when so many of us were present that had an equal right to the spulzie it wadna be a great deal a thousand pounds when divided, still it was worth the looking after. So we just bidit a wee.

Things were brought to a bearing, whosoever, sooner than either themsel's, I daursay, or onybody else present seemed to ha'e the least glimpse of; for just in the middle of their fine going on the sound of a coming fit was heard, and the lassie, taking guilt to her, cried out, "Hide me, hide me, for the sake of gudeness, for yonder comes my old father!"

Nae sooner said than done. In he stappit her into a closet, and, after shutting the door on her, he sat down upon a chair, pretending to be asleep in a moment. The auld faither came bouncing in, and seeing the fellow as sound as a tap he ran forrit and gaed him sich a shake as if he wad ha'e shooken him a' sundry, which sune made him open his een as fast as he had steekit them. After blackguarding the chiel at no allowance, cursing him up hill and down dale, and ca'ing him every name but a gentleman, he haddit his staff ower his crown and, gripping him by the cuff o' the neck, askit him what he had made o' his daughter. Never since I was born did I ever see sic brazen-faced impudence! The rascal had the brass to say at ance that he hadna seen word or wittens o' his daughter for a month, though mair than a hundred folk sitting in his company had seen him daunting her with his arm round her jimpy waist not five minutes before. As a man, as a father, as an elder of our kirk, my corruption was raised, for I aye hated leeing as a puir cowardly sin and an inbreak on the ten commandments, and I fand my neebour, Mr. Glen, fidgetting on the seat as weel as me, so I thocht that whaever spoke first wad ha'e the best right to be entitled to the reward; whereupon, just as he was in the act of rising up, I took the word out of his mouth, saying, "Dinna believe him, auld gentleman, dinna believe him, friend; he's telling a parcel of lees. Never saw her for a month! It's no worth arguing or ca'ing witnesses; just open that press door and ye'll see whether I'm speaking truth or no."

The auld man stared and lookit dumbfoundered, and the young man, instead of rinning forrit wi' his double nieves to strike me, the only thing I was feared for, began a-laughing, as if I had dune him a good turn. But never since I had a being did I ever witness an uproar and noise as immediately took place. The haill house was sae glad that the scoundrel had been exposed that they set up siccan a roar o' lauchter and thumpit away at siccan a rate at the boards wi' their feet that, at lang and last, wi' pushing and fidgetting and hadding their sides, down fell the place they ca' the gallery, a' the folk in't being hurled tapsy-turvy head foremost amang the saw-dust on the floor below, their guffawing sune being turned to howling, ilka ane crying louder than anither at the tap of their voices, "Murder! murder! hand off me; murder! my ribs are in; murder! I'm killed—I'm speechless!" and ither lamentations to that effect; so that a rush to the door took place, in which everything was overturned—the door-keeper being wheeled away like wildfire, the funns strampit to pieces, the lights knockit out, and the twa blind fiddlers dung head foremost ower the stage, the bass fiddle cracking like thunder at every bruise. Siccan tearing, and swearing, and tumbling, and squeeling was never witnessed in the memory of man sin' the building of Babel, legs being likely to be broken, sides staved in, een knocked out, and lives lost—there being only ae door, and that a sma' ane—so that when we had been carried off our feet that length my wind was fairly gane, and a sick dwam cam' ower me, lights of a' manner of colours, red, blue, green, and orange dancing before me that entirely deprived me o common sense till, on opening my een in the dark, I fand mysel' leaning wi' my braid side against the wa' on the opposite side of the close. It was some time before I mindit what had happened, so, dreading scaith, I fand first the ae arm and then the ither to see if they were broken, syne my head, and syne baith o' my legs; but a', as weel as I could discover, was skinhale and scart free—on perceiving which, my joy was without bounds, having a great notion that I had been killed on the spot. So I reached round my hand very thankfully to tak' out my pocket napkin to gi'e my brow a wipe when, lo and behold, the tail of my Sunday's coat was fairly aff and away, dockit by the haunch buttons.

PHILISTINE IN THE COAL-HOLE.

It was about the month of March, in the year of grace anno domini eighteen hunder, that the haill country trummelled, like a man ill of the interminable fiver, under the consternation of Bonapartie and all the French vagabonds emigrating ower and landing in the firth. Keep us a'! the folk, dydit bodies, pat less confidence than became them in what our volunteer regiments were able and willing to do though we had a remnant amang us of the true bluid that with loud lauchter lauched the creatures to scorn, and I for ane keepit up my pluck like a true Hielander. Does ony leeving soul believe that Scotland could be conquered, and the like o' us sold, like Egyptian slaves, into captivity? Fie, fie; I could spit on siccan havers. Are we no descended, faither and son, frae Robert Bruce and Sir William Wallace, having the bright bluid of freemen in our veins and the Pentland Hills, as weel as our ain dear hames and firesides, to fight for? The fief that wadna gi'e cut-and-thrust for his country as lang as he had a breath to draw or a leg to stand on should be tied neck and heels, without benefit o' clergy, and thrown ower Leith Pier to swim for his life like a mangy dog!

It was sometime in the blasty month of March, the weather being rawish and rainy, wi' sharp frosty nights that left all the window soles whitewashed ower with frost-rind in the morning, that as I was going out in the dark, afore lying doun in my bed, to gi'e a look into the hen-house door and lock the coal cellar, so that I might pit the bit key intil my breek pouches, I happened to gi'e a keek in, and, lo and behold, the awfu' apparition of a man wi' a yellow jacket lying sound asleep on a great lump o' parrot coal in a corner.

In the hurry of my terror and surprise at seeing a man with a yellow jacket and a blue foraging cap in such a situation, I was like to drap the guid twopenny candle and faint clean away; but, coming to mysel' in a jiffy, I determined, in case it might be a highway rubber, to thraw about the key, and, rinning up for the firelock, shoot him through the head instantly, if found necessary. In turning round the key the lock, being in want of a feather o' oil, made a noise, and waukened the puir wretch, who, jumping to the soles of his feet in despair, cried out in a voice that was like to break my heart, though I couldna make out ae word of his paraphernally. It minded me, by a' the world, of a wheen cats fufling and feighting through ither, and whiles something that sounded like "Sugar, sugar, measure the cord," and "dabble, dabble." It was waur than the maist outrageous Gaelic ever spoken in the height o' passion by a Hieland shearer.

"Oho!" thinks I, "friend, ye cannot be a Christian from your lingo, that's one thing poz; and I would wager tippence you're a Frenchy. Who kens keeps us all, but ye may be a Bonaparte himself in disguise, come over in a flat-bottomed boat, to spy the nakedness of the land. So ye may just rest content, and keep your quarters good till the morn's morning."

It was a wonderful business, and enough to happen to a man in the course of his lifetime to find Mounseer from Paris in his coal neuk, and have the enemy of his country snug under lock and key; so while he kept rampaging, fuffing, stamping, and diabbling away I went in and brought out Benjie with a blanket row'd round him, and my journeyman, Tommy Bodkin—who, being an orphan, I made a kind of parlour boarder of, he sleeping on a shake-down beyond the kitchen fire—to hold a consultation and be witness of the transaction.

I got my musket, and Tommy Bodkin armed himself with the goose, a deadly weapon, whoever may get a clour with it, and Benjie took the poker in one hand and the tongs in the other; and out we all marched briskly to make the Frenchman that was locked up from the light of day in the coal house surrender. After hearkening at the door for a while, and finding all quiet, he gave a knock to rouse him up and see if we could bring anything out of him by speering him cross-questions. Tammy and Benjie trembled from top to toe, like aspen leaves, but fient a word could we make common sense of it all. I wonder wha edicates thae foreign creatures? It was in vain to follow him, for he just gab, gabbled away like ane o' the stone masons at the tower of Babel. At first I was completely bamboozled and amaist dung stupid, though I kent a word of French which I wantit to pit till him, so I cried through—"Canna you speak Frencha, Mounseer?"

He hadna the politeness to stop and mak' answer, but just gaed on wi' his string of havers, without either rhyme or reason, which we could mak' neither tap, tail, nor main o'.

It was a sair trial to us a', putting us to our wit's end, and hoo to come on was past all visible comprehension, when Tammy Bodkin, gi'eing his elbow a claw, said—"Od, maister, I wager something that he's broken loose frae Pennycuick. We have him like a rotten in a fa'." On Pennycuick being mentioned, we heard the foreign crature in the coal house groaning out, "Och" and "ohone," and "parbleu," and "Mysie Rabbie"—that, I fancy, was his sweetheart at hame, sum bit French queen that wondered he was never like to come frae the wars and marry her. I thocht on this, for his voice was mournfu', though I couldna understand the words; and, kenning he was a stranger in a far land, my bowels yearned within me with compassion towards him.

I wad ha'e gien half-a-crown at that blessed moment to ha'e been able to wash my hands free o' him, but I swithered, and was like the cuddie between the twa bundles of hay. At lang and last a thocht struck me, which was to gi'e the deluded, simple cratur a chance of escape, reckoning that if he fand his way hame he wad see the shame and folly of feighting against us ony mair, and, marrying Maysie Rabbie, live a contented and peacefu' life under his ain feg and bay tree. So, wishing him a sound sleep, I cried through the door—"Mounseer, gooda nighta," decoying away Benjie and Tammy Bodkin into the house and dispatching them to their beds like lamplighters, bidding them never fash their thumbs, but sleep like taps, as I would keep a sharp look-out till morning.

As soon, hoosomever, as I fand a' things snug I slippit awa to the coal-hole, and, gi'ein' the key a canny turn in the lock, I went to my bed beside Nanse.

At the dawn o' day, by cock-craw, Benjie and Tammy Bodkin, keen o' the ploy, were up and astir as anxious as if their life depended on it, to see that all was safe and snug and that the prisoner hadna shot the lock. They agreed to march sentry over him half-an-hour the piece, time about, the ane stretching himsel' out on a stool beside the kitchen fire by way of a bench in the guard-house, while the other gaed to and fro like the ticker of a clock.

The back window being up a jink, I heard the two confabbing. "We'll draw cuts," said Benjie, "which is to walk sentry first. See, here's twa straes; the langest gets the choice." "I've won," cried Tammy, "so gang you in a while, and if I need ye, or grow frightened, I'll beat leatherty patch wi' my knuckles on the back door. But we had better see first what he is about, for he may be howking a hole through aneath the foundations. Thae fiefs can work like moudiewards." "I'll slip forrit," said Benjie, "and gi'e a peep." "Keep to a side," cried Tammy Bodkin, "for, dog on it, Moosey'll maybe ha'e a pistol; and, if his birse be up, he would think nae mair o' shooting ye as dead as a mawkin than I would do of taking my breakfast."

"I'll rin past and gi'e a knock at the door wi' the poker to rouse him up?" askit Benjie.

"Come away then," answered Tammie, "and ye'll hear him gi'e a yowl and commence gabbling like a goose."

As all this was going on I rose and took a vizzy between the chinks of the window shutters, so just as I got my neb to the hole I saw Benjie as he flew past give the door a drive. His consternation, on finding it flee half open, may be easier imagined than described; for, expecting the Frenchman to bounce out like a roaring lion, they hurried like mad into the house, couping the creels ower ane anither, Tammie spraining his thumb against the back door, and Benjie's foot going into Tammie's coat pocket, which it carried away with it like a cloth sandal. What became o' the French vagrant is a matter o' surmise—nae mortal kens.

THE LIFE AND ASTONISHING ADVENTURES

OF

PETER WILLIAMSON

WHO WAS

Carried off when a Child from Aberdeen

AND SOLD FOR A SLAVE.

I WAS born in the parish of Aboyne, Aberdeenshire, of respectable parents, who sent me very early to live with an aunt at Aberdeen. When, under the years of pupilarity, once playing on the quay with others of my companions—being of a stout robust constitution—I was taken notice of by two fellows belonging to a vessel in the harbour employed in the trade called kidnapping—that is, stealing young children from their parents, and selling them as slaves in plantations abroad. Being marked out by those monsters of impiety as their prey, I was cajoled on board the ship by them, where I was no sooner got than they conducted me between the decks to some others they had kidnapped in the same manner. At that time I had no sense of the fate that was destined for me, and spent the time in childish amusements with my fellow-sufferers in the steerage, being never suffered to go upon deck whilst the vessel lay in the harbour.

In about a month's time the ship set sail for America. I cannot forget that, when we arrived on the coast we were destined for, a hard gale of wind sprung up from the S.E., and, to the captain's great surprise (he not thinking he was near land, although having been eleven weeks on the passage), about twelve o'clock at night, the ship struck on a sandbank off Cape May, near the Capes of Delaware, and, to the great terror and affright of the ship's company, in a short time was almost full of water. The boat was then hoisted out, into which the captain and his fellow villains, the crew, got with some difficulty, leaving me and my deluded companions to perish, as they then naturally concluded inevitable death to be our fate. Often in my distresses and miseries since, have I wished that such had been the consequence, when in a state of innocence! But Providence thought proper to reserve me for future trials of its goodness. Thus abandoned and deserted, without the least prospect of relief, but threatened every moment with death, did these villains leave us. The cries, the shrieks and tears of a parcel of infants had no effect on, or caused the least remorse in, the breasts of these merciless wretches. Scarce can I say to which to give the preference, whether to such as these who have had the opportunity of knowing the Christian religion, or to the savages hereinafter described—who profane not the gospel or boast of humanity; and if they act in a more brutal and butcherly manner, yet it is to their enemies, for the sake of plunder and the rewards offered them—for their principles are alike, the love of sordid gain being both their motives. The ship being on a sandbank, which did not give way to let her deeper, we lay in the same deplorable condition until morning, when, though we saw the land of Cape May at about a mile's distance, we knew not what would be our fate.

The wind at length abated, and the captain, unwilling to lose all her cargo, about ten o'clock sent some of his crew in a boat to the ship's side to bring us on shore, where we lay in a sort of a camp, made of the sails of the vessel, and such other things as we could get. The provisions lasted us until we were taken in by a vessel bound to Philadelphia, lying on this island, as well as I can recollect, near three weeks. Very little of the cargo was saved undamaged, and the vessel was entirely lost.

When arrived and landed at Philadelphia, the capital of Pennsylvania, the captain had people enough who came to buy us. He sold us at about £16 per head. What became of my unhappy companions I never knew. It was my lot to be sold to one of my countrymen, whose name was Hugh Wilson, a North Briton, who had in his youth undergone the same fate as myself, having been kidnapped from St. Johnstown, in Scotland.

Happy was my lot in falling into my countryman's power, as he was, contrary to many others of his calling, a humane, worthy, honest man. Having no children of his own, and commiserating my unhappy condition, he took great care of me until I was fit for business, and about the twelfth year of my age, set me about little trifles, in which state I continued until my fourteenth year, when I was more fit for harder work. During such my idle state, seeing my fellow-servants often reading and writing, it incited in me an inclination to learn, which I intimated to my master, telling him I should be very willing to serve a year longer than the contract by which I was sold, if he would indulge me in going to school; this he readily agreed to, saying that winter would be the best time. It being then summer, I waited with impatience for the other season; but, to make some progress in my design, I got a Primer, and learned as much from my fellow-servants as I could. At school, where I went every winter for five years, I made a tolerable proficiency, and have ever since been improving myself at leisure hours. With this good master I continued till I was seventeen years old, when he died; and as a reward for my faithful service, he left me £200 currency, which was then about £150 sterling, his best horse, saddle, and all his wearing apparel.

Being now my own master, having money in my pocket, and all other necessaries, I employed myself in jobbing about the country, working for any one that would employ me, for near seven years, when, thinking I had money sufficient to follow some better way of life, I resolved to settle, but thought one step necessary thereto was to be married; for which purpose I applied to the daughter of a substantial planter, and found my suit was not unacceptable to her or her father, so that matters were soon concluded upon, and we married. My father-in-law, in order to establish us in the world in an easy, if not affluent manner, made me a deed of gift of a tract of land, that lay, unhappily for me, as it has since proved, on the frontiers of the province of Pennsylvania, near the forks of Delaware, in Berks County, containing about two hundred acres, thirty of which were well cleared and fit for immediate use, whereon was a good house and barn. The place pleasing me well, I settled on it, though it cost me the major part of my money in buying stock, household furniture, and implements for out-door work. And happy as I was in a good wife, yet did my felicity last me not long, for about the year 1754, the Indians in the French interest, who had for a long time before ravaged and destroyed other parts of America unmolested, I may very properly say, began to be very troublesome on the frontiers of our province, where they generally appeared in small skulking parties, with yellings, shoutings, and antic postures, instead of trumpets and drums, committing great devastations. The Pennsylvanians little imagined at first that the Indians, guilty of such outrages and violence, were some of those who pretended to be in the English interest, which, alas! proved to be too true to many of us; for, like the French in Europe, without regard to faith or treaties, they suddenly break out into furious, rapid outrages and devastations, but soon retire precipitately, having no stores nor provisions but what they meet with in their incursions. Some, indeed, carry a bag with biscuit or Indian corn therein, but not unless they have a long march to their destined place of action. And those French who were sent to dispossess us in that part of the world, being indefatigable in their duty, and continually contriving and using all manner of ways and means to win the Indians to their interest, many of whom had been too negligent, and sometimes, I may say, cruelly treated by those who pretend to be their protectors and friends, found it no very difficult matter to get over to their interest many who belonged to those nations in amity with us, especially as the rewards they gave them were so great, they paying for every scalp of an English person £15 sterling.

Shocking to human nature were the barbarities daily committed by the savages, and are not to be parallelled in all the volumes of history! Scarce did a day pass but some unhappy family or other fell victims to savage cruelty. Terrible indeed it proved to me, as well as to many others. I that was now happy in an easy state of life, blessed with an affectionate and tender wife, who was possessed of all amiable qualities, to enable me to go through the world with that peace and serenity of mind which every Christian wishes to possess, became on a sudden one of the most unhappy and deplorable of mankind. Scarce can I sustain the shock which for ever recoils on me, at thinking on the last time of seeing that good woman. The fatal 2nd of October, 1754, she that day went from home to visit some of her relations. As I stayed up later than usual, expecting her return, none being in the house besides myself, how great was my surprise, terror, and affright, when, about eleven o'clock at night, I heard the dismal war-cry, or war-whoop of the savages, and to my inexpressible grief, soon found my house was attacked by them. I flew to my chamber window, and perceived them to be twelve in number. They making several attempts to get in, I asked them what they wanted. They gave me no answer, but continued beating and trying to get the door opened. Judge, then, the condition I must be in, knowing the cruelty and merciless disposition of those savages, should I fall into their hands. To escape which dreadful misfortune, having my gun loaded in my hand, I threatened them with death if they should not desist. But how vain and fruitless are the efforts of one man against the united force of so many, and of such merciless, undaunted, and bloodthirsty monsters as I had here to deal with. One of them that could speak a little English threatened me in return, that if I did not come out they would burn me alive in the house, telling me farther, that they were no friends to the English, but if I would come out and surrender myself prisoner, they would not kill me. My terror and distraction at hearing this is not to be expressed by words, nor easily imagined by any person, unless in the same condition. Little could I depend on the promises of such creatures, and yet if I did not, inevitable death, by being burnt alive, must be my lot. Distracted as I was, in such deplorable circumstances, I chose to rely on the uncertainty of their fallacious promises rather than meet with certain death by rejecting them, and, accordingly, went out of my house with my gun in my hand, not knowing what I did, or that I had it. Immediately on my approach, they rushed on me like so many tigers, and instantly disarmed me. Having me thus in their power, the merciless villains bound me to a tree near the door; they then went into the house and plundered and destroyed everything, carrying off what moveables they could; the rest, together with the house, they set fire to, and consumed before my eyes. The barbarians, not satisfied with this, set fire to my barn, stable, and outhouses, wherein were about two hundred bushels of wheat, six cows, four horses, and five sheep, which were entirely consumed to ashes. During the conflagration, to describe the thoughts, the fears, and misery that I felt, is utterly impossible; after this they untied me, and gave me a great load to carry on my back, under which I travelled all that night with them, full of the most terrible apprehensions, and oppressed with the greatest anxiety of mind, lest my unhappy wife should likewise have fallen a prey to those cruel monsters. At daybreak my infernal masters ordered me to lay down my load, when, tying my hands again round a tree with a small cord, they then forced the blood out of my finger-ends. They then kindled a fire near the tree whereto I was bound, which filled me with dreadful agonies, concluding I was going to be made a sacrifice to their barbarity.

The fire being thus made, they for some time danced round me after their manner, with various odd motions and antic gestures, whooping, hallooing, and crying in a frightful manner, as it is their custom. Having satisfied themselves in this sort of their mirth, they proceeded in a more tragical manner, taking the burning coals and sticks, flaming with fire at the ends, holding them near my face, head, hands, and feet, with a deal of monstrous pleasure and satisfaction, and at the same time threatening to burn me entirely if I made the least noise or motion of my body. Thus tortured, as I was, almost to death, I suffered their brutal pleasure without being allowed to vent my inexpressible anguish otherwise than by shedding tears; even which, when these inhuman tormentors observed, with a shocking pleasure and alacrity, they would take fresh coals and apply near my eyes, telling me my face was wet, and that they would dry it for me. How I suffered these tortures I have here faintly described has been matter of wonder to me many times; but God enabled me to wait with more than common patience for a deliverance I daily prayed for.

Having at length satisfied their brutal pleasure, they sat

round the fire and roasted their meat, of which they had robbed my dwelling. When they had prepared it, and satisfied their voracious appetites, they offered some to me; though it is easily imagined I had but little appetite to eat, after the tortures and miseries I had undergone; yet was I forced to seem pleased with what they offered me, lest, by refusing it, they had again resumed their hellish practices. What I could not eat, I contrived to get between the bark and the tree where I was fixed, they having unbound my hands until they imagined I had ate all they gave me; but then they again bound me as before, in which deplorable condition was I forced to continue all that day. When the sun was set they put out the fire and covered the ashes with leaves, as is their usual custom, that the white people might not discover any traces or signs of their having been there.

Going from thence along by the river, for the space of six miles, loaded as I was before, we arrived at a spot near the Apalachian mountains, where they hid their plunder under logs of wood; and oh! shocking to relate, from thence did these hellish monsters proceed to a neighbouring house, occupied by one Joseph Snider and his unhappy family—consisting of his wife, five children, and a young man, his servant. They soon got admittance into the unfortunate man's house, where they immediately, without the least remorse, and with more than brutal cruelty, scalped the tender parents and the unhappy children. Nor could the tears, the shrieks, or cries of these unhappy victims prevent their horrid massacre; for having thus scalped them, and plundered the house of everything that was moveable, they set fire to the same, where the poor creatures met their final doom amidst the flames, the hellish miscreants standing at the door, or as near the house as the flames would permit them, rejoicing and echoing back, in their diabolical manner, the piercing cries, heart-rending groans, and paternal and affectionate soothings, which issued from this most horrid sacrifice of an innocent family. Not contented with what they had already done, they still continued their inordinate villainy, in making a general conflagration of the barn and stables, together with all the corn, horses, cows, and everything on the place.

Thinking the young man belonging to this unhappy family would be of some service to them in carrying part of their plunder, they spared his life, and loaded him and myself with what they had here got, and again marched to the Blue Hills, where they stowed their goods as before. My fellow-sufferer could not long bear the cruel treatment which we were both obliged to suffer, and complaining bitterly to me of being unable to proceed any farther, I endeavoured to condole him as much as lay in my power, to bear up under his afflictions, and wait with patience till, by the divine assistance, we should be delivered out of their clutches; but in vain, for he still continued his moans and tears, which one of the savages perceiving as we travelled on, instantly came up to us, and with his tomahawk gave him a blow on the head, which felled the unhappy youth to the ground, where they immediately scalped and left him. The suddenness of this murder shocked me to that degree, that I was in a manner like a statue, being quite motionless, expecting my fate would soon be the same; however, recovering my distracted thoughts, I dissembled the uneasiness and anguish which I felt as well as I could from the barbarians; but such was the terror that I was under, that for some time I scarce knew the days of the week, or what I did, so that, at this period, life indeed became a burden to me, and I regretted being saved from my first persecutors, the sailors.

The horrid fact being completed, they kept on their course near the mountains, where they lay skulking four or five days, rejoicing at the plunder and store they had got. When provisions became scarce, they made their way towards Susquehana, where still, to add to the many barbarities they had already committed, passing near another house inhabited by an unhappy old man, whose name was John Adams, with his wife and four small children; and, meeting with no resistance, they immediately scalped the unhappy wife and her four children before the good old man's eyes. Inhuman and horrid as this was, it did not satiate them, for when they had murdered the poor woman, they acted with her in such a brutal manner as decency, or the remembrance of the crime, will not permit me to mention, and this even before the unhappy husband, who, not being able to avoid the sight, and incapable of affording her the least relief, entreated them to put an end to his miserable being. But they were as deaf and regardless to the tears, prayers, and entreaties of this venerable sufferer as they had been to those of the others, and proceeded in their hellish purpose of burning and destroying his house, barn, cattle, hay, corn, and everything the poor man a few hours before was master of. Having saved what they thought proper from the flames, they gave the old man, feeble, weak, and in the miserable condition he then was, as well as myself, burdens to carry, and loading themselves likewise with bread and meat, pursued their journey on towards the Great Swamp, where, being arrived, they lay for eight or nine days, sometimes diverting themselves in exercising the most atrocious and barbarous cruelties on their unhappy victim, the old man. Sometimes they would strip him naked and paint him all over with various sorts of colours, which they extracted or made from herbs and roots; at other times they would pluck the white hairs from his venerable beard, and tauntingly tell him he was a fool for living so long, and that they would show him kindness in putting him out of the world; to all which the poor creature could but vent his sighs, his tears, his moans, and entreaties, that, to my affrighted imagination, were enough to penetrate a heart of adamant, and soften the most obdurate savage. In vain, alas! were all his tears, for daily did they tire themselves with the various means they tried to torment him—sometimes tying him to a tree and whipping him, at others scorching his furrowed cheeks with red-hot coals, and burning his legs quite to the knees. But the good old man, instead of repining or wickedly arraigning the divine justice, like many others in such cases, even in the greatest agonies, incessantly offered up his prayers to the Almighty, with the most fervent thanksgivings for his former mercies, and hoping the flames, then surrounding and burning his aged limbs, would soon send him to the blissful mansions of the just, to be a partaker of the blessings there. And during such pious ejaculations, his infernal plagues would come round him, mimicking his heart-rending groans and piteous wailings. One night, after he had thus been tormented, whilst he and I were sitting together, condoling each other at the misfortunes and miseries we daily suffered, twenty scalps and three prisoners were brought in by another party of Indians. They had unhappily fallen into their hands in Cannojigge, a small town near the river Susquehana, chiefly inhabited by the Irish. These prisoners gave us some shocking accounts of the murders and devastations committed in their parts. The various and complicated actions of these barbarians would entirely fill a large volume; but what I have already written, with a few other instances which I shall select from the information, will enable the reader to guess at the horrid treatment the English, and Indians in their interest, suffered for many years past. I shall therefore only mention, in a brief manner, those that suffered near the same time with myself. This party who now joined us, had it not, I found, in their power to begin their wickedness as soon as those who visited my habitation, the first of their tragedies being on the 25th day of October, 1754, when John Lewis, with his wife and three small children, fell sacrifices to their cruelty, and were miserably scalped and murdered, his house, barn, and everything he possessed being burnt and destroyed. On the 28th, Jacob Miller, with his wife and six of his family, together with everything on his plantation, underwent the same fate. The 30th—the house, mill, barn, twenty head of cattle, two teams of horses, and everything belonging to the unhappy George Folke, met with the like treatment—himself, wife, and all his miserable family, consisting of nine in number, being inhumanly scalped, then cut in pieces and given to the swine, which devoured them. I shall give another instance of the numberless and unheard of barbarities they related of the savages, and proceed to their own tragical end. In short, one of the substantial traders belonging to the province, having business that called him some miles up the country, fell into the hands of these devils, who not only scalped him, but immediately roasted him before he was dead; then, like cannibals for want of other food, ate his whole body, and of his head made what they called an Indian pudding.

From these few instances of savage cruelty, the deplorable situation of the defenceless inhabitants, and what they hourly suffered in that part of the globe, must strike the utmost terror to a human soul, and cause in every breast the utmost detestation, not only against the authors of such tragic scenes, but against those who, through perfidy, inattention, or pusillanimous and erroneous principles, suffered these savages at first, unrepelled, or even unmolested, to commit such outrages and incredible depredations and murders; for no torments, no barbarities that can be exercised on the human sacrifices they get into their power, are left untried or omitted.

The three prisoners that were brought with these additional forces, constantly repining at their lot, and almost dead with their excessive hard treatment, contrived at last to make their escape; but being far from their own settlements, and not knowing the country, were soon after met by some others of the tribes or nations at war with us, and brought back to their diabolical masters, who greatly rejoiced at having them again in their infernal power. The poor creatures, almost famished for want of sustenance, having had none during the time of their elopement, were no sooner in the clutches of the barbarians, than two of them were tied to a tree, and a great fire made round them, where they remained till they were terribly scorched and burnt, when one of the villains, with his scalping knife, ripped open their bellies, took out their entrails, and burnt them before their eyes, whilst the others were cutting, piercing, and tearing the flesh from their breasts, hands, arms, and legs, with red-hot irons, till they were dead. The third unhappy victim was reserved a few hours longer, to be, if possible, sacrificed in a more cruel manner. His arms were tied close to his body, and a hole being dug deep enough for him to stand upright, he was put therein, and earth rammed and beat in all round his body, up to the neck, so that his head only appeared above the ground; they then scalped him, and there let him remain for three or four hours in the greatest agonies; after which they made a small fire near his head, causing him to suffer the most excruciating torments imaginable, whilst the poor creature could only cry for mercy in killing him immediately, for his brains were boiling in his head. Inexorable to all his plaints, they continued the fire, whilst, shocking to behold, his eyes gushed out of their sockets; and such agonizing torments did the unhappy creature suffer for near two hours, till he was quite dead! They then cut off his head and buried it with the other bodies, my task being to dig the graves, which, feeble and terrified as I was, the dread of suffering the same fate enabled me to do. I shall not here take up the reader's time in vainly attempting to describe what I felt on such an occasion, but continue my narrative, as more equal to my abilities.

A great snow now falling, the barbarians were a little fearful lest the white people should, by their traces, find out their skulking retreats, which obliged them to make the best of their way to their winter quarters, about two hundred miles farther from any plantation or inhabitants, where, after a long and tedious journey, being almost starved, I arrived with this infernal crew. The place where we were to rest, in their tongue, is called Alamingo. There were found a number of wigwams full of their women and children. Dancing, shooting, and shouting were their general amusements; and in all their festivals and dances they relate what successes they have had, and what damages they have sustained in their expeditions, in which I became part of their theme. The severity of the cold increasing, they stripped me of my clothes, for their own use, and gave me such as they usually wore themselves, being a piece of blanket, a pair of mogganes, or shoes, with a yard of coarse cloth to put round me instead of breeches. To describe their dress and manner of living may not be altogether unacceptable to some of my readers; but, as the size of this book will not permit me to be so particular as I might otherwise be, I shall just observe that they in general wear a white blanket, which in war-time they paint with various figures, but particularly the leaves of trees, in order to deceive their enemies when in the woods. Their mogganes are made of deer-skins, and the best sort have them bound round the edges with little beads and ribbands. On their legs they wear pieces of blue cloth for stockings, some like our soldiers' splatter-dashes. They reach higher than their knees, but not lower than their ancles. They esteem them easy to run in. Breeches they never wear, but instead thereof, two pieces of linen, one before and another behind.

The better sort have shirts of the finest linen they can get, and to these some wear ruffles; but these they never put on till they have painted them of various colours, which they get from the pecone root and bark of trees, and never pull them off to wash, but wear them till they fall to pieces. They are very proud, and take great delight in wearing trinkets, such as silver plates round their wrists and necks, with several strings of wampum, which is made of cotton, interwoven with pebbles, cockleshells, etc., down to their breasts, and from their ears and noses they have rings or beads, which hang dangling an inch or two. The men have no beards, to prevent which they use certain instruments and tricks as soon as it begins to grow. The hair of their heads is managed differently; some pluck out and destroy all, except a lock hanging from the crown of the head, which they interweave with wampum and feathers of various colours. The women wear it very long, twisted down their backs with beads, feathers, and wampum, and on their heads most of them wear little coronets of brass or copper; round their middle they wear a blanket instead of a petticoat. The females are very chaste and constant to their husbands; and if any young maiden should happen to have a child before marriage, she is never esteemed afterwards. As for their food, they get it chiefly by hunting and shooting, and boil or roast all the meat they eat. Their standing dish consists of Indian corn soaked, then bruised and boiled. Their bread is likewise made of wild oats, or sunflower seeds. Their gun, tomahawk, scalping-knife, powder, and shot, they carry with them in time of war. They in war decline open engagements—bush-fighting or skulking is their discipline. They are brave when engaged, having great fortitude in enduring tortures, and are the most implacably vindictive people upon the earth; for they revenge the death of any relation, or any affront, whenever occasion presents, let the distance of time be ever so remote.

After long enduring the greatest of hardships with these Indians, I at last escaped out of their hands, and went to Quebec, where I was put on board a French packet bound for England; and after a passage of six weeks, we at last, to our great joy, arrived at Plymouth on the 6th of November, 1756.

THE FAMOUS EXPLOITS
OF
ROBIN HOOD
LITTLE JOHN AND HIS MERRY MEN ALL.

INCLUDING AN ACCOUNT OF HIS

BIRTH, EDUCATION, AND DEATH.

CHAPTER I.
The Birth and Parentage of Robin Hood.

KIND gentlemen, listen a while to my story, and I will tell you the bold exploits of the famous Robin Hood and his comrade, Little John.

All England was filled with the renown of Robin Hood, and the great and the valiant stood in fear of him. He never harmed the poor, for he pitied their fate, and only spoiled the wealthy and proud, or nobles and slothful bishops, who lived in state on the fruit of the husbandman's toil. Robin was born in the merry town of Locksley, in

Nottinghamshire. His father was a stout forester, and kept the deer of King Richard the First; his mother was niece to the celebrated Sir Guy of Warwick, and was sister to Squire Gamewell, of Great Gamewell Hall.

One day (when Robin was about fourteen years old) his mother thus spoke to her spouse—" Dear husband, to-morrow is Christmas Day, therefore let Robin and I take a ride to Gamewell Hall this morning to see my brother and taste his good ale and pudding. The squire was overjoyed to see his sister, and young Robin learned the use of the bow, and became the best marksman in the place.

CHAPTER II.

Robin's Progress to Nottingham. Being an Account of his Adventures with the Fifteen Foresters.

ROBIN HOOD was now about fifteen years old; in person tall and stout, and of a good countenance; in courage and strength few equalled him. One day he determined to take a journey to Nottingham, hearing that the king had appointed a shooting match in that town, to be disputed by the best archers. When he came thither he happened to fall into company with fifteen stout foresters, who sat drinking and laughing together. "What news, what news?" said bold Robin Hood, "that you drink and talk so merrily." The foresters who despised him on account of his youth, answered roughly, "We are come to win the king's prize, which we are resolved to carry off, in spite of all opposition, and will not be questioned by boys." "I have as good a bow as the best," said Robin Hood, "and will contest the prize with you." "We hold thee and thy bow in scorn," said they; "shall a striplinglike thee bear a bow before the king's archers, that is not able to draw the string?" "I'll lay a bet of twenty crowns," said Robin, "that I win the king's prize, and hit the mark at a hundred yards distance.

" Doubt not I'll make the wager good,
  Or ne'er believe bold Robin Hood."

The mark was a running hart, let loose for the purpose; and when the other bowmen had tried their skill, Robin took his bow, and his well-made arrows, and taking good aim, fairly hit the mark, at a hundred yards distance, the multitude shouted, and hailed the young victor with joy. "The prize is mine," said Robin Hood, "I claim it; the wager, too, is mine, give it me." "The prize is none of thine," said the fifteen foresters, "and the wager shall be none of thine. Take up thy bow, insolent boy, and begone, or we will break thy bones." Robin Hood, full of rage, cried out, "You said I was no archer, but you have found me one, and you now deny me my reward."

He then took up his bow and departed, but having learnt which way the foresters must take at their return home, he repaired to the place where he had left his merry men, and, consulting together, they resolved to lie in ambush in the road. After a while they saw the foresters approaching, shouting and singing, because they had brought off the king's prize; but when Robin Hood and his men presented themselves in battle array, their mirth was quickly changed into terror and amazement. At first they made a show of resistance, but finding the number of their adversaries to be more than treble their own, they threw down their arms and begged for mercy. "You said I was no archer," cried Robin Hood; "now say so again, and let him that chooses it fly for his life, and see if my arrows can overtake him." "We beg for mercy," cried the foresters; "lo! here is the prize that you won, and the wager of twenty crowns." "Well, said Robin, "as you submit quietly, I will grant you your lives, but you shall not escape without some reward for your deeds." He and his men then stripped them of their clothes, leaving them no covering but their trousers, and having cut off their hair and their ears, daubed their faces with a mixture of yellow and red; afterwards they bound their hands, and tied a large pair of antlers on each of their heads, and in this most ridiculous state drove them back into the town, telling them if they offered to return they should not escape with their lives. As soon as they entered the streets the whole place was in an uproar, and, what with the barking of a hundred dogs, the squalling of women, and hooting of boys and men, there was such a hubbub as never before had been known in the town of Nottingham.

Chapter III.

Robin Hood and Little John. Being an Account of their First Meeting, and how their Acquaintance and Friendship began, with their Merry Reception in Sherwood Bower.

When bold Robin Hood was about twenty years old he happened to meet with a jolly stranger, whom he afterwards called Little John. This man, though called little, was a lusty young blade; his limbs were large, and his person seven feet high. Wherever he went people quaked at his name, and he made all his enemies to fly before him. 'Twas thus their acquaintance began:—

Robin and his men had built, in Sherwood Forest, a strong and secret bower, so artfully contrived and hidden among the woods, that none but themselves could ever find them out, and to which they retreated in cases of need. Here Robin once continued fourteen days with his merry bowmen, and then he said to them—"Tarry a while in this grove, my brave men; we have had no sport for these many long days, therefore, I will wander abroad a short way to seek some amusement. But do you be attentive, and hear whenever I blow an alarm with my loud bugle horn, for by this means I will let you know if I want your assistance."

After he had strayed some time near a brook, he espied a tall and lusty stranger coming towards him. They happened to meet on a long, narrow wooden bridge, and neither of them would give way to let the other pass. Robin Hood at length, being enraged, drew an arrow from his quiver, and threatened to shoot at the stranger's breast. "You dare not," said the other, "for if you offer to touch the string, I'll beat out your teeth and tumble you into the brook. You see I have nothing but a staff in my hand, and none but a coward would offer to fight with weapons so different." "The name of a coward," said Robin, "I scorn; I will therefore lay aside my bow and arrows and take a stout staff to prove thy manhood." The stranger accepted the challenge, and the sport was quickly begun. At first Robin gave the man such a stroke that it made his sides ring. The other said, "I must pay you for this, friend, and give you as good as you send, for as long as I am able to handle a staff I scorn to die in your debt." He then gave Robin so hearty a knock on the crown, that the blood ran trickling down to his ears. Robin now engaged more fiercely, and laid on his blows so thick and fast, that he made his adversary's coat smoke as if it had been on fire; but the stranger waxing most furious and strong, at length gave Robin such a terrible side-blow, that it quite beat him down and tumbled him into the brook. Then, in laughter, he called out to his fallen foe, "Prithee, where art thou now, my good fellow?" "Why, faith," said Robin, "I swim with the tide, as every man should do." He now swam along to the bank, and pulled himself out by a thorn, and then said to the conqueror, "Thou art a brave soul, I will contend no longer with thee."

He then took up his horn and blew such a blast with it as made the hills echo all around. Presently they saw coming hastily down the hillside a band of brave archers, clothed in a livery of green. They quickly came up to Robin Hood, and Will Stuckley (their leader) cried out, "Pray, what is the matter, good master? why, you seem wet to the skin?" "No matter for that," said Robin, "the man that stands by has, in fighting, tumbled me into the brook." "If that be the case," said his men, "he shall not escape without a good ducking in the same stream." "Not so, my brave men," said Robin Hood, "he is a stout, hearty fellow, that fought me fairly. My friend," said he to the stranger, pray be not afraid, for no harm shall befall thee; all these are my bowmen, that come at my call, and if thou wilt live with me, and be one of them, thou shalt quickly put on such a dress as theirs; we will teach thee the use of the bow to shoot the fat deer, for we live gloriously, without any restraint, and fear not the laws." "Then here is my hand," replied the stranger, "I'll serve thee with a willing mind, for I perceive you are all brave, hearty fellows. My name is John Little, I am a man of some skill, and at all times will play my part well."

"His name shall be altered," said Will Stuckley, "I like not the sound of John Little, his name shall be called Little John."

CHAPTER IV.
Robin Hood and the Butchers, with his Comical Behaviour to the Sheriff of Nottingham.

ONE day as Robin Hood was taking his walk through the forest, he happened to behold a jolly butcher, sitting between his hampers, on a stout young mare, going to sell his meat at market. "Good morrow, honest fellow," said Robin; "prithee, what food hast thou in thy hampers, and from whence comest thou? for I seem to have a liking to thy company." The butcher replied, "No matter from whence I come, master, nor where I dwell; you may see that I am a butcher, and am going to Nottingham to sell my meat." "Wilt thou sell thy meat to me?" said Robin; tell me the price of it altogether; also, what thou wilt have for the mare that carries thee, and all thy other accoutrements; we will not differ about the cost, for I would fain be a butcher for once." "The price of my meat and the price of my mare," said the butcher, "shall be twenty good marks; and I think they are nothing too dear." Robin agreed, and set out to Nottingham to begin his butcher's trade; and when he came thither, took up his inn next door to the sheriff's house. When other butchers began to open their shops he opened his; but was at a loss how to sell his meat, being so young a butcher; however he was determined not to be undersold, and he found customers plenty. When the other butchers could not sell a joint Robin's trade went on briskly, and no butcher could match him; for he sold more meat for one penny than others could do for five. He sold his meat so fast that the butchers of Nottingham were at a stand to know who this bold fellow was. "Surely," said they, "he is some prodigal that has sold his father's land, and is thus sporting away his money." They then stepped up to him to make acquaintance. "Come, brother," said they, "we are all of one trade, let us go and dine together; the sheriff has provided a treat for the butchers to-day, and you must go with us." "Agreed," said bold Robin, "may that butcher be hanged that can deny the request of his brethren."

After dinner the sheriff said to Robin, "Hast thou any cattle or horned beasts to sell, my good fellow? if thou hast I would fain buy them of thee." "Yes, that I have, Master Sheriff," said Robin; "I have eight or ten score of horned beasts that I long to have sold, and they are fat and fair." The sheriff then saddled his dappled grey horse and set out with Robin Hood to behold his horned cattle, taking with him plenty of gold to complete his bargain. When they came to Sherwood Forest the sheriff began to be apprehensive of some danger, and trembled for fear, saying, "Heaven defend us from a wonderful bold man that is called Robin Hood, who plays a thousand wicked pranks in this country, and empties the pockets of every rich man he meets." They had not gone much farther before they beheld an hundred head of fat deer that came tripping along the road; and then Robin cried out, "Look here, Master Sheriff, behold my herd of horned beasts; how like you their colour and their make? they seem fat and fair to the eye." "What dost thou mean, fellow?" said the sheriff; "I wish I was safe out of this forest, for I like not thy company." "Then will you not buy?" said Robin Hood; "however, since you came hither to buy my cattle, you must pay whether you take them or not." He then put his horn to his mouth and blew a loud blast with it. Quickly Little John and his company appeared, and said, "Pray, what is your pleasure, good master?" Said Robin, "I have brought the sheriff of Nottingham to eat with you to-day, and I hope you will make him right welcome." "He is welcome, kind master," said John; "but I hope he will honestly pay for cooking." Robin now bade the sheriff dismount, and, taking his mantle from his back, quickly told out his gold; then he took him to his bower and feasted him well; afterwards he set him again on his dapple grey horse and brought him back through the wood. "Commend me to your wife at home, my kind sir," said Robin; so he turned and went laughing away.

CHAPTER V.
Robin Hood and Allen Adale, with his Generous Behaviour to Two Distressed Lovers.

As bold Robin Hood one day was standing in the forest just under the green oaken tree, he espied a gallant young man, clothed in scarlet and white, as gay as a lark, who came tripping along the road singing a roundelay. He seemed in great haste and quickly was out of sight. Next morning as Robin Hood stood in the same place he beheld the same young man coming over the plain, but his carriage was totally changed; he now passed slowly along and his head hung drooping upon his breast. Little John stepped towards him, to know who he was, but when the young man saw him coming he bent his bow and said, "Stand off, thou bold forester; what wouldest thou have with me?" "You must come before our master," he replied, "who is standing under the green oaken tree; come without delay and no harm shall befall thee." And when he was come before Robin Hood, Robin said to him, "Hast thou any money to spare for my merry men and me? Come, answer without fear." "Indeed I have no money to spare," said the young man; "I have but five shillings and a little gold ring, and this ring I have kept for these seven long years to present to my bride on my wedding day. Yesterday I should have married the maid that I love, but she was chosen to be an old knight's wife, and taken from me by force; therefore my heart is nearly broken?"

Robin Hood now set out, with fifty stout archers in his train, nor did they stop till they came near to the church where Allen should have been married. He then concealed his men while he went boldly into the church. "What dost thou here, bold man?" said the bishop. "I am a merry harper," said Robin, "as good as any in the north." "O, welcome then," said the bishop, "for that music is my delight." Presently there came in a wealthy old knight leading a young damsel by the hand, of a fair though sorrowful countenance, dressed in her glittering attire. "This is not a fit match," said bold Robin Hood, "the bridegroom is much too old and uncomely; but since I am here, and the bride is prepared, she shall now choose her own mate."

Robin then applied the horn to his mouth, and blew twice and thrice with it, at the sound of which his fifty stout bowmen came leaping over the churchyard, and the first man was Allen Adale, who gave bold Robin his bow. "This is thy true lover," said Robin; "come, take her, and be married before we depart." "That never shall be," said the bishop; "thy speech is too bold, and the law of our country requires that they be three times asked in the church." Robin Hood then pulled off the bishop's rich apparel, and put it upon Little John, and made him appear like a priest. "By my faith," said Robin, laughing, "that clothing becomes thee well; thou now lookest like a man and a bishop; therefore begin thy office." When Little John went to the desk the people began to laugh and seemed to enjoy the joke; he asked them full seven times over to make the bauns sure, lest three times should not be enough. "Who gives this fair maid to Allen Adale for a wife?" said Little John. "I give her to him with all my heart," said Robin Hood, "and he that dare to oppose, or take her away from her spouse, shall buy her dearly."

Thus ended this merry wedding, and the new married pair returned with Robin Hood to Sherwood bower.

Chapter VI.

Robin Hood and his Kinsman. Showing how he met and fought with a Stranger, who afterwards proved to be his Cousin Scarlet.

As Robin walked about the forest one day he met with a comely young man, dressed in a doublet of silk, with scarlet hose, travelling boldly along with a stout bow in his hand. A herd of fat deer happened to be feeding not far distant, which, when the stranger saw, he bent his bow, and shot the best of them through the heart. "Well shot, well shot," said Robin Hood, "thy aim was good and sure; I like a bold archer well; and if thou wilt be one of my comrades, and live in my bower, I will treat thee with noble entertainment, and pay thee well besides." "Go, talk with thy grandame," said the stranger, "and make no such wild offers to me, or else I shall use thee somewhat rudely." "Thou hadst better be quiet," said Robin, "for if thou shouldest offer to make an assault, thou wilt dearly repent of the deed; my arm is not weak, and thou mayest see that I carry a bow; besides, though I am now alone, should I blow an alarm with my loud bugle-horn, I should quickly have at my command a hundred brave men." "I defy all thy power," said the other, "and if thou offerest to touch thy horn, my good broadsword shall cut it in two, and strike thee to the dust." Bold Robin

Hood then bent his stout bow, and stood ready to shoot at his foe. The stranger also took his strong bow and as readily stood on his guard. "Prithee, let us hold our hands," said Robin Hood, "for if we attempt to shoot, one of us must infallibly die; let us now lay aside our bows and try each other's skill with bucklers and good broadswords." These rivals in skill then fought stoutly and boldly, and many a hard blow resounded upon their bucklers. They aimed their strong blows above and below, from the head to the feet, but neither of them could make the other give way. Robin Hood at length gave the stranger such a mighty stroke that it made the fire fly from his eyes, and almost deprived him of his senses. "I hope to give thee a blow," said the stranger, "that shall shame all the rest, and put an end to the fray." Then presently, taking good aim with his sword, he struck Robin upon the head with such force, that the blood soon appeared and ran trickling down his cheeks. "By my faith," said Robin Hood, "I must now beg for quarter; prithee, my brave fellow, tell me who thou art, and what is thy name, for I love and respect a brave man." The stranger answered, "I was born and bred in the town of Maxfield, and my name is Gamewell; I am forced to fly from home and to hide myself for having killed my father's steward, who had falsely accused me; and I came to this forest to seek a bold uncle of mine, who goes by the name of bold Robin Hood." "Art thou then a cousin of bold Robin Hood's?" answered he; "had I known it before, our fight would have been sooner done." "On my life," said the stranger, "I am his first kin, and son to his mother's second brother, who now lives at court with the king, and for gallant deeds he performed in Palestine he is soon to be made a noble peer." When Robin heard this he embraced him with great joy, and soon let him know that he himself was his uncle Robin Hood. They then set out for the green shady bower, and met Little John by the way.

Chapter VII.

Robin Hood and Bishop of Hereford. Robin Hood in Distress changes Clothes with an old Woman to Escape from the Bishop, whom he afterwards takes Prisoner, and obliges him to sing Mass.

Robin Hood and all his men were now outlawed, because they had broken the forest laws (which were very severe), and had killed the king's fat deer.

As Robin walked out one fine summer's day, when the fields were pleasant and green, and the birds sang sweetly in the bushes, he was tempted to wander beyond the skirts of the forest, far away from his bower; and as he was thinking of going back he was espied by the proud bishop of Hereford, who was passing along with a great company. "Oh, what shall I now do?" said Robin to himself. "If the bishop should take me I shall be hanged without mercy." Then Robin turned nimbly about and ran with full speed to the house of an old woman whom he knew. "Good woman," said Robin, "I pray you let me in, for yonder is the bishop and all his men, and if I am taken, I must die." "Why, who art thou," said the old woman, "that comest hither in such a fright?" "I am Robin Hood," he replied; "canst thou not recollect me?" "I think I now do," said the old woman, "and if thou art even Robin Hood, I will provide for thy safety and hide thee from the proud bishop and his company." "Then give me thy gown and thy female attire," said Robin, "and put thee on my livery of green: give me also thy distaff and spindle, and take my arrows and bow."

When Robin Hood was thus arrayed he went forth without fear, and returned to his men in the wood. When Little John saw him thus dressed, coming over the forest, he cried, "Behold, who is yonder, that seems approaching this way; the old woman looks like a witch, and I will send an arrow to meet her." "Hold thy hand, hold thy hand," said Robin Hood, "I am thy master in disguise, and this habit I was forced to put on to escape from a strong enemy who had me in chase."

Now, in the meantime, the bishop went to the old woman's house, and with a loud, furious voice, cried, "Bring that traitor, Robin Hood, that I may take him along with me and make him pay the forfeit of all his bad deeds." The old woman then came out dressed like Robin, and the bishop placed her upon a grey steed, while he rode along laughing for joy that he had seized upon bold Robin Hood. But as they were riding through the forest in which their road lay, the bishop espied a hundred tall men, stout and brave, coming out of the wood, with their arrows in their hands. "Oh, who are all these bowmen?" said the bishop, "and who is that man that leads them towards us so boldly?" "In good faith," said the old woman, "I think it is bold Robin Hood." "Then who art thou," said the bishop, trembling with fear. "I am only a poor old woman, proud bishop," said she: "hast thou any occasion for me now?" Robin Hood coming up, took the bishop by the hand, and placing him upon the stump of a tree made him tune his voice and sing a full mass to all the company; afterwards they brought him through the wood, and having set him upon his horse with his face towards the tail, they charged him for ever after to pray for Robin Hood, and putting the tail in his hand, bid him begone.

CHAPTER VIII.

Robin Hood and the Three Yeomen. Robin delivers Three Yeomen from Nottingham Gallows, who were going to be Hanged for Killing the King's Deer.

As Robin Hood wandered about the fields one day he met a fair lady who came weeping along the road in great distress. "Oh, why do you weep so pitifully," said Robin, "and what is the cause of your great distress?" "I weep," she replied, "for the sorrowful fate of three brothers, the bravest and dearest of men, who are all condemned to die." "What church have they robbed?" said Robin, "or what parish priest have they killed? or have they in treason been caught against the rightful king?" "Woe is me!" said the lady, "for my brothers must die, and only for killing the king's fallow deer." "They shall not die," said bold Robin Hood; "therefore go your way quickly home, and I will hasten to Nottingham for the sake of your three hapless brothers."

Robin Hood then set out to Nottingham, and in his way met with a poor beggar man, who came walking slowly and mournfully along the highway. "What news, my old man?" said Robin, "what news dost thou bring from the town?" "Oh! there is weeping and wailing in Nottingham town," cried the old beggar man, "for the sake of three yeomen who are condemned to die, for they are greatly beloved."

The beggar had a tattered old coat upon his back which was neither green, yellow, nor red, but some of every colour; and Robin Hood thought it would be no disgrace, for once, to be in the beggar's dress. "Come, pull off thy coat, my old beggar," said he, "and thou shalt put on mine, and thirty shillings beside I will give thee to buy bread and beer." When Robin was thus arrayed, away he went to the town, and when he came thither he soon found the sheriff and his men, and likewise the three sorrowful yeomen who were going to die. "One favour I humbly beg," said bold Robin Hood to the sheriff, "that I may be the hangman when the three yeomen are to die." "'Tis granted with free goodwill," said the sheriff; "therefore go and prepare thyself for thine office, for they have but few hours to live."

Robin then returned to his brave band of archers, whom he brought and placed in ambush near the field where the gallows was fixed; afterwards going again to the sheriff, the three yeomen were led to the appointed spot. "Now, begin thine office, my jolly hangman," said the sheriff, "for these yeomen no longer must live: and thou shalt have all their good clothing, and all their money besides."

Then Robin mounted the gallows, with his horn in his hand, and he made it sound loud and shrill, when quickly came marching over the field a hundred and more of his faithful bowmen, all clothed in green. "Whose men are all these," said the sheriff, "that come marching so boldly this way?" "Oh, these are all Robin Hood's men," said he, "and they are come to fetch me, and likewise to take the three yeomen, who are going to die." "Oh, take them, pray take them, without more ado," said the sheriff; "for there is not a man in all Nottingham that can do the like of thee."

CHAPTER IX.
Robin Hood and the Tinker of Banbury.

In summer time when the leaves were green and birds sang merrily upon every tree, Robin Hood set out to Nottingham in disguise, and as he went along the road he overtook a jolly tinker. Robin greeted him kindly, and after some discourse, said, "Tell me whence thou comest, my jolly fellow, and in what town thou wast bred, for I hear there is sad news in Nottingham, and when thou knowest it thou may not choose to go thither." "I come from Banbury," said the other, "where I was born and bred, and am a tinker by trade; now tell me the news thou hast heard." "My news is only this," said Robin, "two tinkers were yesterday set in the stocks for drinking ale and strong beer." "If that be all," said the tinker, "I value not your news a farthing; for in drinking good ale and beer I am sure never to be outdone, and resolve to have my share; and if I may judge by your looks, you often take a good part." "Now," said Robin Hood, "tell me what news has come to thy ears, for, as thou travellest from town to town, thou canst never be in want of good stories." "All the news that I lately have heard," said the tinker, "relates to a bold outlaw who is called Robin Hood; the king has given out warrants to apprehend him, and I have one in my pocket to take him, whenever I can find him; and if thou canst tell me where he is, and assist me to seize him, it will make us rich men, for a hundred pounds, or more, will be our reward." "Let me see the warrant," said Robin, "that I may know if it be good, and I will do the best that I can to assist thee in taking him this very night." "My warrant I shall not let thee see," said the tinker, "for I dare not trust it out of my hand."

As soon as they came to Nottingham they went to a good inn, and calling for strong ale and wine, the tinker drank so much that he forgot what he had to do, so that at night Robin made haste away, taking the tinker's warrant, and left him in the lurch to pay all the reckoning. When the tinker awoke in the morning and found that his comrade was gone, he called for the host and said, "I had a warrant from the king that might have done me good, for it was to take a bold outlaw called Robin Hood; but now my warrant is stolen away from me, and I have not money enough to pay the score, for the man that came with me last night is fled away; therefore tell me what I have got to pay, and I will leave my tools with thee in pledge till I return."

The tinker then went his way, and soon learnt in the town that the only way to find out bold Robin Hood was to seek him in the parks, killing the king's deer. Away then he went, and made no delay till he found Robin Hood chasing the deer through the woods. "What bold knave is that," said Robin, "that comes so freely to hinder my sport." "No knave am I," cried the tinker, "and that you soon will know to your cost; which of us have done wrong my crab-tree shall decide." The tinker and Robin then fought manfully, and the fray lasted three hours, or more, but at length the tinker thrashed Robin's bones so sore, that he made him cry out for peace. "One favour I have to beg," said Robin Hood, "and I pray thee to grant it me." "The only favour I will grant," said the tinker, "is to hang thee on a tree." But while the tinker turned round, Robin blew his horn, at the sound of which Little John and Will Scarlet quickly appeared, and said, "What is the matter, dear master, that you look so forlorn?" "Here is a tinker standing by," said Robin, "that has thrashed my bones sore." When they heard this they were going to seize him by the throat, but Robin said, "Let our quarrel now cease, that henceforth we may be friends with the tinker, and he with us; and if he will consent to be one of us, I will yearly give him fifty pounds, as long as he lives, which he may spend in the way which he likes best." So at last the tinker consented, and went along with them to their bower.

Chapter X.
Robin Hood's Death.

And now I must bring my stories to a close, and the unhappy death of valiant Robin Hood.

Robin fell ill, and because he required to be treated with skill, he went to Kirkley Abbey, where they sent for a monk to bleed him, and this monk being eager to get the reward that King Henry had set upon Robin Hood's head, most treacherously bled him to death.

Thus he that never feared a sword or a bow, or any man that lived, was basely killed, in letting of blood, and died without a friend to close his eyes. As soon as his men heard of his death they were filled with grief and dismay, and fled away in haste. Some of them crossed the seas and went to Flanders, some to France, and some to Spain and Rome.

> Robin, Earl of Huntingdon,
> Lies underneath this marble stone;
> No archer ever was so good—
> His name it was bold ROBIN HOOD.
> Full thirty years, and something more,
> These northern parts he vexed sore.
> Such outlaws as he, in any reign,
> May England never see again.

HISTORY OF
DR. FAUSTUS
SHOWING

His wicked Life and horrid Death, and how he sold himself to the Devil, to have power for twenty-four years to do what he pleased, also many strange things done by him with the assistance of

MEPHISTOPHELES.

With an account how the Devil came for him at the end of twenty-four years, and tore him to pieces.

CHAPTER I.
Dr. Faustus' birth and education, with an account of his falling from the Scriptures.

DR. JOHN FAUSTUS was born in Germany. His father was a poor labouring man, not able to bring up his son John; but he had a brother in the same country, who was a very rich man, but had never a child, and took a great fancy to his cousin, and he resolved to make a scholar of him; and in order thereunto, put him to the Latin school, where he took his learning extraordinary well. Afterwards he put him to the University to study divinity; but Faustus could in no ways fancy that employment; wherefore he betook himself to the studying of that which his inclination is most for, viz., necromancy and conjuration, and in a little time few or none could outstrip him in the art. He also studied divinity, of which he was made Doctor; but within a short time fell into such deep fancies and cogitations that he resolved to throw the Scriptures from him, and betake himself wholly to the studying of necromancy and conjuration, charms and soothsaying, witchcraft, and the like.

Chapter II.
How Dr. Faustus conjured up the Devil, making him appear at his own house.

FAUSTUS, whose mind was to study conjuration, the which he followed night and day, he took the wings of an eagle, and endeavoured to fly over the world, to see and know all the secrets of heaven and earth; so that in a short time he attained power to command the Devil to appear before him when he pleased. One day as Dr. Faustus was walking in a wood near to Wurtemberg, in Germany, he having a friend with him who was desirous to know of the doctor's art, he desired him to let him see if he could then and there bring Mephistopheles before him; all which the doctor immediately did, and the devil upon the first call made such a noise in the wood as if heaven and earth would have come together; then the devil made such a roaring as if the wood had been full of wild beasts. The doctor made a circle for the devil, the which circle the devil ran round, making a noise as if ten thousand waggons had been running upon paved stones. After this it thundered and lightened, as if the whole world had been on fire. Faustus and his friend, amazed at this noise, and the devil's long tarrying, thought to leave his circle; whereupon he made him such music, the like was never heard in the world. This so ravished Faustus that he began again to conjure Mephistopheles in the name of the prince of the devils to appear in his own likeness; whereupon in an instant hung over his head a mighty dragon. Faustus calls again after his former manner, after which there was a cry in the wood as if hell had opened, and all the tormented souls had been there. Faustus, in the meanwhile, asked the devil many questions, and commanded him to show many diabolical tricks.

Chapter III.

How Mephistopheles came to Dr. Faustus' house, and what happened between them.

Faustus commanded the spirit to meet him at his house by ten of the clock the next day. At the hour appointed he came into his chamber asking Faustus what he would have. Faustus told him it was his will and pleasure to conjure him to be obedient to him in all points of those articles, viz. :—

First, That the spirit should serve him in all things he asked, from that time till his death.

Secondly, Whatsoever he would have, he should bring him.

Thirdly, Whatsoever he desired to know, he should tell him.

The spirit answered him and said he had no such power of himself, until he had acquainted his prince that ruled over him. "For," said he, "we have rulers over us that send us out, and command us home when they please; and we can act no farther than our power is, which we receive from Lucifer, who, you know, for his pride, was thrust out of heaven. But," saith the spirit, "I am not to tell you any more except you make yourself over to us."

Whereupon Faustus said, "I will have my request! but yet I will not be damned with you." Then said the spirit, "You must not, nor shall not have your desire, and yet thou art mine, and all the world cannot save thee out of my hands." Then said Faustus, "Get thee hence, and I conjure thee that thou come to me at night." The spirit then vanished. Faustus then began to consider how he might obtain his desire, and not give his soul to the devil.

And while Faustus was in these his devilish cogitations night drew on, and this hellish spirit appeared to Faustus, acquainting him that now he had got orders from his prince to be obedient to him, and to do for him whatsoever he desired, provided he would promise to be his, and withal to acquaint him first what he would have of him? Faustus replied that his desire was to become a spirit, and that Mephistopheles should be always at his command; that whatsoever he called for him, he shall appear invisible to all men, and that he should appear in what shape he pleased, to which the spirit answered that all his desires should be granted if he would sign those articles he should wish or ask for. Whereupon Dr. Faustus withdrew and stabbed his wrist, receiving the blood in a small saucer, which cooled so fast, as if it forewarned him of the hellish act he was going to commit; nevertheless he put it over embers to warm it, and wrote as follows:—

"I, John Faustus, approved doctor of divinity, with my own hand do acknowledge and testify myself to become a servant to Lucifer, Prince of Septentrional and Oriental, and to him I freely and voluntarily give both soul; in consideration for the space of twenty-four years, if I be served in all things which I shall require, or which is reasonable by him to be allowed; at the expiration of which time from the date ensuing, I give to him all power to do with me at his pleasure; to rule to retch and carry me where he pleases body and soul. Hereupon I defy God and Christ, and the hosts of angels and good spirits, all living creatures that bear his shape, or on whom his image is imprinted; and to the better strengthening the validity of this covenant and firm agreement between us, I have writ it with my blood, and subscribe my name to it, calling all the powers and infernal potentates to witness it is my true intent and meaning.   JOHN FAUSTUS."

CHAPTER IV.

What happened to Faustus after the signing of the articles.

WHEN Faustus had made an end of his writing he called Mephistopheles to him, and delivered him the bond; whereupon the spirit told him if he did not repent of what he had done, he should enjoy all the pleasure his thoughts could form, and that he would immediately divert him. He caused a kennel of hounds to run down a hart in the hall, and vanished; then a bull danced before Faustus, also there was a lion and a bear, which fell to fighting before Faustus, and the lion destroyed the bear; after that came a dragon and destroyed the lion. And this, with abundance of more pastime, did the spirit present to the doctor's view, concluding with all manner of music, with some hundreds of spirits, which came and danced before Faustus. After the music was over, and Faustus began to look about him, he saw ten sacks full of silver, which he went to dispose of, but could not, for none could handle it but himself, it was so hot. This pastime so pleased Faustus, that he gave Mephistopheles the will that he had made, and kept a copy of it in his own hands. The spirit and Faustus being agreed, they dwelt together, and the devil was in their house-keeping, for there was never anything given away to poor, which before Faustus made this contract was frequently done, but the case is now altered.

CHAPTER V.
How Faustus served the Duke of Bavaria.

FAUSTUS having sold his soul to the devil, it was reported among his neighbours, so that none would keep him company but his spirit playing merry tricks for to please him. Not far from Faustus' house lived the Duke of Bavaria, the Duke of Saxony, and the Bishop of Salisburgh, whose houses and cellars Mephistopheles used to visit, and to bring the best of everything they had. One day the Duke of Bavaria invited most of the gentry of the country to dinner, for whose entertainment there was abundance of provision got ready. The gentry being come, and ready to sit down to dinner, in an instant Mephistopheles came and took all away with him, leaving them full of admiration. If any time Faustus had a mind for wild fowl, the spirit would call whole flocks in at a window; also the spirit did teach Faustus to do the like so that no lock nor key could keep them out. The devil also taught Faustus to fly in the air, and to act many things that are incredible and too large for this small book to contain.

Chapter VI.
How Dr. Faustus dreamed of Hell in his Sleep and what he saw there.

AFTER Faustus had a long conference with his spirit concerning the fall of Lucifer, and the state and condition of all the fallen angels, he, in a vision or dream, saw hell and all the devils and souls that were tormented there; he saw hell divided into several cells, or deep holes; and for every cell, or deep ward, there was a devil appointed to punish those that were under his custody. Having seen this sight, he much marvelled at it; and at that time Mephistopheles being with him, he asked him what sort of people they were that lay in the first dark pit; then Mephistopheles told him they were those who pretended themselves to be physicians, and who had poisoned many thousands to try practice; "and now," saith the spirit, "they have just the same administered to them which they gave to others, though not with the same effect, for they will never die here," saith he. Over their heads was a shelf laden with gallipots full of poison. Having passed them he came to a long entry exceeding dark where there was a mighty crowd. He asked him what those were? and the spirit told him they were pick-pockets, who loved to be in a crowd, when they were in the other world, and to content them they put them in a crowd there. Amongst them were some padders on the highway, and those of that function. Walking farther he saw many thousands of vintners, and some millions of tailors, in so much that they could not feel where to get stowage for them; a great number of pastry cooks with peels on their heads. Walking farther, the spirit opening a great cellar door, from which arose a terrible noise, he asked what they were. The spirit told him they were witches, and those who had been pretended saints in the other world; but how they did squabble, fight, and tear one another! Not far from them lay the whoremongers and adulterers, who made such a hideous noise that he was very much startled. Walking down a few steps he espied an incredible number almost hid with smoke. He asked what they were? The spirit told him they were millers and bakers; but good lack, what a noise was there among them! The millers crying to the bakers, and the bakers crying to the millers for help, but all was in vain, for there was none to help them. Passing on still farther, he saw thousands of shopkeepers, some of whom he knew, who were tormented for defrauding and cheating their customers. Having taken this prospect of hell, the spirit Mephistopheles took him in his arms, and carried him home to his own house, when he awaking, he was amazed at what he saw in his dream. So being come to himself, he asked the spirit in what place hell was, and who made it? Mephistopheles answered, "Knowest thou, that before the fall of Lucifer, there was no hell, but upon his fall was hell ordained. As for the substance of hell, we devils do not know. It is the wrath of God that makes hell so furious, and what we procured by our fall; but where hell is, or how it is governed, and whatsoever thou desirest to know, when thou comest there thou shalt be satisfied as far as we know ourselves."

CHAPTER VII.
Containing some Tricks of Dr. Faustus.

DR. FAUSTUS having attained the desire of his spirit, had now full power to act or do anything whatever he pleased. Upon a time the Emperor had a desire to see him, and likewise some of the doctor's tricks; whereupon he was requested by the Emperor to do somewhat to make him merry; but the doctor in the meanwhile looking around him he at last espied a great lord looking out at a window, and the doctor calling his spirit to help him, he in an instant fastened a large pair of horns upon the lord's head, that he could not get his head in till Faustus took off the horns again, which were soon taken off invisibly. The lord whom Faustus served so was extremely vexed, and resolved to be revenged on the doctor, and to that end lay a mile out of town for Faustus' passing by, he being that day to depart for the country. Faustus coming by a wood side, beheld that lord mounted upon a mighty warlike horse, who ran full drift against Faustus, who, by the assistance of his spirit, took him and all, and carried before the Emperor's palace, and grafted a pair of horns on his head as big as an ox's, which he could never be rid of, but wore them to his dying day.

CHAPTER VIII.
How Faustus ate a load of Hay.

FAUSTUS upon a time having many doctors and masters of arts with him, went to walk in the fields, where they met with a load of hay. "How now, good fellow," saith Faustus, "what shall I give thee to fill my belly with hay?" The clown thought he had been a madman to talk of eating hay, told him he should fill his belly for one penny, to which the doctor agreed, and then fell to eating, and quickly devouring half of the load; at which the doctor's companions laughed, to see how simply the poor country fellow looked, and to hear how heartily he prayed the doctor to forbear. So Faustus pitying the poor man, went away, and before the man got near his house all the hay was in the cart that the doctor had eaten, which made the country fellow very much admire.

CHAPTER IX.
How he struck a parcel of Students, who were fighting together, blind; and how he served a parcel of Clowns who were singing and ranting at an inn.

THIRTEEN students meeting with seven more near Dr. Faustus' house, fell to, extremely, first in words and at last to blows. The thirteen being too hard for the seven, and Dr. Faustus looking out at his window and seeing the fray, and how much they were overmatched, conjured them all blind, so that the one could not see the other, and in this manner they fought one another, which made all that saw them laugh. At length the people parted them, and led them to their chambers, they instantly received their sight. The doctor coming into an inn with some friends, was disturbed by the hallowing and bawling of a parcel of drunken clowns, whereupon, when their mouths were wide open, he so conjured them, that by no means they could shut them again : and after they had stared one upon another, without being able to speak, thinking they were bewitched, they dropped away in a confused fear, one by one, and never could be got to the house afterwards.

CHAPTER X.

How Faustus helped a Young Man to a Fair Lady.

THERE was a gallant young gentleman who was in love with a fair lady, living at Wurtemberg, near the doctor's house. This gentleman had long sought this lady in marriage, but could not attain his desire, and having placed his affections so much upon her, he was ready to pine away, and had certainly died with grief, had he not made his address to the doctor, to whom he opened the whole matter. Now no sooner had the gentleman told his cause to the doctor, but he told him that he need not be afraid, for his desire should be fulfilled, and that he should have her whom he so much desired, and that this gentlewoman should have none but him, which was accordingly done, for the doctor so changed her mind that she could think of nothing else but him whom before she hated; and Faustus' desire was this: He gave him an enchanted ring which he ordered him to put into the lady's hand, or to slip it on her finger, which he did; and no sooner had she got the ring than her heart burned with love to him. She, instead of frowns, could do nothing but smile upon him, and not be at rest till she asked him if he thought he could love her, and make her his wife? He gladly answered with all his heart. So they were married the next day, and all by the help of Dr. Faustus.

CHAPTER XI.
How Faustus made Seven Women dance naked in the Market-place.

FAUSTUS walking in the market-place, saw seven women sitting all in a row, selling eggs, butter, etc. Of every one he bought something and departed. No sooner was he gone but all the eggs and butter were gone out of their baskets, and they knew not how. At last they were told that Dr. Faustus had conjured their goods away. They thereupon ran speedily to the doctor's house, and so demanded satisfaction for the ware. He resolving to make himself and the town's people merry by his conjuring art, made them return to their baskets naked as ever they were born; and having danced a while in the market-place every one's goods were conjured into their baskets again, and they set at liberty.

CHAPTER XII.
How Faustus served a Country Fellow who was driving Swine.

DR. FAUSTUS, as he was going to Wurtemberg, overtook a country fellow driving a hundred swine, who were very headstrong, some running one way and some another; so that the driver could not tell how to get them drove along. The doctor taking notice of it, so by his conjuring art he made every one of them dance upon their two hind legs, with a fiddle in one of their fore feet, and with the other fore foot they played upon the fiddle, and so they danced and fiddled all the way until they came into Wurtemberg market, the driver of them dancing all the way before them, which made the people wonder. After the doctor had satisfied himself with the spirit he conjured all of the fiddles away, and the driver then offered them for sale, and quickly sold them all, and took the money; but before he was gone out of the house Faustus had conjured all the hogs out of the market-place, and sent them all home to the driver's house. The man who bought them, seeing all the swine gone, stopped the man who sold them and would have his money, which he was forced to pay, and so returned home sorrowful, and not knowing what to do; but, to his great surprise, found all the swine in their sties.

Chapter XIII.
How Faustus begun to bethink himself of the near approach of his End.

Faustus having spun out his twenty-four years, within a month or two, began to consider what he should do to cheat the devil, but could not find any way to prevent his miserable end, which was now near, whereupon he thus cries out to himself, "Oh! miserable wretch that I am, I have given myself to the devil for a few years' pleasure, and now I must pay full dear. I have had my desires; my filthy lusts I have satisfied, and I must be tormented for ever and ever."

A neighbour of his, a very good old man, hearing of his way of living, in compassion to his soul came to him, and with tears in his eyes besought him to have more regard to his most precious soul, laying before him the promise of God's grace and mercy, freely offered to repenting sinners, and spake so feelingly that Faustus shed tears, and promised to him that he would try to repent. This good man was no sooner gone away than Mephistopheles found him pensive and on his bed. Now Mephistopheles mustering what had happened, began to reproach him with breach of covenant to his lord Lucifer, and thereupon almost twisted his neck behind him, which made him cry out very lamentable; in the meantime threatening to tear him to pieces unless he renewed his obligation, which for fear, with much sorrow he did, in a manner the same as the former, which he confirmed by the latter.

Chapter XIV.

How Dr. Faustus was warned of the Spirit to prepare for his End.

FAUSTUS' full time being come, the spirit appeared to him, and showed him his writing, and told him that the next night the devil would fetch him away, which made the doctor's heart to ache. But to divert himself, he sent for some doctors and master bachelors of arts, and other students to take dinner with him, for whom he provided great store of varieties, with music and the like. But all would not keep up his spirits, for the hour drew near; whereupon his countenance changing, the doctors and masters of arts inquired of him the reasons of his melancholiness? to which Faustus answered, "My friends, you have known me these many years, and how I have practised all manner of wickedness. I have been a great conjurer, which devilish art I obtained of the devil; and also to obtain power to do whatever I pleased I sold myself to the devil for twenty-four years' time, which full time being out this night, makes me full of horror. I have called you, my friends, to see this my dreadful end; and I pray let my miserable death be a warning to you all how you study the devilish art of conjuring; for if once you begin it, a thousand to one but it will lead you to the devil, whither I am this night to go, whether I will or not." They hearing of this sad story blamed him for concealing it so long, telling him if he had made them acquainted before that they thought it might have been prevented. He told them he had a desire several times to have disclosed this intrigue; but the devil told him that if he did he would presently fetch him away. He also told them he had a desire to join with the godly, and to leave off that wicked course; but immediately the devil used to come and torment him, etc. "But now," saith Faustus, "it is but in vain for me to talk of what I did intend, for I have sold myself to the devil; body and soul is his." No sooner had he spoken these words, but suddenly it fell a thundering and lightning, the like was never heard; whereupon Faustus went into the great hall, the doctors and masters staying in the next room intending to hear his end. About twelve o'clock the house shook so terribly that they thought it would have been down upon them, and suddenly the house windows were broken to pieces, so that they trembled and wished themselves elsewhere, whereupon a great clap of thunder, with a whirlwind the doors flew open, and a mighty rushing of wind entered with the hissing of serpents, shrieks and cries, upon which he lamentably cried out "Murder," and there was such roaring in the hall as if all the devils in hell had been there. When daylight appeared they took the boldness to enter into the room, and found his brains beaten out against the wall and the floor sprinkled with blood; but missing his body, they went in search of it, and found it on the dunghill mangled and mashed to pieces. So ended this miserable wretch's life, forsaking God and all goodness, and given up to his implacable enemy, which we hope may stand not only as a fearful, but lasting monument and warning to others.

THE WHOLE LIFE AND DEATH
OF
LONG MEG
OF
WESTMINSTER.

Chapter I.
Where Meg was Born, her coming up to London, and her Usage to the Honest Carrier.

In the reign of Henry VIII. was born in Lancashire a maid called Long Meg. At eighteen years old she came to London to get her a service—Father Willis, the carrier, being the waggoner—and her neighbour brought her up with some other lasses. After a tedious journey, being in sight of the desired city, she demanded why they looked sad. "We have no money," said one, "to pay our fare." So Meg replies, "If that be all, I shall answer your demands," and this put them in some comfort. But as soon as they came to St. John's Street, Willis demanded their money. "Say what you will have," quoth she. "Ten shillings a piece," said he. "But we have not so much about us," said she. "Nay, then, I will have it out of your bones." "Marry, content," replied Meg, and, taking a staff in her hand, so belaboured him and his man that he desired her for God's sake to hold her hand. "Not I," said she, "unless you bestow an angel on us for good luck, and swear e'er we depart to get us good addresses."

The carrier, having felt the strength of her arm, thought it best to give her the money and promised not to go till he had got them good places.

Chapter II.

Of her being placed in Westminster, and what she did at her Place.

The carrier, having set up his horses, went with the lasses to the Eagle in Westminster, and told the landlady he had brought her three fine Lancashire lasses; and seeing she often asked him to get her a maid, she might now take her choice. "Marry," said she, "I want one at present, and here are three gentlemen who shall give their opinions." As soon as Meg came in they blessed themselves, crying,

"Domine, Domine, vice Originem."

So her mistress demanded what was her name. "Margaret, forsooth," said she briskly. "And what work can you do?" She answered she had not been bred unto her needle, but to hard labour, as washing, brewing, and baking, and could make a house clean. "Thou art," quoth the hostess, "a lusty wench, and I like thee well, for I have often persons that will not pay." "Mistress," said she, "if any such come let me know, and I'll make them pay I'll engage." "Nay, this is true," said the carrier, "for my carcase felt it;" and then he told them how she served him. On this Sir John de Castile, in a bravado, would needs make an experiment of her vast strength; and asked her "if she durst exchange a box o' the ear with him." "Yes," quoth she, "if my mistress will give me leave." This granted, she stood to receive Sir John's blow, who gave her a box with all his might, but it stirred her not at all; but Meg gave him such a memorandum on his ear that Sir John fell down at her feet. "By my faith," said another, "she strikes a blow like an ox, for she hath knocked down an ass." So Meg was taken into service.

Chapter III.

The method Meg took to make one of the Vicars pay his Score.

Meg so bestirred herself that she pleased her mistress, and for her tallness was called Long Meg of Westminster.

One of the lubbers of the Abbey had a mind to try her strength, so, coming with six of his associates one frosty morning, calls for a pot of ale, which, being drank, he asked what he owed. To which Meg answers, " Five shillings and threepence."

" O thou foul scullion, I owe thee but three shillings and one penny, and no more will I pay thee." And, turning to his landlady, complained how Meg had charged him too much. "The foul ill take me," quoth Meg, "if I misreckon him one penny, and therefore, vicar, before thou goest out of these doors I shall make thee pay every penny"; and then she immediately lent him such a box on the ears as made him reel again. The vicar then steps up to her, and together both of them went by the ears. The vicar's head was broke, and Meg's clothes torn off her back. So the vicar laid hold of her hair, but, he being shaved, she could not have that advantage; so, laying hold of his ears and keeping his pate to the post, asked him how much he owed her. "As much as you please," said he. "So you knave," quoth she, " I must knock out of your bald pate my reckoning." And with that she began to beat a plain song between the post and his pate. But when he felt such pain he roared out he would pay the whole. But she would not let him go until he laid it down, which he did, being jeered by his friends.

Chapter IV.

Of her fighting and conquering Sir James of Castile, a Spanish Knight.

All this time Sir James continued his suit to Meg's mistress, but to no purpose. So, coming in one day and seeing her melancholy, asked what ailed her, for if anyone has wronged you I will requite you. "Marry," quoth she, " a base knave in a white satin doublet has abused me, and if you revenge my quarrel I shall think you love me." " Where is he?"

quoth Sir James. "Marry," said she, "he said he would be in St. George's Fields." "Well," quoth he, "do you and the doctor go along with me, and you shall see how I'll pummel the knave."

Unto this they agreed, and sent Meg into St. George's Fields beforehand. "Yonder," said she, "walks the fellow by the windmill." "Follow me, hostess," said Sir James; "I will go to him." But Meg passed as if she would have gone by. "Nay, stay," said Sir James; "you and I part not so. I am this gentlewoman's champion, and fairly for her sake will have you by the ears." With that Meg drew her sword, and to it they went.

At the first blow she hit him on the head, and often endangered him. At last she struck his weapon out of his hands, and, stepping up to him, swore all the world should not save him. "O save me, sir," said he; "I am a knight, and it is but a woman's matter; do not spill my blood." "Wert thou twenty knights," said Meg, "and was the king here himself, I would not spare thy life unless you grant me one thing." "Let it be what it will, you shall be obeyed." "Marry," said she, "that this night you wait on my plate at this woman's house and confess me to be your master."

This being yielded to and a supper provided, Thomas Usher and others were invited to make up the feast, and unto whom Sir James told what had happened. "Pho!" said Usher jeeringly, "it is no such great dishonour for to be foiled by an English gentleman since Cæsar the Great was himself driven back by their extraordinary courage." At this juncture Meg came in, having got on her man's attire. "Then," said Sir James, "this is that valiant gentleman whose courage I shall ever esteem." Hereupon, she pulling off her hat, her hair fell about her ears, and she said "I am no other than Long Meg of Westminster, and so you are heartily welcome."

At this they all fell a-laughing. Nevertheless, at supper time, according to agreement, Sir James was a proper page; and she, having leave of her mistress, sat in state like her majesty. Thus Sir James was disgraced for his love, and Meg was counted a proper woman.

Chapter V.

Her Usage to the Bailiff of Westminster, who came into her Mistress's and arrested her Friend.

A BAILIFF, having for the purpose took forty shillings, arrested a gentleman in Meg's mistress's house, and desired the company to keep peace. She, coming in, asked what was the matter. "O," said he, "I'm arrested." "Arrested! and in our house? Why this unkind act to arrest one in our house; but, however, take an angel and let him go." "No," said the bailiff, "I cannot, for the creditor is at the door." "Bid him come in," said she, "and I'll make up the matter." So the creditor came in; but, being found obstinate, she rapped him on the head with a quart pot and bid him go out of doors like a knave. "He can but go to prison," quoth she, "where he shall not stay long if all the friends I have can fetch him out."

The creditor went away with a good knock, and the bailiff was going with his prisoner. "Nay," said she, "I'll bring a fresh pot to drink with him." She came into the parlour with a rope, and, knitting her brows, "Sir Knave," said she, "I'll learn thee to arrest a man in our house. I'll make thee a spectacle for all catchpoles;" and, tossing the rope round his middle, said to the gentleman, "Sir, away, shift for yourself; I'll pay the bailiff his fees before he and I part." Then she dragged the bailiff unto the back side of the house, making him go up to his chin in a pond, and then paid him his fees with a cudgel, after which he went away with the amends in his hands, for she was so well beloved that no person would meddle with her.

CHAPTER VI.

Of her meeting with a Nobleman, and her Usage to him and to the Watch.

Now it happened she once put on a suit of man's apparel. The same night it fell out that a young nobleman, being disposed for mirth, would go abroad to see the fashions, and, coming down the Strand, espies her; and, seeing such a tall fellow, asked him whither he was going. "Marry," said she, "to St. Nicholas's to buy a calve's head." "How much money hast thou?" "In faith," said she, "little enough; will you lend me any?" "Aye," said he; and, putting his thumb into her mouth, said, "There's a tester." She gave him a good box on the ear, and said, "There's a groat; now I owe you twopence." Whereupon the nobleman drew, and his man too; and she was as active as they, so together they go. But she drove them before her into a little chandler's shop, insomuch that the constable came in to part the fray, and, having asked what they were, the nobleman told his name, at which they all pulled off their caps. "And what is your name?" said the constable. "Mine," said she, "is Cuthbert Curry Knave." Upon this the constable commanded some to lay hold on her and carry her to the compter. She out with her sword and set upon the watch, and behaved very resolutely; but the constable calling for clubs, Meg was forced to cry out, "Masters, hold your hands, I am your friend; hurt not Long Meg of Westminster." So they all stayed their hands, and the nobleman took them all to the tavern; and thus ended the fray.

CHAPTER VII.

Meg goes a shroving, fights the Thieves of St. James's Corner, and makes them restore Father Willis, the Carrier, his hundred marks.

Not only the cities of London and Westminster, but Lancashire also, rung of Meg's fame, so they desired old Willis, the carrier, to call upon her, which he did, taking with him the other lasses. Meg was joyful to see them, and it being Shrove Tuesday, Meg went with them to Knightsbridge, and spent most of the day with repeating tales of their friends in Lancashire; and so tarried the carrier, who again and again inquired how all did there, and made the time seem shorter than it was. The night growing on, the carrier and the two other lasses were importunate to be gone, but Meg was loath to set out, and so stayed behind to discharge the reckoning, and promised to overtake them.

It was their misfortune at St. James's Corner to meet with two thieves who were waiting there for them, and took a hundred marks from Willis, the carrier, and from the two wenches their gowns and purses. Meg came up immediately after, and then the thieves, seeing her also in a female habit, thought to take her purse also; but she behaved herself so well that they began to give ground. Then said Meg, "Our gowns and purses against your hundred marks; win all and wear all." "Content," quoth they. "Now, lasses, pray for me," said Meg. With that she buckled with these two knaves, beat one and so hurt the other that they entreated her to spare their lives. "I will," said she, "upon conditions." "Upon any condition," said they. "Then," said she, "it shall be thus—

"1. That you never hurt a woman nor any company she is in.

"2. That you never hurt lame or impotent men.

"3. That you never hurt any children or innocents.

"4. That you rob no carrier of his money.

"5. That you rob no manner of poor or distressed.

"Are you content with these conditions?" "We are," said they. "I have no book about me," said she, "but will you swear on my smock tail?" which they accordingly did, and then she returned the wenches their gowns and purses, and old Father Willis, the carrier, a hundred marks.

The men desiring to know who it was had so lustily beswinged them, said—"To alleviate our sorrow, pray tell us your name." She smiling replied—"If anyone asks you who banged your bones, say Long Meg of Westminster once met with you."

Chapter VIII.

Meg's Fellow Servant pressed; her Usage of the Constable; and of her taking Press Money to go to Boulogne.

In those days were wars between England and France, and a hot press about London. The constables of Westminster pressed Meg's fellow servant, and she told them if they took him her mistress was undone.

All this could not persuade the constable, but Harry must go, on which she lent the constable a knock. Notice being given to the captain, he asked who struck him. "Marry," quoth Meg, "I did, and if I did not love soldiers I'd serve you so too." So, taking a cavalier from a man's hand, she performed the exercise with such dexterity that they wondered, whereupon she said—"Press no man, but give me press money and I will go myself." At this they all laughed, and the captain gave her an angel, whereupon she went with him to Boulogne.

Chapter IX.

Of her Beating the Frenchman off the Walls of Boulogne, for which gallant behaviour she is rewarded by the King with Eightpence per Day for Life.

King Henry, passing the seas, took Boulogne. Hereupon the Dauphin with a great number of men surprised and retook it. Meg, being a laundress in the town, raised the best of the women; and, with a halberd in her hand, came to the walls, on which some of the French had entered, and threw scalding water and stones at them that she often obliged them to quit the town before the soldiers were up in arms.

And at the sally she came out the foremost with her halberd in her hand to pursue the chase.

The report of this deed being come to the ears of the king, he allowed her for life eightpence a day.

Chapter X.

Of her fighting and beating a Frenchman before Boulogne.

During this she observed one who in a bravado tossed his pike. She, seeing his pride, desired a drum to signify that a young soldier would have a push at pike with him. It was agreed on, and the place appointed life against life.

On the day the Frenchman came, and Meg met him, and without any salute fell to blows; and, after a long combat, she overcame him, and cut off his head. Then, pulling off her hat, her hair fell about her ears.

By this the Frenchman knew it was a woman, and the English giving a shout, she, by a drummer, sent the Dauphin his soldier's head, and said, "An English woman sent it."

The Dauphin much commended her, sending her a hundred crowns for her valour.

Chapter XI.

Of her coming to England and being Married.

The wars in France being over, Meg came to Westminster and married a soldier, who, hearing of her exploits, took her into a room, and, making her strip to her petticoat, took one staff and gave her another, saying, "As he had heard of her manhood, he was determined to try her." But Meg held down her head, whereupon he gave her three or four blows, and she in submission fell down upon her knees desiring him to pardon her. "For," said she, "whatever I do to others, it behoves me to be obedient to you; and it shall never be said, if I cudgel a knave that injures me, Long Meg is her husband's master; and therefore use me as you please." So they grew friends, and never quarrelled after.

Chapter XII.
Long Meg's Usage to an angry Miller.

Meg going one day with her neighbours to make merry, a miller near Epping looking out, the boy they had with them, about fourteen years old, said—" Put out, miller, put out." " What must I put out?" said he. " A thief's head and ears," said the other.

At this the miller came down and well licked him, which Meg endeavoured to prevent, whereupon he beat her. But she wrung the stick from him, and then cudgelled him severely; and having done, sent the boy to the mill for an empty sack, and put the miller in all but his head; and then, fastening him to a rope, she hauled him up half way, and there left him hanging. The poor miller cried out for help, and if his wife had not come he had surely been killed, and the mill, for want of corn, set on fire.

Chapter XIII.
Of her keeping House at Islington, and her Laws.

After marriage she kept a house at Islington. The constable coming one night, he would needs search Meg's house, whereupon she came down in her shift with a cudgel, and said—" Mr. Constable, take care you go not beyond your commission, for if you do I'll so cudgel you as you never was since Islington has been." The constable, seeing her frown, told her he would take her word, and so departed.

Meg, because in her house there should be a good decorum, hung up a table containing these principles:—

First. If a gentleman or yeoman had a charge about him, and told her of it, she would repay him if he lost it; but if he did not reveal it, and said he was robbed, he should have ten bastinadoes, and afterwards be turned out of doors.

Secondly. Whoever called for meat and had no money to pay should have a box on the ear and a cross on the back that he might be marked and trusted no more.

Thirdly. If any good fellow came in and said he wanted money, he should have his belly full of meat and two pots of drink.

Fourthly. If any raffler came in and made a quarrel, and would not pay his reckoning, to turn into the fields and take a bout or two with Meg, the maids of the house should dry beat him, and so thrust him out of doors.

These and many such principles she established in her house, which kept it still and quiet.

THE FAMOUS HISTORY

OF THE LEARNED

FRIAR BACON

GIVING

A Particular Account of his Birth, Parentage, with the many Wonderful Things he did in his Lifetime, to the amazement of all the World.

CHAPTER I.

Friar Bacon's Birth and Parentage, and by what means he came to be so great a Scholar. How the King sent for him from Oxford, and in what wonderful manner he pleased the King's Five Senses; also the Comical Pranks he played with a Courtier sent to fetch him.

THE famous Friar Bacon, whose name has spread through the world, was born in Lancashire; his father's name was Ralph Bacon, and his name Roger. From his infancy he was observed to have a profound, pregnant wit; as he grew up, a great reader of books and desirous of learning, which to admiration he took so fast that his schoolmaster could teach him no further, and being about to send him home, with commendations, to his father, he, fearing the worst, humbly besought him to prevail, if possible, with his father that he might be sent to the University, where he had a desire to go and learn the liberal sciences.

His schoolmaster denied him not his request, but went home with him, and, taking the old man aside, told him he had learned his son as far as he was able, that he took it in extremely well, and was willing to improve it at the University, and that he was verily persuaded, by the promptness he perceived in him, if he would be at a little charge with him there, he would be so great a proficient as would advance him to an eminent station.

The old man heard this with some indignation, but concealed his anger till the schoolmaster was gone, and then, taking his son to task, said, "How now, sirrah! have not I been at cost enough already, but are you itching to put me to more? Methinks I have given you such learning as to enable you, in time, to be a constable or churchwarden of the parish, and far outdo those in the office that can neither read nor write; let that suffice. As for the rest of your business for the future, it is to learn horse language and whistle well, that you may be dexterous at driving the plough and cart and managing the sheep and oxen; for, sirrah," continued he, "have I anybody else to leave my farm to but you, and yet you take upon you, forsooth, to be a scholard, and consequently a gentleman; for they all profess themselves so, though never so beggarly, living lazily, and eating up the fat of other men's labours, marry gaup! Goodman Twoshoes, your great-grandfather, your grandfather, and I, have thought it no scorn to dig and delve; and pray what better are you than us? Here, sirrah, take this whip and go with me to plough, or I'll so lace your fine scholarship that you had better this had never been mentioned to me."

Young Bacon was much displeased and highly grieved, but durst not reply, knowing his father to be a very hasty, choleric old man; however, this sort of living so little agreed with his sprightly genius that in a short time he gave him the slip, and going to a monastery, making his desires known to the superior, he kindly entertained him, and made him a brother of the Augustin Friars. There he profited so much that in a few years he was sent to Oxford to study at their charge, where he soon grew such a proficient that his fame soon spread, not only in the University, but also over all England, and came to the ears of King Edward the Third, who then reigned; and he, taking a progress with his queen and nobles, was desirous to see him, and have an experiment of his art; so that, being at a nobleman's house within four miles of the city of Oxford, he sent a gentleman of his bedchamber to desire him to come to him. The knight delayed not the message, and, finding him at his study, did his errand. The friar told him he would be with his majesty, and bid him make haste or he should be there before him. At this he smiled, being well mounted, saying scholars and travellers might lie by authority. "Well," said Friar Bacon, "to convince you, I will not only be there before you, ride as fast as you can, but I will there show you the cook-maid you lay with last, though she is now busy dressing the dinner at Sir William Belton's, a hundred miles distance from this place." "Well," said the gentleman of the bedchamber, "I doubt not but one will be as true as the other"; so, mounting, rode laughing away, and thinking to be at the king's quarters in a short space, he spurred his horse valiantly; but suddenly a mist arose, that he knew not which way to go, and, missing the way, he turned down a bye-lane and rode over hedge and ditch, backwards and forwards, till the charm was dissolved.

When the friar came into the king's presence he did him obeisance, and was kindly welcomed by him. Then said the king, "Worthy Bacon, having heard much of your fame, the cause of my sending for you was to be a spectator of some fine curiosities in your art." The friar excused at first; but the king pressing it, promised on his royal word no harm should come to him, he bid all keep silence, and, waving his magic wand, there presently to their great amazement, ensued the most melodious music they had ever heard, which continued very ravishing for nearly half an hour. Then, waving his wand, another kind of music was heard, and presently dancers in antic shapes at a masquerade entered the room, and having danced incomparably well, they vanished. Waving his wand the third time, louder music was heard, and whilst that played, a table was placed by an invisible hand, richly spread with all the dainties that could be thought of. Then he desired the king and queen to draw their seats near, and partake of the repast he had prepared for their highnesses: which, after they had done, all vanished. He waved the fourth time, and thereupon the place was perfumed with all the sweets of Arabia, or that the whole world could produce. Then waving the fifth time, there came in Russians, Persians, and Polanders, dressed in the finest soft fur, silks, and downs of rare fowls, that are to be found in the universe, which he bid them feel, and then the strangers, having danced after their own country fashion, vanished.

In this sort Friar Bacon pleased their five senses, to their admiration and high satisfaction; so that the king offered him money, but he refused it, saying he could not take it. However, the king pressed on him a jewel of great value, commanding him to wear it as a mark of his favour. Whilst this was doing, the gentleman of the bedchamber came in, puffing and blowing, all bemired and dirty, and his face and hands scratched with the bushes and briars. The king, at this sight, demanded why he stayed so long, and how he came in that condition? "Oh, plague," said he, "take Friar Bacon and all his devils! they have led me a fine dance, to the endangering of my neck. But is the dog here? I'll be revenged on him!" Then he laid his hand on his sword, but Bacon, waving his wand, charmed it in his scabbard, so he could not draw it out, saying, "I fear not your anger; 'tis best for you to be quiet, lest a worse thing befall you." Then he told the king how he gave him the lie, when he told him he would be there before him.

Whilst he was thus speaking, in came the cook-maid, brought by a spirit, at the window, with a spit and a roasted shoulder of mutton on it, being thus surprised as she was taking it from the fire; and wishfully staring about her, and espying the gentleman, she cried, "O my sweet knight, are you here? Pray, sir, remember you promised to provide linen and other necessaries for me. Our secret sins have grown, and I've two months to reckon," and hereupon she ran towards him to embrace him; but he turning aside, she was carried out at another window to her master's house again.

This was the cause of both amazement and laughter, though the gentleman was much ashamed and confounded to be thus exposed, still muttering revenge; but Friar Bacon told him his best way was to put up all, since he had verified all his promises, and bid him have a care how he gave a scholar the lie again.

The king and queen, well pleased with the entertainment, highly commending his art, and promising him their favour and protection, took their leave of the friar, returning to London, and he to his study at Brazen Nose College.

Chapter II.

How Friar Bacon put a Comical Trick upon his man Miles, who, pretending Abstinence on a Fast Day, concealed Victuals in his Pocket to eat in a Corner.

Friar Bacon kept a man to wait on him who, though but a simple fellow, yet a merry droll and full of waggeries. His name was Miles, and though his master and those of the order often fasted on set days, Miles loved his guts too well to pinch them, and though outwardly he seemed to fast for compliance, he always kept a private reserve to eat in a corner, which Bacon knew by art, and resolved to put a trick upon him. It so happened on Good Friday, in Lent, a strict fast was held, and Miles seemed very devout; for when his master bid him, however, take a bit of bread and a sip of wine early in the morning to keep him from fainting, he refused it, saying he was a great sinner, and therefore ought to do more than this for his mortification, and to gain absolution, making a great many pretences of sanctity, and how well he was inclined to keep the holy fast. "'Tis well," said the friar, "if I catch you not tripping." Hereupon Miles went to his cell, pretending to pray, but indeed to eat a fine pudding he had concealed: which he had no sooner put into his mouth at one end, but it stuck there; he could neither eat it nor get it out. The use of his hands failed, and he was taken with a shivering all over, so that, thinking he should have died presently, he cried piteously out for help; whereupon Friar Bacon, calling the scholars together, went in to see what was the matter, and perceiving him in that plight said, smiling, "Now I see what a penitent servant I have, who was so conscientious he would not touch a bit of bread, but would willingly have devoured two pounds of pudding to have broke his fast." He piteously entreated him to dissolve the charm and deliver him, and he would never do so again. "Nay," said the friar, "you shall do penance for this"; so, taking hold of the end of the pudding, he led him out to the scholars, saying, "See, here's a queasy-stomached fellow, that would not touch a bit of bread to-day!" When they saw him in this plight, they all fell heartily a-laughing; but Friar Bacon, not so contented, led him to the college gate, and by enchantment fixing the end of the pudding to the bar, he was made so fast to it as if it had been by a cable rope, and on his back were placed these lines:—

"This is Friar Bacon's man, who vow'd to fast,
But, dissembling, thus it took at last;
The pudding more religion had than he;
Though he would eat it, it will not down, you see.
Then of hypocrisy pray all beware,
Lest like disgrace be each dissembler's share.

Miles all the while was jeered and sported with by all the scholars and town's people, but, after four hour's penance, his master dissolved the charm, and released him, and he ever after kept the fasts, not so much out of religion as for fear that a worse trick should be put upon him.

Chapter III.

How Friar Bacon saved a Gentleman who had sold himself to the Devil for Money, and put a Trick upon the Old Deceiver of Mankind.

When Friar Bacon flourished at Oxford, a young gentleman, by his prodigality, having run out his estate and involved himself in debt, grew exceeding pensive and melancholy, purposing to make himself away, in order to put an end to his miseries and the scorns that were put daily upon him by his former companions, being also utterly cast off by his friends; so, walking by a wood side, full of sorrow, he met, as he thought, an old man in good clothing, who saluted him and demanded the cause of his melancholy, and why he walked so solitary. At first he refused to tell him, as thinking he could do him no good; but the other urging it, promised to assist him if he wanted anything. He said, "I am in want. I want fine clothes, as I used to have; I want money to buy food, pay debts, redeem my mortgaged land, and many things more. Can you help me to enough to do it?" "I can," said the old man, "on one condition." "What's that?" said the gentleman. "If it be anything tolerable I shall not refuse it, for I cannot be well worse or in greater hardship than I am now." "Why," said the other, "the matter is not so much; you shall only oblige yourself when I have furnished you with money to do all you have named and you have paid every one you owe a farthing to, to become obedient to me, and be disposed of at my pleasure." Now the young man, taking him for a usurer, and very rich, supposed this obligation was only a fetch to marry his daughter or some kinswoman of his, which he could be well contented to do, not doubting to have a good portion, and therefore scrupled not to do as he desired. Upon this he bid him meet him the next morning, about the same time, when he would have the writing ready; and on signing he should have the money. So they parted, and the gentleman delayed not coming, without asking advice, and was as punctually met; but when he saw the writing in blood he was startled a little, but the old man told him it was only a whim of his own to have it so written to distinguish it from other men's, and put his debtors more in mind to repay the money he lent them. Upon this speech, and the gentleman's seeing store of gold and silver brought by three or four of whom he supposed to be servants, he believed it. "But how," said he, "shall I write with the same?" "Oh," said he, "let me see. I'll prick your right vein," which he did, whilst the gentleman found an unusual trembling and an inward remorse in his mind. However, taking the bloody pen in his hand, he desperately subscribed and sealed the writing. Then, telling the money into a cloak bag, he laid it on his horse, and they, with much ceremony, took leave of each other. The gentleman laughed in his sleeve to think how he would find him out, seeing he had not asked, nor himself told him, where he lived.

Soon after he summoned all his creditors, paid them to a farthing, redeemed his land, went gallant, and recovered his esteem in the world; but one evening as he was looking over his writings in his closet, he heard somebody rap at the door, when, opening it, he saw the party he had borrowed the money of, with the writing in his hand, who told him he was now come to demand him, and he must now go along with him; for to his knowledge he had paid his debts, and done whatever was agreed to. The gentleman, wondering how he should know this so soon, denied it. "Nay," replied he, fiercely, "deny it not, for I'll not be cheated of my bargain," and thereupon changed into a horrible shape, struck him almost dead with fear, for now he perceived it was the devil. Then he told him if he did not meet on the morrow, in the same place he had lent him the money, he would come the next day and tear him to pieces. "And," says he, "if I prove not what I say, you shall be quiet"; and so vanished out of the window in a flash of flame, with horrible bellowings. The gentleman, seeing himself in this case, began to weep bitterly, and wished he had been contented in his sad condition, rather than have taken such a desperate way to enrich himself, and was almost at his wits' end.

Friar Bacon, knowing by his art what had passed, came to comfort him, and having heard the whole story, bid him not despair, but pray and repent of his sins, and he would contrive to show the devil a trick that should release him from his obligation. This greatly comforted the gentleman, and he promised to do whatever the friar should order him. "Then," says he, "meet at the time appointed, and I will be near. Offer to put the decision of the controversy to the next that comes by, and that shall be myself, and I will find a way infallibly to give it on your side. Accordingly he met, and the devil consented to put it to arbitration. Then Friar Bacon appearing, " Lo," said the gentleman, " here's a proper judge. This learned friar shall determine it, and if it goes against me, you have free liberty to do with me as you please." " Content," said the devil. Then each of them told their story, and the writing was produced, with all the acquittances he had taken; for the devil, contrary to his knowledge, had stolen them and the other writings belonging to his estate out of his closet. The friar, weighing well the matter, asked the gentleman whether he had paid the devil any of the money he borrowed of him. " No," replied he, " not one farthing." " Why then," said he, " Mr. Devil, his debts are not discharged; you are his principal creditor, and, according to this writing, can lay no claim to him till every one of his debts are discharged." " How! how!" replied the devil, " am I outwitted then? O friar, thou art a crafty knave!" and thereupon vanished in a flame, raising a mighty tempest of thunder, lightning, and rain; so that they were wet through before they could get shelter. Then Bacon charged him he should never pay the devil a farthing of his debt, whatever shape he came in, or artifice he used to wheedle him out of it, and then he could have no power over him. The gentleman on this, living a temperate frugal life, grew very rich, and leaving no children at his death, bequeathed his estate to Brazen Nose College, because Friar Bacon, a member of it, had delivered him from so great a danger of body and soul.

Chapter IV.

How Friar Bacon framed a Brazen Head which, by Enchantment, was to Speak; by that means all England had been walled with Brass, if the Folly of his man Miles, who was set to watch the Head, had not disappointed it, not timely calling his Master to answer it, for which he was struck Dumb many Days.

Friar Bacon, being now a profound proficient in the art of magic and many other sciences, contrived, with one Friar Bungey, who was his pupil, to do something memorable for the good of his country, and many things they cast in their minds. At last they remembered that England had often been harassed and invaded by the Romans, Saxons, Danes, Normans, and other nations at sundry times, to the great effusion of blood, and often alteration of the constitution of governments; and if anything might be contrived to prevent the like for the future, they should thereby raise a lasting monument to their names.

Bacon, upon this, concluded to frame a head of brass, and if, by their art, they could cause it to speak, and answer their demands, they required that all the sea-girt shores of England and Wales should be walled with brass, and brazen towers be raised on the frontiers of Scotland, to hinder the incursions and rovings of the hardy Scots.

They laboured to do this by art, but could not; so they conjured up a spirit, to inquire of the infernal council whether it might be done or not. The spirit, however, was unwilling to answer, till Friar Bacon threatened with his charms to bind him in chains in the Red Sea or to a burning rock, and make him the sport of wrecking whirlwinds.

Terrified by this means, he said of himself he could give no answer, but must inquire of his lord, Lucifer. They granted him two days for an answer. Accordingly he returned this:—" If they for two months would carefully watch the head, it should in that time speak, but the certain time should not be known to them, and then, if they did hear it, they should be answered."

At this they much rejoiced, and watched by turns very carefully for six weeks, and no voice was uttered. At length, tired out, and broken for want of their natural rest, they concluded some other might watch as well as they, till they refreshed themselves in repose, and call them when the head began to speak, which would be time enough; and because this was a secret they did not care for having it known till they saw what they should make of it. Bacon thereupon proposed his man Miles, and Bungey approved of it; so they called Miles, told him the nature of the brazen head and what was intended, by giving him a strict charge on his life, to awake them as soon as ever he heard it speak.

"For that, master," said he, "let me alone. I warrant you I'll do your business effectually, never fear it." So he got him a long sword by his side, and a tabor and pipe to play, and keep him awake if any drowsiness or the like should overtake him.

The charge being given, and he thus accoutred, the two friars went to rest in the next apartment. Miles then began to pipe and sing songs of his sweethearts and frolics:—

> "Bessy, that is so frolic and gay,
> Like a cat she loves with her tail to play;
> Though sometimes she'll pant and frown,
> All's well when her anger goes down.
>
> She'll never say nay, but sport and play;
> O, Bessy to me is the queen of the May;
> For Margery she is peevish and proud;
> Come, fiddlers, then, and scrape the crowd."

Whilst his merriment passed, after a hoarse noise, like

thunder almost spent, the head spoke distinctly, "TIME IS." "Oh ho!" says Miles, "is this all the news you can tell me? Well, copper nose, has my master taken all this pains about you, and you can speak no wiser? Dost thou think I am such a fool to break his sweet slum for this? No, speak wiser, or he shall sleep on. Time is, quotha! Why, I know time is, and that thou shalt hear, goodman kettle jaws.

"Time is for some to gain,
　　Time is for some to lose;
Time is for some to hand,
　　But then they cannot choose.

Time is to go a score,
　　Time is when one should pay:
Time is to reckon, too,
　　But few care for that day.

Time is to graft the horn
　　Upon another's head;
Time is to make maids' hearts swell,
　　Oh, then 'tis time they're wed.

"Hear'st thou this, goodman copper nose? We scholars know when time is, without thy babbling. We know when time is to drink good sack, eat well, kiss our hostesses, and run on the score. But when time is to pay them is indeed but seldom."

While thus he merrily discoursed, about half an hour after the same noise began as before, and the head said, "TIME WAS." "Well," said Miles, "this blockish head is the foolishest thing my wise master ever troubled himself about. How would he have laughed, had he been here, to hear it prat so simply! Therefore, thou brazen-faced ass, speak wiser, or I shall never trouble my head to awake him. Time was, quotha! thou ass thou! I know that, and so thou shalt hear, for I find my master has watched and tutored thee to a fine purpose.

> "Time was when thou, a kettle,
>   Was wont to hold good matter;
> But Friar Bacon did thee spoil
>   When he thy sides did batter.
>
> Time was when conscience dwelt
>   With men of each vocation;
> Time was when lawyers did not thrive
>   So well by men's vexations.
>
> Time was when charity
>   Was not denied a being;
> Time was when office kept no knaves;
>   That time was worth the seeing.

"Ay, ay, and time was for many other things. But what of that, goodman brazen face? I see my master has placed me here on a very foolish account. I think I'd as good go to sleep, too, as to stay watching here to no purpose." Whilst he thus scoffed and taunted, the head spoke a third time, and said, "TIME IS PAST!" and so, with a horrid noise, fell down and broke to pieces. Whereupon ensued lamentable shrieks and cries, flashes of fire, and a rattling as of thunder, which awaking the two friars, they came running in, in great disorder found Miles rolling on the floor, in a stinking pickle, almost dead with fear, and the head lying shattered about the room in a thousand pieces. Then, having brought him to his senses again, they demanded how this came. "Nay, the devil knows better than I," said Miles, "I believe he was in this plaguy head: for when it fell, it gave a bounce like a cannon." "Wretch that thou art!" said Bacon, "trifle not with my impatience. Didst thou hear it speak, varlet? answer me that."

"Why, truly," said Miles, "it did speak, but very simply,

considering you have been so long a-tutoring it. I protest I could have taught a jackdaw to have spoke better in two days. It said, 'TIME IS.'" "Oh, villain!" says Bacon, "had'st thou called me then, all England had been walled with brass, to my immortal fame." "Then," continued Miles, "about half an hour after, it said, 'TIME WAS.'" "O, wretch! how my anger burns against thee. Had you but called me then, it might have done what I desired." "Then," said he, "it said, 'TIME'S PAST'"; and so fell down with the horrid noise that waked you and made me, I am sure, befoul my breeches; and since here's so much to do about time, I think it's time for me to retire and clean myself." "Well, villain," says Bacon, "thou has lost all our cost and pains by thy foolish negligence." "Why," said Miles, "I thought it would not have stopped when it once began, but would have gone on and told me some pleasant story, or have commanded me to have called you, and I should have done it; but I see the devil is a cunning sophister, and all hell would not allow him tinkers and brass enough to do the work, and therefore has put this trick upon us to get off from his promise." "How, slave," said the friar, "art thou at buffoonery, now thou hast done me this great injury? Sirrah! because you think the head spake not enough to induce you to call us, you shall speak less in two months' space," and with that, by enchantment, he struck him dumb to the end of that time, and would have done worse had not Bungey had compassion on the fellow's simplicity and persuaded him from it.

And thus ends the history of that famous Friar Bacon, who had done a deed which would have made his fame ring through all ages yet to come, had it not been for the simplicity of his man Miles.

THE HISTORY

OF

THE BLIND BEGGAR

OF BETHNAL GREEN,

CONTAINING

His Birth and Parentage; how he went to the Wars and Lost his Sight, and turned Beggar at Bethnal Green; how he got Riches, and educated his Daughter; of her being Courted by a rich, young Knight; how the Blind Beggar dropt Gold with the Knight's Uncle; of the Knight and the Beggar's Daughter being Married; and, lastly, how the famous Pedigree of the Beggar was discovered, with other Things worthy of Note.

CHAPTER I.

How Monford went to the Wars of France, where he lost his Sight; how he was accompanied with his Wife, who preserved his Life, and of his Return to England, etc.

IN former days, when the rose of England eclipsed the lilies of France, and true English valour made that nation stoop, among other brave gallants that went over to try their fortune, Monford was one, a person well descended, who, being naturally inclined to war and greedy of fame, neither the entreaty of friends nor the marriage he had contracted with a kind, beautiful woman, could alter his purpose; but taking his wife Margaret with him, he, with many hundreds more, crossed the seas, and with the help of a prosperous wind, arriving at Calais, marched to the royal standard, accompanied with his loving wife, who, in manlike attire, became his inseparable companion, and was the cause of saving his life; for many skirmishes happened between the English and French, wherein young Monford behaved himself with wondrous courage; and in one, following too hot the pursuit, was, with divers others, entrapped into ambush, late in the evening; and though he manfully disputed it, making great slaughter of the enemy, yet in spite of resistance he was beaten from his horse by a forcible stroke, and left in the field for dead among the dying men; where he had undoubtedly perished through loss of blood, and the anguish of his wounds, had not his tender-hearted love, upon hearing what had happened and his not returning, hasted to the field, where, among the slain, she by moonlight discovered him, stripped and struggling for life, and by the help of a servant brought him to a shepherd's cottage, where she carefully dressed his wounds and administered such cordials as brought him to himself, to her unspeakable joy; though this joy was something abated when she found he had lost his sight, but true love working in her heart, the alteration or disfigurement of his countenance did not alter her affection; but comforting him in the best manner she could, though his natural courage would not admit of any dejection, she procured him a homely suit of apparel, and brought him (unfit for service) back to England, of whose entertainment and settlement at Bethnal Green, in the county of Middlesex, and course of life, you shall hear in the following chapter.

CHAPTER II.

How Monford arrived in England and of the Cold Entertainment he found among his relations.
How he settled in Bethnal Green, where he continued to beg for his Living.

MONFORD, having escaped a dreadful storm at sea, landed with his wife on the coast of Essex, where he had some considerable relations, to whom, in his necessity, they applied themselves for succour; but they, who, after the death of his parents, had wasted much of his patrimony, or fearing he might be chargeable to them, would not know him, and those that were convinced he was the same Monford that went over to France gave him but cold entertainment; insomuch that, scorning to rely upon their charity, he told his wife that he intended, early in the morning, to haste towards London, and that he would rather trust to Providence than the ingratitude of those who, in his prosperous days, had caressed him. His wife declared she would labour at her spinning-wheel or do what she was capable for a living. In two days travelling they spent what little money they had saved, so necessity obliged them to ask charity of the people as he passed through the country towns and villages; who, understanding that he came by his misfortune in fighting for the honour of his country, gave liberally to him; and considering that the loss of his sight had rendered him incapable of business, he resolved to embrace what providence had cast in his way, which was to live upon charity. Whereupon, arriving at Bethnal Green, near London, he hired a small cottage for his wife and himself, and daily appearing publicly to crave alms, was from thence called "The Beggar of Bethnal Green," and in a short time found it a thriving trade, insomuch that his bed of straw was changed into down, and his earthen platters and other utensils into a better sort of decent furniture.

Chapter III.

How Monford happened to meet with Snap, an old, experienced Beggar, who gave him an Insight into the Mystery of the Canting Tribe; and how he invited him to the Rendezvous.

Monford resolving in this kind of way to spend the remainder of his days, being very well contented with his trade, having played it with great success in the place where he lived, one day he was encountered by an old proficient in the art of begging, who, seeing him very diligent, did greatly covet his acquaintance, and to know what gang he did belong to. He therefore accosts him in their canting method, which is a sort of speech or rather a gibberish peculiar to themselves. Monford, being ignorant, could make him no direct answer, which the other, whose name was Snap, perceiving, and thereby knowing him to be a young beginner, invited him to their feasts or rendezvous in Whitechapel, whither he having promised to come, and they between them tripped off four black pots of rum, they parted that time.

Chapter IV.
How Monford went to the Beggars' Feast, and of his Entertainment, and also the Presents they made.

Monford, upon his coming home, declared to his wife what a merry companion he met with, and what discourse he had, and likewise what he had promised, entreating her to get things in readiness, that she might conduct him thither, where appeared, instead of a ragged regiment of lame, blind, and dumb, there was a rout of jovial dancers, as gay as the spring, and as merry as the maids; which made them imagine they were mistaken in the place or was imposed upon, and therefore turned to go away, had not Snap started from his chair, where he sat as supervisor, in all his gallantry, and taking him by the hand, let him know who it was introduced him into the assembly, where he was received as brother of their society, every member saluting him with a compliment, and, that he might not want a guide for the future, Snap, in the name of the society, presented him with a dog and a bell trained to the business. So his wife and he, being splendidly entertained, were dismissed, upon his promise that he would not be absent at their yearly meeting.

Chapter V.

What Success he had in the Begging Trade. How his Wife was brought to Bed of a Daughter, and Christened by the Name of Elizabeth.

The blind beggar soon became master of his trade, and, by the help of his dog, trudged often to London, and having the perfect tone, had the luck to return with his pockets well lined with chink. His way of begging became so pleasing to him that he would often sing as follows—

> A beggar lives a merry life,
>   And has both wealth and ease;
> His days are free from care and strife,
>   He does whate'er he please.
>
> While others labour, sweat, and toil,
>   His tongue does get him pelf;
> He travels with his dog and bell,
>   And brings home store of wealth.

He being by this time in a warm condition, to add further to his joy, his loving wife fell in labour, and was delivered of a daughter, whose birth made him think he was the happiest man alive, and hundred times he kissed her and dandled her in his arms, whom he christened by the name of Elizabeth, and as she increased in years, so her beauty and modesty caused her to be called "Pretty Betty." Some began to dote upon her admirable perfections, and the better to qualify her gave her such learning as was suitable to her degree, which she improved; so that her beauty and wit, her skill in singing, dancing, and playing on instruments of music, procured her the envy of the young maidens thereabouts, who supposed themselves much superior in birth and fortune, would often reflect upon her birth, and call her a beggar's brat. She bore all their ill language without returning it, and endeavoured to win them to her by gentle persuasions; but not prevailing, and her patience spent, she said, "I never injured any of you, but have strove to do you all the good offices which I was capable of doing; why, then, do you envy and abuse me? What if my parents are in a mean station, yet they pay for my education of dancing and singing which they bestow upon me, and though, perhaps, I am not so well descended as some of you, though you may be mistaken, yet Heaven might have made your case the same had it thought fit." Yet, finding that they did not cease to rail at her, and being by this time about fifteen years of age, she prevailed with her parents to grant her leave to seek her fortune.

CHAPTER VI.
How handsome Betty took Leave of her Parents, and the Entertainment she met with.

Now the time of Betty's departure being come, her parents furnished her with clothes and other necessaries, whereupon she fell upon her knees and craved their blessing, which being given, with many prayers for her prosperity, they took a sad farewell.

Pretty Betty, having now left her father's house, or rather smoke-loft, went pensive along the road towards Stradford, relying only on Providence to direct her. Having walked all night, at sunrise she came to Rumford, in Essex and being ready to faint, betook herself to an inn, and called for something to refresh her. The mistress of the house, taking notice of her garb, beautiful face, and modest behaviour, though dejected, began to ask her from whence she came, and whither she was bound. Betty replied, "I am going to seek my fortune. I am very well educated by my indulgent parents, who live near London; but I am now obliged, contrary to my former expectation, to get my livelihood in some honest way of working." The good woman, being more and more taken with her carriage, demanded if she would be content to stay with her till she could better provide to her advantage, and that she would use her as a daughter rather than a servant. Betty thankfully accepted the offer, and in the performance of whatever she undertook discharged herself so well that she gained the love and applause of all that observed her, insomuch that her name for beauty and ingenuity began to spread, and abundance of young men resorted to the house, which created a great trade, on purpose to see her, who generally took a liking to her; for nature had made her so lovely and charming that she could not but be admired, insomuch that many of them, as they found opportunity, began to buzz love stories in her ears, to which she gave but little heed, till four suitors of greater worth beat off these little assailants, and laid close siege, as in the following chapter will appear.

CHAPTER VII.
How Pretty Betty, living at an Inn at Rumford, was Courted by Persons of Fortune.

IT being whispered about that pretty Betty must needs be some great person's daughter, it highly increased her reputation. At last the innkeeper's son, a very rich London merchant, courted her. But she modestly declined his offers, as also the offers of all other suitors, by representing to them the inequality of her fortune to theirs; but this served only to increase their passions. And being every day importuned, she at last resolved to discover who her parents were, judging that way to be the most sure means to try the sincerity of their love and affection which they pretended to have for her.

CHAPTER VIII.
How Pretty Betty being Woo'd by her Master's Son, a Merchant, a Gentleman, and a Knight; how, upon her declaring her Parentage, was slighted by all but the Knight; and of their Agreement.

OUR beautiful virgin, being hardly pressed for love and

enjoyment, found herself obliged to take a course that might rid her of her lovers, or allot one of them to her share; wherefore she told them she was not really at her own disposal, her parents being alive; therefore, if they loved her as they said, and seeing but one could enjoy her, she was contented her father should choose one for her, of whose choice she would approve.

This set them almost at daggers drawing, who should get thither first, but whither to go they knew not, therefore desired to be informed, every one's heart being filled with joy, not doubting to carry the prize; when thus she began:—"My parents, worthy sirs, live on Bethnal Green. My father is left with a dog and a bell, living upon the charity of good people, and my mother a poor woman that spins for bread. Thus I have declared to you my parents, and though I might have the richest person in the world for a husband, yet I would not marry him without their consent, which I think myself bound in duty to obtain."

Most of her suitors seemed thunderstruck at this plain declaration, every one, except the knight, despising her now as much as they seemed to love her before, each of them swearing they would not undervalue themselves to marry a beggar's child. But the knight was more inflamed than ever, and having a large estate, did not regard interest or a portion so much as he did the pleasing of his fancy with a beautiful, modest, young, and virtuous maid, all of which centred in Pretty Betty. Therefore, after he had paused a while took the blushing virgin by the hand, and said, "You see, fair creature, how they that pretended to love you did it only in expectation of your being descended from wealthy parents, and that they might get a large portion. Though they have left you, if you will accept of me for a husband, who truly love you on account of your virtue and beauty, I will make you my wife and settle on you a jointure." To this she replied, "Alas, sir, I dare not hope for so much happiness, or, if I durst, yet would not dispose of myself without my parents' consent; though I must confess," says she, blushing, "I ever did esteem you above all the gentlemen who did make love and offer themselves to me." This modesty kindled his passion more, and therefore, after many vows of constancy, it was agreed that he should provide horses and servants, and conduct her the next morning to Bethnal Green, to ask and obtain her father's consent; yet this affair was not so secretly managed but spies being abroad soon discovered it, who not only discovered to the knight's uncle, who was guardian and trustee for him, and had the sole care of his estate, but to most of the young men in Rumford who were her admirers, as the following chapter will inform you.

Chapter IX.

How Pretty Betty rid behind the Knight to her Father's House, and what happened on the Road; also what happened between the Knight's Uncle and Betty's Father.

Pretty Betty, having met the knight according to appointment, did not scruple to ride behind him; but they had scarce got out of town when his uncle came to the inn, but not finding either of them there, was confirmed that what had been told him was true, and therefore he followed them to prevent the match, being accompanied with several of Betty's lovers, who suspected the knight had taken her away by force. Their hurry and confusion was great, and the townsmen going a nearer way, overtook and fell foul upon the knight and his servants, without giving him leave to speak for himself or suffering his mistress to excuse him, so that a sharp conflict ensued, till at length divers persons that were travelling the road came and parted them, whereby they came to a right understanding, which made those that had misused him beg his pardon, which he granted, and, dismissing them, kept on his way till, coming to the old man's door, they alighted; which made him, upon hearing the noise of horses trampling, being a thing very unusual, start from the fire, and put his head out of the window, and not understanding the meaning of it, ere the knight's uncle came puffing and blowing at a strange rate crying, "Why, how now nephew? what's this I hear of you? Are you mad to disgrace your family by marrying a beggar's brat? For shame, for shame! consider better than to make yourself a laughing stock to the world by such an unseemly match." Then, turning about to Pretty Betty, said, "Pray how came this about, you baggage you? But, however, I say, nephew, leave her and come along with me and I will provide a rich wife for you suitable to your condition."

To this the young knight would have replied, but the blind beggar Monford, not being able to bear his taunts and reproaches any longer, said, "I cannot see you at all, but sir, whatever you are I hear you too much, and more than becomes a civil gentleman; nor do I count my girl so mean to suffer her to be railed on at my door; therefore, pray sir, hold your prating, or I shall fell you with my staff. I have seen the day when a taller fellow than you durst not put me in a passion. If your kinsman does not think my child a fit match for him, let him let her alone and welcome. I am satisfied she hath her share of beauty and good breeding, and those are enough to recommend her. But know, sir, that I, her father, am willing and ready to lay down as many guineas for my child as you are to drop for your nephew, and therefore care not how soon you begin." The knight's uncle was something surprised at this speech of the blind beggar's; but, however, he accepted of the challenge, and sent to London for a bag of gold. As soon as it was brought, Monford pulled out two large cat skins stuffed with gold from under a bundle of rags, whereby it appeared his trade had been advantageous. Both parties being ready, they rained a golden shower so plentifully that the gentleman's stock failed him, and the beggar, not hearing it chink, fell into laughter and said, "How, sir, is your money done so soon? I thought at first you had more words than money. Pray, for your credit's sake, try your friends, for I have three or four cat skins with golden puddings in their bellies yet." "Indeed," said the gentleman, "I am content to own you have outdone me, and think you have the philosopher's stone, or keep a familiar to bring it to you from the golden mountain. But seeing the world goes so well with you, I shall no further go about to persuade my nephew from being your son-in-law, but beg pardon for what I have done." "Oh, do you so," said the beggar, "then may things be better, perhaps, than you expect." Then, turning to the knight, "Gather up," said he, "the loose coin I have scattered, and here's a cat skin filled which will make up the sum of three thousand pounds, beside a hundred more to buy her a wedding gown. Take this as her present portion, and, as you behave yourself, expect more hereafter. I give her to you, and with her a blessing. Go to church and be married, in God's name, and I wish you both success and prosperity." When he had thus spoken, the knight and bride fell upon their knees, and gave him a thousand thanks and departed, whilst those that had been suitors, hearing what had happened, were ready to hang themselves for madness.

CHAPTER IX.

How Pretty Betty was Married to the Knight, and her true Pedigree discovered.

THINGS being come to pass, great preparations were made for the wedding. The bride and bridegroom were dressed in rich apparel, and as soon as the ceremony was ended they went to the place appointed for keeping their wedding dinner. Hither resorted abundance of persons of distinction, who had been invited, yet none of them surpassed the bride in modesty and beauty. At length her father and mother came in, dressed in silks and embroidered velvets. The company was pleased with the entertainment, which was very costly, and when the music, dancing, and masquerading was ended, the old man Monford sung a song, wherein he discovered his pedigree and his valour in the wars of France, which also filled the company full of admiration.

OLD MONFORD'S SONG.

You gallants all, that here are come
    To make this day more happy prove;
Know, though I'm blind, I am not dumb,
    But wish you happiness and love.

The bride, although her birth seems mean,
    Is born of a noble race;
Her predecessors great have been,
    If you her pedigree do trace.

Know she is Monford's daughter fair,
    Who lost his sight in the wars of France,
Who ever since, in begging here,
    Did take this happy, thriving chance.

Consider, bridegroom, then her birth,
    Which some think mean and low,
As much of honour can bring forth
    As you have power to show.

The name of Monford, which had been held so famous for virtue and valour in those days, did not a little cause wonder in the hearers, who, desiring him to explain himself, and give the company a particular account of all his adventures from his youth till the present time, and immediately a profound silence ensued, the noble company sitting in full expectation of being diverted with the surprising achievements and glorious exploits of old Monford, especially his son-in-law, who was more desirous than all the rest to hear this seemingly so much pleasing relation, and his beautiful bride was no less anxious to hear more of her pedigree; for till now she had been kept in the dark with regard to her high birth. Monford, hearing all were silent, begun to relate first, his marriage; second, his going over to France, accompanied by his beloved spouse, his adventures there; and, lastly, how he lost his sight in an engagement, with his return to England, and the success he had by begging; all which caused a general joy, since those who had formerly known him by that name supposed him to be dead; and the bridegroom was pronounced now more happy than ever, whose lovely bride in both birth and fortune equalled his in all degrees, and her father, for the credit of his daughter, promised to leave off his begging trade and live upon what he had got. This day was concluded to the joy and satisfaction of all parties.

THE
PLEASANT HISTORY
OF
POOR ROBIN
THE
MERRY SADDLER OF WALDEN

SHOWING

The Merry Pranks he played during his Apprenticeship,
and how he Tricked a rich Miser, etc.
Very diverting for a Winter Evening Fireside.

CHAPTER I.

The birth of Poor Robin, how he was bound Apprentice to a Saddler, and what a trick he served his Master.

POOR ROBIN was born in Saffron-Walden, in the county of Essex, of honest, plain parents, who brought him up not as our nice dames do now-a-days, by directing him how much he should eat, but, as the fashion was then, full fed with gross meat, so that in a few years he grew a sturdy lad; and considering his growth and manners, a man might well say better fed than taught. His father being willing he should be able to live in the world another day, bound him an apprentice to a Saddler, one who fitted poor Robin's humour to a hair: for the master loving drink, he thought it should go hard if the man likewise did not also wet his lips with it. It fortuned one time his master had brewed a barrel of beer stronger than ordinary, to the drinking of which poor Robin one night invites five or six of his comrades, who, before the next morning, drank it all up. Poor Robin to excuse himself, draws the spiggot out, and throws a pailful of small beer and two or three pails full of water under the tap, and by a wile gets a great sow into the cellar; so the next morning when his master arose all was quiet, and the sow was blamed for what the boar pig had done.

CHAPTER II.
How Poor Robin served his Master for sitting up late at Nights.

POOR ROBIN'S master had gotten a custom that the man did not at all like, which was, that after he had tippled all day, sometimes till ten or eleven o'clock at night, he would then come home and fall asleep in a chair, during which time his man must not go to bed, but wait until his master awakened. Poor Robin to break him of this evil custom, one night when his master came home soundly fuddled, and falling asleep in his chair as usual; so he made a great fire, and then drew his master's legs so near thereto, that his toes touched some of the coals; which being done, he sits him down in the other corner to observe the sequel. He had not sat long till his master's shoes began to fry, whereupon he suddenly awakes, and jumps about as if he had been mad. The man all the while counterfeits himself asleep, and seemed not to awake for a good space. At last, seeming much to pity his master's misfortune, they went to bed. But never after that would his master sit up to sleep in his chair.

CHAPTER III.
How Poor Robin served a rich Miser.

IN the same town lived a rich miser who had wealth enough to have been treasurer of the town, and wisdom answerable to a beadle of a parish. This man, fuller of faith than good works, would neither feast the poor nor relieve their wants, nor hold brotherly unity with any. Poor Robin being resolved to put a trick upon him, it being then Christmas, made it fit for his purpose; and so counterfeiting himself to be the gentleman's man, about ten or eleven o'clock at night, just when people were in bed, he calls at sundry men's doors, inviting them the next day to his master's (naming the gentleman's name) to dinner. Whereupon the next day appeared the number of two and twenty in their roast-meat apparel; but, contrary to their expectations, finding small preparations towards a dinner, they began to wonder wherefore he had invited them; the gentleman as much wondered wherefore they came. At last the truth was cleared on both sides, some laughed, and some frowned; and so they all departed home.

Chapter IV.

How Robin Married and set up for Himself.

Poor Robin having served out his apprenticeship would needs set up for himself, and thereupon hires a house and shop; yet thinking it inconvenient for him to live alone, and that two heads were better than one, he resolved to do as many others did, marry in haste though he should repent at leisure. But his fortune was better than his deserts, for though she was but a homely woman, with whom he joined in matrimony, yet she was provident to live in the world, and for his own part he stood not much on beauty, but had rather have a fat purse than a fair wife, seeing there was great profit in the one, and less danger of being made a cuckold by the other. Never did a couple more lovingly agree together than did this pair at first, insomuch that duck and lamb were the ordinary terms he bestowed upon her; whereupon a wit of the town hearing this loving language betwixt them, made this epigram to be read by any that can understand it.

> Poor Robin thinks his wife excels most dames,
> And calls her duck and lamb, with such kind names,
> A duck's a bird, a lamb's a beast we know,
> Poor Robin's wife's a foul beast then I trow.

Chapter V.

How Poor Robin served one of his Companions a Slovenous Trick.

POOR ROBIN having set up for himself (as you have heard), he would oftentimes travel abroad in the country to get acquaintance amongst the gentry. It happened one time, being belated homeward, and his brain intoxicated with the juice of Bacchus, that he took up his quarters in a country ale-house, where notwithstanding he had gotten a lusty jug before, yet fell he to drinking of beer and cider, as if his belly was bottomless; at last growing sleepy he went to bed, where it was his chance to be lodged in the same chamber where one of his acquaintances was already in bed, who as he lay down sooner than poor Robin, so the next morning was he no sooner got up providing a pot and toast ready against poor Robin arose, but a foul mischance befel poor Robin in the meantime, for the wine, beer, and cider not agreeing in his belly, he very mannerly, sir-reverence vomited on the bed. Whereupon not knowing what to do, and being loth to be discredited, a crotchet came into his crown, which he presently put in execution. He takes the dirty sheets from off his own bed, and lays them on his friend's, and then takes his and lays them on his own bed, so spreading the coverlet as if nothing was amiss, he makes himself ready and downstairs he goes. No sooner was he below but his friend arrests him at Mr. Fox's suit, and by all means would make him pay his groat for being drunk. Poor Robin excused himself as well as he could, and would be judged by the landlord whether he was fuddled or no; whilst they were wrangling about paying the groat, the maid went up into the chamber to make the beds; but finding one of them in a pitiful pickle, she came chafing down, calling the man beastly fellow and nasty knave, with other Billingsgate language, such as came first to her tongue's end. The man thought her mad, thus to scold for nothing, till at last she told him plainly he had vomited the bed. "Nay," quoth poor Robin, "I will be judged by my landlord which of us was most fuddled last night." "Truly," said the host, "I can judge no otherwise but that he was, or he would not have played such a nasty trick." Whereupon it was judged by all the company that the man should pay his groat, and poor Robin got free.

CHAPTER VI.

Of a sad Disaster that befel Poor Robin.

It happened on a time, during the late unhappy wars, that all the Essex Trainband were assembled at Walden, to resist the king's forces, who, in a bravado, had made their excursions as far as Huntington. Amongst other military weapons of destruction, they brought a drake, which they planted under poor Robin's chamber-window, to be shot off at nine o'clock at night, for a warning for all people to repair home. Poor Robin and his wife were at that time newly gone to bed; now it is to be understood, the chamber where they lay went out half over the room below, a rail of about four feet high being set up by the side to keep them from falling, close by the rail was poor Robin's bed. But whilst they were going to sleep, the drake was shot off, which poor Sarah, his wife, hearing, with the fright gave a sudden start, and threw poor Robin quite over the rail into the room below. Poor Robin was much bruised in body and half dead. At length he got up, but his courage was so cooled with the greatness of his fall that he had more need of a doctor than a sleep.

Chapter VII.

How Poor Sarah was cheated of her Mutton Pie.

Poor Sarah on a time made a very great pie, into which she had put a whole loin of mutton besides other things, so that it was valued worth five or six shillings at least. This pie she sent to the common oven to bake, which, being perceived by three or four merry blades, they resolved, if they could possibly, to cheat her of the pie, which at last they brought to pass on this manner. At such time as the baker used to draw, two of them went and held poor Sarah in a tale, whilst the other sent one of her neighbour's boys to the baker's with a pail, a napkin, and money to pay for the baking. The baker mistrusting no knavery, delivered the boy the pie, which was presently carried to the next alehouse, whether inviting some more of their companions unto them, with much mirth and laughter; and because the jest should be publicly known they set the crier to work, who published the same in every corner of the town.

Chapter VIII.

How Poor Robin ate Dog-stones instead of Lamb-stones.

As Poor Robin was more addicted to flesh than fish, so of all sorts of flesh he loved a dish of lamb-stones best. A merry disposed companion knowing his appetite, resolved to put a trick upon him. A gentleman of the town who kept a pack of hounds, having gelt his dogs, he gets the stones, and with a few sweet breads presents them to poor Robin as a dainty dish. Poor Robin very thankful for so great kindness would not stay, but presently had them dressed, making all the haste he could, for fear any should come in to be partakers with him in his dinner. But having eaten them, and understood the truth, he fell a-spewing as if his gall would come up with it. Poor Sarah, in like manner, disgorged her stomach, so that who should have seen them, would have concluded them drunk with eating.

Chapter IX.

A witty Jest that Poor Robin gave a Sergeant.

The Blue Regiment of Train-Soldiers being on a time at Walden, one of the sergeants, to show his bravery, had gotten a great blue scarf about his middle, being as much or more than the ensign had in his colours. Poor Robin thinking him too fine to fight, would venture to put a jeer upon him, and calling him, asked if he wanted any work? "Why," said the sergeant, "what makes you ask?" "Pray your pardon," quoth poor Robin, "I was mistaken in you, I took you for a shoemaker, because you had gotten your blue apron before you."

Chapter X.

How Poor Robin won Five Shillings by kissing his Hostess.

Poor Robin, with some other of his mates, being drinking in an ale-house, where was an exceeding tall hostess, one of them offered to lay five shillings (because Poor Robin was low) that he should not kiss her as he stood on the ground. Poor Robin accepted the challenge, and covered the money. But when he went to kiss her, his mouth would not reach higher than her apron string. Whereupon dropping a shilling on the ground he made her stoop to lift it, then he clasped his arms round her neck, gave her a kiss, and so won the wager.

Chapter XI.

Poor Robin's sayings of Ambitious Men.

Poor Robin, being in company with some gentlemen who were talking of the ambition of some men now-a-days, that would venture the loss of their souls for the possession of a kingdom: "Yea," quoth poor Robin, "but the success of many of them is far different from King Saul's, for he seeking asses found a kingdom, and they seeking a kingdom find themselves to be asses."

Chapter XII.
Poor Robin's Journey to London.

Poor Robin having never been in London in his life, and being very desirous to see the city whose fame rang so loud in every man's mouth, he resolved to make a journey thither, and spend some time in viewing the rarities of the same; but because he was unacquainted with the city customs, he got a companion of his to go along with him. No sooner were they past Aldgate, but poor Robin seeing such a number of signs, he whispered with his friend, "Certainly," quoth he, "they must needs be all drunkards that live in this place. I never saw so many ale-houses together in my life." And thereupon beckoning to his companion, enters one of the shops and calls for a jug of beer; but they making him acquainted with his error, how they sold no drink, but if he wanted anything else they could furnish him with it. He presently without any studying asks them to show him a pair of hedging gloves, whereupon changing their opinion, instead of a fool they took him for a jeering companion; and to fit him for his gloves had him to the pump and soundly bedrenched him from head to foot. And having occasion to go through Birching Lane, and being asked by the salesmen, "Countrymen, what lack you?" "Marry," quoth he, "that which I fear you cannot furnish me withal," and being importuned of them to know what it was: "Why," quoth he, "that which you have none of I want, honesty." Night approaching, poor Robin and his walking mate repaired to their inn, where, after they had supped and drunk five or six jugs of beer with the host of the house, and some of his men (for inn-keeper's servants drink most of their beer at other men's cost), his friend loving no tobacco, and poor Robin desiring the heathenish weed to pass away the time, they agreed among themselves that every one of the company should either tell a tale or sing a song. Poor Robin, who first mentioned the same, beginning in this manner.

Chapter XIII.
A Tale of a Pair of Cards.

Not many ages since a parson of a country village was accused to a committee that he was a great gamester at cards, being so addicted thereunto that he would ofttimes play on Sundays. The committee thus informed, sent for the parson to answer this accusation; who receiving the warrant made no excuse nor delay, but with all haste made his appearance before them; with him also came the informer to justify his accusation. Being thus met together, the committee began to reprove the parson for being addicted to such a vice, as to be noted for a common player at cards. "Indeed," said the parson, "I am so far from it, that I know not what a pair of cards meaneth." "Sir," quoth the informer, "if you please to search his pockets, I believe you will find a pair there at present, for he seldom goeth without such tackling." Whereupon the committee commanding his pocket to be searched, they found a pair of cards there indeed, but the parson denied them to be cards, saying, "They may be cards to you, but to me they are an almanack." And being demanded how he could make it appear, he answered thus: "First," quoth he, "here is as many suits of cards as there be quarters in a year, and as many court cards as there be months in a year, and as many cards as there be weeks in a year, and as many spots as there be days in a year. Then when I look upon the king it puts me in mind of the allegiance that I owe to my sovereign lord the king; looking upon the queen puts me in mind of the allegiance that I owe to the queen; the ten puts me in mind of the Ten Commandments; the nine, of the nine muses; the eight, of the eight altitudes; the seven, of the seven liberal sciences; the six, of six days we ought to labour in; the five, of the five senses; the four, of the four evangelists; the three, of the Trinity; the two, of the two sacraments; and the ace, that we ought to worship but one God." Quoth the committee, "If this be all the use you make of them we can find no fault with you. But Mr. Parson, of all the cards you have nominated, you have forgot the knave; pray, what use make you of him?" "O sir," said he (pointing to his accuser), "that is your worship's informer."

"Poor Robin having ended his tale," says his friend, "I suppose that was the same parson that used to read his litany every day of the week excepting Sunday, and I being constant hearer of him, learnt it as perfectly as my pater noster."

Chapter XIV.
Poor Robin's Litany.

From being turned out of doors,
From town-rats, and ale-house scores,
From lowsie queans and pocky bores,
    Libera nos.

From tailors' bills and drapers' books,
From sluttish maids and nasty cooks,
From froward wives and crabbed looks,
    Libera nos.

From breaking pipes and broken glasses,
From drinking healths and drunken asses,
From lying lubbers and lisping lasses,
    Libera nos.

From paying of lawyers' fees,
From mouldy bread and musty cheese,
From trotting jades and scorning shes,
    Libera nos.

From fetters, chains, bolts, and gyves,
From pointless needles and broken knives,
From thievish servants and drunken wives,
    Libera nos.

From tailors' bodkins and butchers' pricks,
From tenpenny nails and headless spikes,
And from attorneys' knavish tricks,
   Libera nos.

From being taken in disguise,
From believing of a poet's lies,
And from the devil and the excise,
   Libera nos.

From brown bread and small beer,
From being taken stealing deer,
From all that hath been named here,
   Quesemus te.

The litany being ended the tapster comes for his reckoning, but poor Robin made answer that he should do as the rest had done, either tell a tale or sing a song. Says he, "Sing I cannot, but I will tell you how they marry in Scotland, as a Scotch priest told me that lay here, and got me to engage for him to my master for twenty shillings, and he running away, I was forced to pay his score for him.

Chapter XV.

A Scotch Marriage.

We don't use to wad in Scotland as you wad in England. Jockey comes to the kirk and takes Sir Donkyn by the rocket, and says, "Good morn, Sir Donkyn." "What's the matter, Jockey, what's the matter?" "A wadding, a wadding," says he, "don't you see the hoppers and the skippers, and all the lads of the gang?" "I'se don't, I'se come to you belyve." Then Sir Donkyn gangs to the kirk, "I spee and I spee, wha a deil do you spee; Jockey of the high lane, and Jenny of the long cliff; if any know why these twa may not be wadded together, let them now speak or hold their tongue in the deil's name. Jockey wilt thou ha'e Jenny to thy wadded wife? I say, Jockey, say after me, Jockey wilt thou ha'e Jenny to thy wadded wife, forsaking all loons, lubberloons, swing-bellied calves, black lips, and blue noses? Ay, forsooth. If these twa be not as well wadded as e'er I wadded twa these seven years, the deil and St. Andrew part them."

The wedding being ended, all the company went to bed, where we will leave them till the next morning, to relate poor Robin's perambulation about the city.

Chapter XVI.
Poor Robin's perambulation about the City.

No sooner did Apollo begin to appear in the eastern horizon, but poor Robin, shaking off melancholy sleep, roused his companion to prepare himself for their intended perambulation; and having armed themselves with a pot of nappy ale, they took their first walk to see the Royal Exchange, a most magnificent structure, built by Sir Thomas Gresham. From thence they went to take a view of Leadenhall, but the exceeding bravery of the Exchange had so dimmed the beauty of the place, that it was nothing pleasing to poor Robin's eye. He made no tarrying there, but went presently down to the Tower, where having seen the lions, and from the wharf taken a superficial view of the bridge, as also the ships upon the river Thames, he became weary of beholding so many surprising objects. He had, however, far more content in seeing the ships, so admirably pleasing to his fancy it was to see how these little pretty things hopped about. But lest he should take a surfeit with such ravishing delights, his friend persuaded him to go to see the ancient cathedral of St. Paul's, being at present made a horse-guard by the soldiers, which poor Robin beholding, "What a blessed reformation," quoth he, "have we here! For in our country we can scarce persuade men to go to church, but here come men and horses too." Having satisfied himself with the sight of St. Paul's, they would in the next place go to visit Westminster, the rather because it was at term time, where, beholding so great a number of lawyers in their gowns, he cried out, "Oh, let us begone from this place, for if two or three make such a quarrel in our town, certainly there is no abiding here for men in their wit." A country gentleman overhearing him, "I remember," quoth he, "once I heard a story of a man that went down to hell, wherein he beheld men of all professions, ages, and conditions, saving only lawyers, which made him the more to wonder, because he imagined them all there, and asking the devil the reason, he made this reply, 'We have them here though you see them not, but we are forced to keep them in a room by themselves lest they should set all the devils in hell at variance.'" Poor Robin laughed very heartily at this tale, and having now satisfied his inn, and having discharged all reckonings, his friend and he returned home.

Chapter XVII.

Many odd Whimsies and Conceits of Poor Robin.

Poor Robin daily frequenting the tavern and ale-house had learned of his companions many drunken whimsies and other odd conceits, as the five properties that belong to an host, that he must have the head of a stag, the bag of a nag, the belly of a hog, skip up and down like a frog, and fawn like a dog. As also the four ingredients whereof a woman's tongue is made, viz.: The sound of a great bell, the wagging of a dog's tail, the shaking of an aspen leaf tempered with running water.

When poor Robin had gotten a cup in his crown, as it oftentimes happened, he would then be playing the poet, and nothing but rhymes could then come out of his mouth; for as one writes:

> Poet and pot doth differ but one letter,
> And that makes poets love the pot the better.

Amongst other of his conceits, this following comparison was much used by him:—

> Like a purse that hath no chink in't,
> Or a cellar and no drink in't,
> Like a jewel never worn,
> Or a child untimely born,
> Like a song without a foot,
> Or a bond and no hand to't,
> Such doth she seem unto mine eyes,
> That lives a virgin till she dies.
>
> The money doth entice the purse,
> The drink in the cellar quencheth thirst,
> The jewel decks, if worn it is,
> The child soon dies, abortive is;
> The end o' the song doth sweetest sound,
> The hand doth make the party bound.
> So she that marries e'er death takes her,
> Answers that for which Nature makes her.

"Women," said he, "are all extremes, either too willing, or too wilful; too forward or too froward; too courteous or too coy; too friendly or too fiendly." This made Arminius, a ruler in Carthage, refuse to marry, saying, "If I marry a wife, she will be wilful; if wealthy, then wanton; if poor, then peevish; if beautiful, then proud; if deformed, then loathsome; and the least of these is able to plague a thousand men."

THE END.